RESTLESS NATION

RESTLESS

STARTING OVER IN AMERICA

JAMES M. JASPER

NATION

THE UNIVERSITY OF CHICAGO PRESS · CHICAGO AND LONDON

James M. Jasper is the coauthor of *The Animal Rights Crusade* and author of *Nuclear Politics* and *The Art of Moral Protest*, the last also published by the University of Chicago Press.

The University of Chicago Press, Chicago 60637
The University of Chicago Press, Ltd., London
© 2000 by The University of Chicago
All rights reserved. Published 2000
Printed in the United States of America
10 09 08 07 06 05 04 03 02 01 00   5 4 3 2 1

ISBN (cloth): 0-226-39478-6

Library of Congress Cataloging-in-Publication Data

Jasper, James M., 1957–
   Restless nation : starting over in America /
  James M. Jasper.
      p.   cm.
   Includes bibliographical references (p.   ) and
  index.
   ISBN 0-226-39478-6 (alk. paper)
    1. United States—Emigration and immigration.
  2. Migration, Internal—United States. I. Title.
  JV6450 .J37 2000
  325. 73—dc21   00-009053

In memory of

Dorothy Howard Engle, Helen Howard Ireland,

Beatrice Howard Pyles, and Lucie Galleher Howard,

and for 350 years of Howards who resisted

restlessness and stayed put in Maryland

CONTENTS

PREFACE

Iwas doing research on Americans' faith in movement when my own life forced me to weigh the risks and payoffs of relocating. I lost my job and faced the prospect of either moving to another part of the country or changing career paths. My wife and I had just married and bought a house, and we liked the New York neighborhood where we lived. My wife would have had to relocate as well, which she was willing to do even though she was flourishing in her tenured professorship at a nearby university. Many American men would have moved, either dragging their wives with them or leaving them behind. For me the choice was just as obvious: I stayed where I was, and shifted careers from professor to writer, of which *Restless Nation* is the first fruit. But in fact, I had simply played one American trump card, that of starting over, against a closely related one, that of moving. The two usually go together, but not always. This book is about the peculiarity in American character that encourages us to see moving as a solution to most of our problems.

Americans move in order to do better economically, to get in touch with the higher things in life, including their own souls, to adjust or flee their family ties, to pursue physical health, to escape what constrains them. This restlessness is especially characteristic of American men, who believe in a true inner self untouched by civilization, other people, or organized social life—a self they can move intact to a new location. Loyalty to place, like loyalty to people, feels like a trap. Yet I hope to show that restlessness can also be a trap, distorting our sense of the world around us and the possibilities it holds for us, raising expectations that cannot always be filled.

A New Yorker may seem an unlikely spokesman for loyalty to place, but that is only because of Americans' nostalgic sense that rural places are "good," while cities are treacherous. Different places have different virtues, and New Yorkers have shown enormous attachment to their neighborhoods, sometimes their blocks. Time after time they have marched into the streets to fend off some threat to their proud communities. Identities can be developed even on the basis of being "city people." Any place can feel like home, and that's a feeling we need to cultivate. My allegiance to New York is especially strong because I have lived in a lot of other places, and eventually chose the one I liked most. This is what I will later call the "search then settle" pattern, which I see as a way of moderating American restlessness.

This is a book about national character. If you spent your life in a dark box in the cellar, you might believe there is no such thing as national character. But if you have ever watched the news, read a novel, or traveled abroad, you have noticed national traits. This does not mean that everyone in a country is identical: not every American has to be the same for there to be a recognizable "American" character. Despite their impressive diversity, Americans are, on average, different from other people. Even though they and their ancestors have come from all around the world, from a staggering range of countries, Americans tend to share a number of recognizable traits that make them American. One reason is that certain kinds of people from all around the world have come here because they thought this was the best country for people like them: a self-fulfilling belief. *Restless Nation* attempts to describe and understand those similarities of vision and character. All countries are unique, but some are uniquer than others. The United States is at the top of the list.

Essays on American character have become unfashionable in recent years. Under pressure from streamlining deans, academic social scientists have been concerned to prove that they were doing science of much the same sort as physicists and biologists. Few really believed this, but social scientists set out to mimic the methods and units of the "hard" sciences, with the result that they began to study "brains" rather than minds, "semiotics" rather than cultures, "formal organizations" rather than societies, and "bureaucratic elites" rather than politics. There was no room any more for the subtleties of character, which result from the complex interplay of psychology, culture, national institutions, and a variety of social processes. And there was no "discipline," in the new scientific division of labor, assigned to such soft things. Even those in the humanities today study texts and narratives, not the people who write and read them.

National character studies, when they were last popular in the 1950s, had a variety of flaws that made them vulnerable to "scientific" attacks.

They did not always distinguish clearly between individuals and institutions, making the latter seem like a mysterious emanation from citizens' essential qualities, or from "the land." Scholars also frequently collapsed individual attitudes and broader cultural meanings, as though they were talking about some kind of group mind with a will of its own. There was little room for disagreement and conflict within a culture, little room for individual divergence from "the" national character. Finally, studies of American character in the 1950s had an annoying air of self-congratulation. American civic culture, having saved the world from fascism, was the ideal toward which other national cultures, if they matured properly, were supposedly headed. American freedoms represented everything good.

Radical critics of the 1960s made American institutions—big business, the military, government, universities—into symbols of everything bad. The people themselves disappeared, often assumed to be inherently good but corrupted by the false consciousness of mass culture and corporate advertising. Many of these critics eventually landed jobs in universities, where they discovered that the scientific side of marxism, rather than its political and critical side, offered nice career opportunities. Neither their structural critique nor their scientific pretensions allowed much room for something as delicate as national character.

Just as it was obvious in the 1950s, if poorly articulated, that people of different nations tended to have contrasting characters, it is clear today that the majority of Americans have not been duped by big business or Richard Nixon. If they vote conservatively, it is not because they have been tricked into it or because the poor (presumed to be radical) are excluded from voting. There is something in Americans' character that leads them—as it has throughout their history—to dislike socialism, to mistrust government, to fear and despise poor people, to dislike but also admire the rich. The concern with freedoms that observers half a century ago admired is still there, but it has a dark side the boosters did not wish to see: an individualism that sees markets as just, the poor and the rich as equally responsible for their fates, and the natural environment as a resource to be used up in pursuit of our own opportunities. Americans believe that people can start over, at any time, and make the kind of life they desire. This is a powerful ideal but also a dangerous trap.

I do not view national character as comprising primordial feelings and beliefs shared by all the people in a nation, which bubble up to color all their actions and institutions. There is nothing so mysterious about what makes Americans American. We have institutions, culture, and traditions shaping us in all sorts of traceable ways. Ideas are important, too, as in the images of the United States strong enough to motivate foreigners to travel thousands of hard miles to come here. The United States differs from other countries in several ways: the almost constant flow of immigrants, enormous natural wealth, and a history of wretched black-white relations are the most obvious. In this book I concentrate on the first two, saving the third for a later volume.

It's trendy to disparage the myth of the United States as a melting pot in which a single culture is created out of diverse immigrant traditions, but I think we do a surprisingly good job of Americanizing new immigrants and especially their children. I worry more about the kind of culture we socialize them into, one in which Americans have little attachment to either place or other people. One thing most immigrants share is a belief in America as a land of freedom and opportunity where their lives will be better, where individuals are free to forge their own destinies. "Restlessness" is my label for these beliefs, which center around physical migration as the key to material and spiritual salvation. The story of America is a story about movement.

Recent debates over immigration have either looked at its economic effects or slipped into racist overtones suggesting that people who look different must somehow act and "be" different. I trace the cultural and psychological effects of immigration as they ripple outward from the new arrivals. They teach us that the world is open to individual effort, especially in the form of starting over. For a variety of reasons, this is a lesson most Americans have absorbed, even those who have never met an immigrant (although that is hard to avoid). Ironically, some of the sharpest critics of immigration believe in a conservative individualism that is one of immigration's deepest legacies.

The same scientific movement that banished studies of national character almost destroyed geography as an academic discipline. Its characteristic intuition that place matters disappeared from intellectual agendas. If we do not ask why or how place matters to humans, we can never see what Americans might be missing in their nomadic disregard for it, what roots might mean for individuals and communities. Americans hold on to placelessness with a peculiar but proud embrace.

Every potential reader of this book must wonder, Do we need another study of American character? For reasons I hope to show, this is the language we use to discuss most moral issues, transforming them into questions about what is "truly" American, and what is un-American. By the end, I hope the reader will understand why national character is so important to Americans, and why we can never fully give up our intuition that we are different. We *are* different.

Most studies of national character single out one cause to explain everything. The obvious problem with such explanations is that they are wrong. The world is never that simple. The restless movement of Americans does not explain all our history and attitudes. But I think it accounts for a lot of them, perhaps more than any other single factor. With some qualifications and supplements, we can use restlessness to understand much of what has happened in the United States over the last four hundred years.

Restless Nation is only a first step in exploring what it is to be American, focusing on what gets people here and moves them around once here—especially men. But migration and masculinity are not the whole of American character. In a sequel, tentatively entitled *Yearning for Connection*, I hope to examine those Americans who have been more ambivalent about restlessness and the markets with which it is especially associated. Any number of American countertraditions have felt uneasy with the modern world's emphasis on change and movement, seeking either to manage the uncertainties of markets or to escape from them. Southern agrarians have lapsed into antebellum nostalgia; nineteenth-century women created a culture of domesticity sheltered from markets; a few religious traditions have claimed to find bedrock in the unseen world; many African Americans have forged a more communal culture of solidarity. Even many members of the white middle class have tried, especially through science, to find ways to manage the vicissitudes of markets. Only a few, beginning with Thoreau, have searched for a connection to the land around them.

Restless Nation contains some facts and figures. But statistical averages are of little help in understanding dreams and identities. For this we need autobiographies, novels, poems, letters, and a good deal of interpretation. We need to reconstruct those interior lives that are so important to Americans. Only one in ten Americans may be foreign born, but what a symbolic impact they have! Perhaps only one man in ten abandons his job and family to start life anew out west. But what do the other nine think about?

Almost one thousand undergraduates at New York University and Columbia endured the lectures out of which this book slowly emerged, and they deserve my deepest appreciation. One of them, Elisabeth Troni, became my research assistant until she gave in to restlessness one day. Drew Halfman took over and did a fine job of checking quotes and searching for figures, until he too went off to do field work. In the end,

Nitsan Chorev tracked down most of the photographs and tied up loose ends, also giving me commentary on the manuscript draft. The first four times I taught the course, I did so with Mark Roelofs, who helped shape the way I think about American politics and character. Nick and Bill Demas graciously shared their recollections—and a family photograph—of their father, whose story opens chapter 2. I would also like to thank Dorothy Nelkin, Wolf Heydebrand, Willie Jasso, Barbara Heyns, Juan Corradi, Alan Wolfe, Jess Benhabib, and Duncan Rice for helping to free me from the constraints of academic life so that I could pursue my own dream of becoming an independent writer. Sometimes starting over requires a push.

Mary Waters, one of the world's greatest experts on immigration, read two drafts of the book and aided me with sensible criticism and advice. On the kind of short notice only a dear friend can ask for, Chip Clarke also proved a ferocious critic, especially when it came to weak passages that needed excision. Sven Steinmo also commented on a draft. Others have read individual chapters, including Judy Gerson and the West Village Writers' Group. Once again Doug Mitchell has shown why he is a legendary editor—among other duties driving me many miles in his Dodge Caravan across dark countryside in search of good food. Robert Devens, Barbara Fillon, and Nick Murray were also both charming and helpful. Sarah Rosenfield again proved she is a brilliant sociologist and critic as well as the world's greatest spouse; my thanks for everything, including comments on yet another manuscript.

INTRODUCTION

An American will build a house in which to pass his old age and sell it before the roof is on; he will plant a garden and rent it just as the trees are coming into bearing; he will clear a field and leave others to reap the harvest; he will take up a profession and leave it, settle in one place and soon go off elsewhere with his changing desires. . . . At first sight there is something astonishing in this spectacle of so many lucky men restless in the midst of abundance.
—*Alexis de Tocqueville*

In the most widely read of American novels, Huckleberry Finn and an escaped slave named Jim float hundreds of miles down the Mississippi River, eluding suspicious and unsavory characters along the way. Set in the 1830s, the novel features Huck's struggle with his conscience over whether to turn Jim in to the authorities. He is convinced that he will go to Hell if he does not, for all the rules of his society support slavery and condemn escape. In the end, though, this young adolescent follows his personal impulses and fondness for Jim. The community that Jim and Huck have created on their little raft, despite the occasional tricks that Huck plays on his superstitious companion, exists outside the pressures of the "sivilized" world both are fleeing. Huck and Jim are not only apart from but better than the scoundrels they meet during their odyssey, superior to the social life they observe in a peculiar setting that is part South, part frontier. At the end of the novel, Jim settles down with his wife as a free man. But Huck is still on the move, famously declaring, "I reckon I got to light out for the Territory ahead of the rest, because Aunt Sally she's going to adopt me and sivilize me and I can't stand it. I been there before."[1] Tom Blankenship, Samuel Clemens's childhood companion and real-life model for Huck Finn, ended up in Montana.

In 1838, a real youth named Frederick Bailey also went on a journey, north instead of south, gaining his freedom by fleeing his native Maryland. Unlike Huck, Bailey had no moral qualms to overcome, for he clearly saw that slavery was evil. His only quandary was one of means, not ends. Some of his voyage was also by boat, in disguise as a sailor. His journey was filled with dangers, and he saw some of his companions killed for their efforts. Having changed his last name several times to avoid detection, upon settling into a new life in New Bedford, Massachusetts, he adopted the name Douglass. In reconstructing his thoughts years later, in the first of several autobiographies, he contrasted the push and pull of migration: "On the one hand, there stood slavery, a stern reality, glaring frightfully upon us,—its robes already crimsoned with the blood of millions, and even now feasting itself greedily upon our own flesh. On the other hand, away back in the dim distance, under the flickering light of the north star, behind some craggy hill or snow-covered mountain, stood a doubtful freedom—half-frozen—beckoning us to come and share its hospitality."[2]

Douglass kept moving and remaking himself. At a meeting one evening in Nantucket, when he was only twenty-three, he stood, and spoke, and was reborn as a gifted abolitionist speaker. He was soon paid to travel Massachusetts, then New England, and eventually the world to deliver his message. Although rarely at home, he moved his wife and growing family, first to Lynn, Massachusetts, then Rochester, and finally to Washington, D.C., moving through a series of bigger and better homes in each place. He remade himself in print as well, reworking the details of his life in three successive autobiographies, four if you count a major revision of the last one (they were the only books he wrote). He embodied his own message, of how a slave could become a man.

Here are two teenagers, one black and one white, one real and one fictional, one extremely mature and the other still a child. Both, however, found self-transformation through flight. Both left a society they found oppressive or evil; both expected something better somewhere else. For each of them, the journey was treacherous, full of con men and vendettas and mobs for Huck, posses, informants, and brutal punishments for Fred. In the end, each of them had to make a choice on his own, with no guidance from—in fact contrary to—society's institutions, rules, and authorities. For each, the turning point came in rejecting the organized life of society through movement. Both managed to start fresh new lives in a new part of the United States.

Huck and Fred illustrate several American traits I hope to unravel in this book. Our most important yet personal moments often come through movement, usually propelled by some form of escape, but also drawn by some kind of dream. The rich connotations of freedom—less doubtful to other migrants than it was to Fred—get embodied in a physical place: the territories for Huck, the North for Fred, the West for other Americans, America itself for potential immigrants around the world. A trip to that place means a new, better life. Most Americans also have a romantic belief that the individual is whole and untarnished outside of organized social life—neither Huck nor Fred learned much about himself or changed significantly during his trip. Whether you seek wealth or autonomy or inner peace, you can be true to yourself only by fleeing and starting over, leaving friends and jobs and sometimes even family. Our famous American individualism arises from movement. That restless motion begins with immigration, but it affects all of us—even those who stay put. Finally, as Americans, we exaggerate—just as they themselves did—the degree to which Huck and Fred journeyed as individuals. We forget how thoroughly Jim protected and guided Huck at all times. And to shield the underground movement, Douglass in his published account skipped over the dense network of slaves and abolitionists who helped him move north as well as the wife who financed his journey. In our minds, these are stories of individuals.

The imagination was just as active in Douglass's autobiographies, in which he reworked the details of his own life, as in Sam Clemens's work of fiction. Both men drew on common American themes in order to craft what they thought was a good or representative American life. They articulated very popular dreams: *Huckleberry Finn* is the most successful American novel, and Douglass the most widely read African American writer in college surveys of American literature. But the restless lives they crafted are not necessarily good for all Americans: these are the lives of men, and very young men at that. The restless life of self-creation has had less appeal to most women, who have often laughed at their men's dreams even as they accompanied them.

Faith in movement and actually moving are not the same thing. One lies in the realm of fantasy, movies, dreams, and novels like *Huckleberry Finn;* the other takes place in the world of economics and demographics and "real life." American men tend to be restless in both ways, since the two are closely related. If you believe in starting over, you are more likely to try it. And if you do it, especially if it works out well, you will believe in it and celebrate it. Movement and fantasies of movement are

logically distinct, but we'll see how they reinforce each other. Throughout American history there have been plenty of both.

Here's my recipe for the United States. Take an enormous territory, rich
with deep forests, the blackest soil, every manner of animal, vegetable,
and mineral, and endless navigable rivers and coasts. Exterminate most
of its native people. Then, over four hundred years, repopulate it with
immensely diverse folk, from all around the globe, whose only common
feature is their restlessness. They are the ones with the stamina, resources, health, and desire to get here despite immense obstacles. Many
are escaping social rigidities and political oppression at home, but almost all are pulled by a wondrous image of opportunity awaiting them
here. The liberties symbolized by the famous statue in New York harbor
cannot be divided neatly into political or religious, economic or cultural; immigrants may strive for any manner of freedom, from all constraints, whether by law, government, business, or custom.

Once here, they don't stop moving. They continue to migrate all over
this huge land. They put their families in Conestoga wagons and move
to California. They toss their clothes into Dodge Caravans and go to
Texas in search of jobs. They sell their belongings, fly to Hawaii, and live
on a boat to get away from it all, to start over. The literal frontier, with
free land for homesteads, disappeared one hundred years ago, but
Americans still treat their country as a figurative frontier with resources
to exploit in pursuit of their dreams. Just as they or their ancestors began their lives anew when they came to this country, Americans are willing to do it again and again until they get it right. Constraining families,
unsavory reputations, bankruptcy, dead-end jobs, and oppressive social
ties can all be left behind. The automobile—which was invented in Europe but found its first mass market in the United States—is the perfect
embodiment of this restlessness, the most seductive means of individual movement except for those archetypal dreams where you glide
along without trying—better, perhaps, since cars are enclosed spaces,
little homes you can take with you, where you can play music as loudly
as you want, eat dinner, spend the night, even have sex.

Samuel Clemens, for example, was on the move most of his life. The
only job that held him longer than a year as a young man was one that
kept him moving constantly as a Mississippi riverboat pilot. He left his
hometown of Hannibal, Missouri, at age seventeen, telling his mother
he would remain in St. Louis but all the time intending to go to New
York. He lasted about two months in each of those cities before moving

to Philadelphia, where he stayed only a bit longer before fleeing to Washington, D.C. Then back to Philadelphia, then west to return to his family, who had themselves in the meantime moved to Muscatine, Iowa. His adventures returned him to St. Louis, thence to Keokuk, Iowa (rejoining his family, who moved almost as frequently as he), and eventually to Cincinnati. Three months there, and he was on his way to New Orleans, barely twenty-one years old. He would spend much of the rest of his life traveling the world, fulfilling his teenage vow that he would never be trapped by a place.

You can be restless, of course, without going anywhere—maybe even more so. We don't all move West. But we think about it. We reassure ourselves that we could, that we always have an escape if we need it. And we weigh this option against others. If our boss fired us or family responsibilities overwhelmed us, we could always get in the car and go. Like Huck, we could light out for the territory, whatever literal or figurative frontier attracted us. It's a fantasy—and mostly a man's fantasy— but fantasies have real effects. We believe in the possibility of fresh starts even when we don't pursue them. There's always California.

The ability to escape the burden of the past, both collective and individual, is the central dream of the modern world. Over the past several hundred years, modernizing cultures have freed individuals from all sorts of constraints: a man need no longer follow the occupation of his father; status and lifestyle too are no longer hereditary; economic innovation is respected and rewarded; we are free to choose our associates, our residences, even (some of us) our political leaders. In many versions of the modern dream, economic markets symbolize the freedom to maneuver that individuals crave. The Americas were discovered and colonized just as this modern vision of freedom was first blossoming, especially in that nation most responsible for settling North America. The English of the seventeenth century boasted of their love of freedom, in contrast to Continental despotism, and the full vision, in its most radical form, could be transplanted here. This tight fit between America's self-image and the excitement of modernity is the reason this single country has been such a powerful symbol throughout the world: of freedom for those who believe in the modern project, of evil chaos for those who fear it. From cultures around the world, America has always attracted those most interested in these modern freedoms and eager to take advantage of them. The hopes and circumstances of the country's founding continue to resonate.

There has been migration and travel throughout human history. But most of the migrations, like the one that brought humans to the

Americas fifteen thousand years ago, involved nomads in pursuit of game or refugees from starvation or war. Few had specific destinations in mind. Travel and adventure have also been celebrated in world literature, usually as a source of new information and understanding. The heroes of epics and romances went off to test themselves, but their goal was always to return home. In one of the most famous cases, home was an obsession with Odysseus, who had never wanted to leave Ithaca in the first place. (It is easier to be loyal to a place when you are king of it.) The adventures of Herakles, Odysseus, and Jason were primarily a form of torture imposed by unfriendly gods. In the picaresque novels of the early modern period, travel was part of one's education. The point was to grow and learn, but eventually to find a role for oneself in the society (and social class) one was born into. Even the Portuguese, Spanish, and other explorers who mapped the Americas and so many other places intended to return home, hopefully richer for their discoveries. International, one-way migration to start a new life in a new land was something different and relatively new to the modern world; it is the dream upon which America was founded.

The novelty of the Americas was nothing short of startling and wondrous to Europeans. They first hoped that some of the cultures here might embody a sound alternative to what many perceived as sclerotic and corrupt European nations, that the noble savages here might be more noble than savage. When the Indians proved uncooperative or opaque, Europeans began to view the new land mass as a blank slate upon which they could build their own utopian visions, new cultures which could be rationally constructed from scratch in a way that would prevent the religious wars, economic scarcities, and political oppressions of the Old World. Utopian communities, especially religious ones, have been part of American culture ever since. They have proven short-lived, however, since individual members regularly decide that they can do even better, founding a newer sect or leaving for the latest frontier. The same centrifugal impulse that leads people to found new cults then encourages them to leave those cults.

The United States has always been distinctive and celebrated for its sheer size, its sparse settlement, and its great raw wealth. But geography is not destiny. What matters is how the land and its riches are felt and interpreted through culture. Immigrants arrive with certain intentions. Americans expect certain kinds of room to maneuver, especially to start over. They are afraid of many kinds of ties and obligations, especially to place. They make certain assumptions about how individuals are related to society or how government is related to the economy.

Their individualistic worldview is encouraged by the land but not determined by it. A range of cultural signals send the same message: that individuals are in control of their lives because they can get up and move. Far from being an emanation of or adaptation to the land and conditions that immigrants encountered, this expectation was part of what they brought with them. America was a symbol in world culture before it was a destination, and its image as the land of liberty was first crafted elsewhere, out of the psychological needs of foreigners. Like many great Americans themselves, our national character is an import.

America has remained the land of the dream, capable of stirring all sorts of ambitions in those who wish to come here and those who have arrived. America's famous optimism comes from the confidence that you can always find a new place that is right (or at least better) for you, a place where you can start over on a better track. Sometimes this confidence has been reinforced by religious images of the promised land; sometimes it has been linked to a notion of historical progress and technological advance. It has frequently led Americans to try things that others would not. One result has been a vibrant and flexible economy, always changing to meet new needs, thanks especially to immigrants who are not bound to old ways of doing things.

The movement and freedom of the American dream also have their dark side. The natural environment was one of the first victims of restlessness, since few Americans grow loyal to the places they inhabit. A handful of pioneers like Daniel Boone may have adopted Indian ways, but the dominant view saw the land and its resources as something to be used up in creating a new society. For men, land was merely a means, especially of getting rich, even if it was destroyed or made fallow in the process. It was not a habitat in which to settle down permanently. With the first colonists, the entire country took on the feel of a boomtown, full of rowdy young men (and a few women) hoping to strike it rich and then move on when the soil was depleted or the gold mined. Even today, when boomtowns are more likely to be oilfields or construction sites, they feel transitory. They are filled with drinking, gambling, and violence—apparently what young men do when women are scarce. Throughout most of American history the frontier and the immigrant cities were similar in being crowded with young men hoping to make their way, visualizing their surroundings as a means to this end.

But disregard for the physical landscape is echoed by disrespect for the social, for people as well as places. There is a surprising anxiety at the heart of restlessness, for American restlessness is economic and cultural as well as geographic. People want to move up as they move around. In fact that's the main reason for moving around. Americans not only hope but expect to advance, for this is a long-standing feature of our self-definition. We believe, against most evidence, that the United States has more social mobility than other countries. This is the reason, we say to ourselves in self-congratulation, that immigrants wish to come here. Almost all commentators have recognized this as the crux of the American dream: a faith that hard work will pay off with material (and sometimes spiritual) rewards. Many studies of American character have confused the dreams with the reality, with a self-congratulatory ring to them.

The hidden costs of this dream of mobility are considerable. The route upward is rarely as easy as we expect it to be. Most Americans fail to move very far through the hierarchy; some

Critics of American culture are always saying we are not as connected as we used to be: we no longer feel family and community obligations, no longer join clubs and associations, or feel the same loyalties to the people and places around us. American society, they say, is fragmenting. As one recent critic put it, Americans are "bowling alone." These accusations of individualism are accurate enough in their descriptions of contemporary life. But they are nostalgically wrong in thinking that this lack of connection is a new thing. Americans, especially American men, have always been willing to sneak off in the middle of the night. How else explain the fact that this same "communitarian" tradition of criticism has been around for four hundred years?

even go down. Our economic aspirations, as a result, encourage cultural anxiety. Americans constantly look for signs of how far they have come by examining how they dress, what they drive, where they live. Their lifestyles become yardsticks for their upward mobility, but only when compared to how others live. Sometimes they emulate the tastes of those above them on the rung they hope to occupy next. Even more, they condemn the styles of those below them, who turn out to be uncomfortably close. Unlike geographic restlessness, this interior anxiety can never be alleviated. You can never be rich enough. Our very expectations breed disappointment. "Every little ragged boy," a nineteenth-century critic complained, "dreams of being President or a John Jacob Astor. The dream may be a pleasant one while it lasts, but what of . . . the excited, restless, feverish life spent in the pursuit of phantoms?" The "everlasting struggle for wealth" leaves "little of recreation and enjoyment of life."[3]

Our uneasiness leads us to moralize lifestyles, so that culture becomes a moral gauge for placing ourselves and others. We look upwards at "the rich." We admire them and let them keep a large proportion of their incomes. But we are also concerned that they succeed in the "right" way, through virtuous hard work rather than luck or ruthlessness, and even while we envy them, we may condemn them for moral transgressions. Because we believe that economic markets are composed of small individuals, not government and big corporations, we are inclined to think that they are fair in how they distribute society's rewards. We blame the rich for what they do with their gains, not for making them. They have won the great lottery. They are living out our fondest dreams. We also cast our moralizing vision downwards, toward the poor, who embody our nightmares. We can reassure ourselves by despising others. Those at the bottom, we insist, must be there because of their own traits. The underside of American history is that we blame those we leave behind (or hope to) in our upward and outward movement.

The unfamiliar lifestyles of immigrants have always made them useful targets, and the same stereotypes appear again and again. At the same time that employers advertised in China to lure workers to the United States, popular imagery portrayed the Chinese as lazy opium addicts, unable to care for themselves and inevitably dependent on the rest of us. In the latter part of the nineteenth century there was the same talk of collapsing standards in the schools so familiar today. There was nostalgia for a simpler time and place, the homogeneity of small towns where everyone knew each other (a situation that had never existed in America)—before "they" arrived. The same things were said about Irish and German immigrants in the 1850s, the Chinese in the 1870s, the Jews and Italians in the 1890s, and poor, inner-city immigrants today. Once they have made it, immigrants are valuable proof of the American dream; until then we dismiss them as hopeless and unworthy.

Culture tells us how to look at the world—what to see and what to ignore. Immigration shapes American culture, not only by giving us people to fear at the bottom, but by showing that upward movement is possible. Stories about immigrants help focus our attention on individual movement through society, for no one has done more to take active control of their destinies. As a culture we readily understand stories which concentrate on individual choices, actions, and rewards. Americans have a hard time seeing economic, social, or demographic structures, the opportunities and constraints that affect everyone's life chances; we see only the individuals moving through these structures.

Our notorious individualism does not mean that we care about our-selves most—Americans can be extremely altruistic—but that we view the world as composed of individuals. We see markets as composites of individual choices; we see culture as individual creativity; we see in-comes as rewards for individual effort. Anything else—governments, corporations, organizations—is an artificial intrusion to be ignored or resisted. Because we attribute most of what happens to people to their own traits and choices rather than to their structural position, much less luck, we often fall back on distorted stereotypes: Irish immigrants are poor because they won't work; Mexicans are dirty because they don't care about hygiene; Italians live five to a room because they lack basic decencies; African Americans in the inner city are poor because they have babies at too young an age. How can they remain poor in the land of opportunity?

The deep, interior self—the "real" foundation of the individual—is the starting point for how Americans understand the world. Like the Puritans, who hoped to decipher people's predetermined destiny in the afterlife by examining their behavior and relative success in this life, we care most about a deep moral character we can never see. We assume that all Americans control their own lives, create their own destinies. Inner character leads to choices, and personal choices determine how someone fares in life. The individual self has a deep reality, out of which other traits and actions arise.

Markets fit neatly with this view of the world; governments do not. Americans want to believe that markets consist of individuals making untrammeled choices, and so we have trusted markets to do things such as allocate wealth. Americans fear government as intrusive bureau-cracy, capable only of thwarting our desires. Markets enable restless movement; governments constrain it. One represents our dreams; the other, our nightmares.

Immigrants, who have been arriving in North America almost contin-uously for four hundred years, have reinforced cultural and moral feel-ings like these. New arrivals, still at the bottom, give shape to our fears and anxieties, give us concrete targets for expressing our dislikes. In con-trast, older, more successful immigrants reassure us that we live in the land of opportunity and mobility, that the dream is alive. In both cases, we see individuals and their families making strategic choices and taking charge of their lives. Forget the recurrent debates over the economic ef-fects of immigration; the deepest effects are on our cultural images.

Our grandparents, the family legend often goes, came to this country penniless and yet worked their way up and out in the face of vicious prejudice. They lived on the Lower East Side so that we could live in Westchester. They worked hard so that we could go to City College or Harvard. And this legend is often true. Immigrants are unusual people, with special drive, ambition, and talent. Many families and towns around the world have chosen their most promising young men and then pooled their resources to send them to America. They in turn have saved enough to bring others here, establishing elaborate social networks that are an important but invisible structural resource. The historical photographs of Ellis Island, the cramped tenements of the Lower East Side, the tales of discrimination and appalling first jobs—all these bits of collective memory emphasize the hardships of coming to America. To vindicate such suffering, this country just *had* to be a golden land of opportunity. Many immigrants have overcome initial poverty and prejudice to succeed in America. Their stories are dramatic, moving, and memorable. Americans are right to be proud of them.

But these stories about our forebears suggest that anyone else who works hard can achieve the same success. Clawing one's way out of poverty is the essence of Americanization, a step away from the stigma of being poor in the consummate land of opportunity and wealth. The myth of successful immigrant ancestors—myth because the truth and the exaggeration interweave seamlessly—overlooks the unusual things that restless immigrants bring with them: sometimes material resources, more often cultural ones like education or job skills, and always a restlessness that translates into tough, driven, and often "difficult" personalities. They come to America in pursuit of economic success and single-mindedly win it—at least the ones we hear about, the ones who stay to raise families. Most of the losers return home.

Americans have come to believe that migration and starting over are normal. Yet the norm, throughout the world, is to stay put, to heed the demands of family, community, and identity. Less than 2 percent of the world's population today consists of people who have had the drive to migrate. We easily forget how unusual American restlessness is. We condemn anyone who remains poor because they are unwilling to uproot themselves in pursuit of improvement. Only with the constant presence of immigrants throughout our history could we have maintained such unnaturally high expectations of ourselves.

Immigrants have sustained both the dream and the nightmare of American mythology. They were the ones who, able to compare the new land with the old, created an "American" identity at a time when the native-born were more likely to think of themselves as Virginians or Yankees rather than Americans. Their transformation from unwashed mass to successful tycoons is the essence of America. The lower they be-gin, the more impressive their ascent. The greater the sin, the grander the salvation.

Our culture does little to alleviate our restlessness. The United States is the most anxious and the most unequal of the industrial societies, but also the most religious—an ironic development for the first country to cut off official government support for religion. The very competition that "disestablishment" created in the early nineteenth century sparked an era of remarkable Christian fervor that saw the rapid growth of Bap-tists and Methodists and the founding of many new churches, from the Church of Jesus Christ of Latter-Day Saints to the African Methodist Episcopal Church. Instead of curbing our strident individualism, itin-erant preachers and fractious sects reinforced the idea that each per-son's religious feelings were as important as another's, so that no central authority should tell us what to believe. Once again, Americans were re-sponsible for their own souls and their own destinies. Religion has pumped up our anxieties, not assuaged them.

Nor have the arts been helpful in challenging the American myth of self-made success, for they have regularly glorified flight. From Cooper and Whitman to Kerouac and Pynchon, the characters of our fiction have despised organized social life, not to mention the formal authori-ties who represent it. But instead of fighting them, they flee them. Huck Finn gets on the raft and floats off. John Updike's Rabbit gets in his Toyota and drives up Route 95, rejecting the demands of family and civ-ilization. This romantic view of the individual, who is most natural and good when avoiding formal organizations, social commitments, and government, only reinforces our restlessness. Men's heroes wear furs and live on the fringes of society. Today, when they can't be Daniel Boone or Cooper's deerslayer, Natty Bumppo—and very few ever could—men use therapeutic language and drums to discover a wild man within them. The languages of the Idaho survivalist and Upper West Side ther-apist differ enormously, yet they are based on similar visions of the place of the individual in society. Individuals are good, institutions bad. Since Emerson, religion and the arts have frequently criticized Ameri-can materialism, but in the name of an even deeper individualism, an internal spiritual restlessness.

Art creates its own reality, and we rarely confuse it with the world of the everyday. But the realm of drama and dreams affects us deeply. In it we work out who we would like to be, what our deepest dilemmas are, what our range of feelings can be, who our heroes and villains are. Art builds character—especially for Americans, who take their art very seriously as a lesson. For us, it is more a form of moral education than a source of pleasure. Recent debates over school curricula, after all, are not about kids having fun through reading, but about the sources of American moral character and our deepest identity. Americans go to museums to improve themselves, not for the sheer fun of it.

While the arts preach to the upper classes that individuals come first, both morally and factually, fundamentalist Christians and other religious leaders deliver the same message to the lower classes. Core beliefs that individuals create their own destinies and that civilization's institutions are corrupt, persisting throughout American history, have sometimes been mobilized by the Left and sometimes by the Right. They have been used to assail the authority of priests, lawyers, doctors, business, and the rich (as they were in the 1790s, 1890s, and 1930s) as well as to attack immigrants, the poor, and government (as in the 1850s, 1920s, and 1980s). In classic American populism, our anger went in both directions at once. We can hate the top and the bottom of society and even see them as united in a sinister alliance. We hate authority and vote for politicians who rail against it. We use our government to fight government.

Restlessness is not the whole of American history. It is especially the story of American men. Throughout our history, women's sensibilities have provided a counterpoint, and occasionally a brake, on men's restlessness. Until the twentieth century, though, men made the important decisions, established our political and economic institutions, and rarely consulted their wives in doing so. Women have only recently begun to make inroads into this dominance. Only in 1946 did women begin to outnumber men in the American population, a situation long the norm in other industrialized countries.

There may be some truth to ancient images—fertility goddess, Mother Earth, Mother Nature, and so on—that tie women to the land. Few women were enthusiastic about moving west, following the frontier; many stayed home, even without their husbands, and most of the rest wished they had. When they went, they were more interested in planting a garden, having a view, and settling down, even while their husbands plowed the land right up to the door and looked for opportunities to move again. Until the 1930s, the majority of immigrants were men, hoping to establish themselves before trying to find or fetch a bride, or send for a family left behind. Only since World War II have women had the political clout to implement, now and then, their view of their surroundings as a place to settle down and raise a family. In the last twenty years women have founded thousands of "not in my backyard" groups to protect their neighborhoods and environments from corporations and governments that see only profit in them. Where men recognize an opportunity for making money, women envision a place to live. Women are more likely than men to feel rooted or, as many feminists say, connected.

Women are no longer as tied to the home as they once were; most have jobs and the independence that working brings. But they are still the ones who usually raise children and care for aging parents. They are encouraged from an early age to be sensitive to those around them. Their desire for connection—perhaps weaker than in the past—is no innate, biological trait; it is learned every day from their surroundings.

Men have tried hard to ignore women's influence. His mother and wife get short mentions in Frederick Douglass's autobiographies, since they are irrelevant to his theme of taking control of his own life. In *Huckleberry Finn*, women represent everything Huck is fleeing, a theme that tends to hide the fact that Jim is escaping to reunite with his wife. Huck has no sexual interest in women, and Clemens ridicules the women's culture of sentimental novels and maudlin poetry. American men insist they are making their lives on their own, so they either ignore women's aid or fear women's overtures of connection and stability. Restless individuals find it safer to pay for sex and avoid expectations and entanglements.

Restlessness depends on fantasy: optimism about a new start, the vision of a new self, a new utopian world. Men have always been the dreamers, able to concoct elaborate visions in their minds. Whether those alternative worlds were mathematics or music, politics or religion, science fiction or material ambition, they involve some disconnection from the immediate world around one, from the immediate obligations and emotional bonds of daily life. Men have usually been more ready than women to sever these bonds in pursuit of something new.

Women offer connections—to people as well as to places. This is what restless men fear, at least when they are young. But connections turn out to be what life is all about, and no one dies happy who dies alone. Huck and Fred were teenagers when they made their famous journeys. Most immigrants have been men in their teens and twenties. By the time they are old enough to think about roots, it is often too late. The trees have been cut, the house sold. A lifetime of anxious restlessness has rarely offered much happiness, even to those who have "made it." What is more, economic success at the dawn of the new millennium depends on human relations more than on continual movement, on bonds with clients more than on mining gold. American culture desperately needs new habits and sentiments. The geographic frontier officially closed one hundred years ago. Perhaps it is time to close it culturally.

But how? How do we encourage a sense of connection to place? We can begin by removing the many ways our government subsidizes migration, from tax breaks for relocation to the enormous subsidies given to highway construction. Increased awareness of local bioregions, accompanied by the kind of respect that environmentalists promote, might also help. Connections to place and to people go hand in hand, and strengthening one may strengthen the other. And if nothing else, we could at least push our nation to live up to its attractive ideals instead of using those ideals to mask a very different reality. Social mobility is a powerful dream, worthy of fulfillment. To the extent that we wish to continue our movement, we should at least make sure it has the payoffs we expect.

Fortunately, there are signs that Americans are beginning to settle down and grow up. Fewer of us are immigrants, and more of us are women. We are twice as old, at the median, than in the colonial period. Fewer jobs depend on boomtown exploitation of the natural world, and more on symbols and interpersonal skills in services, information, communications, and entertainment industries. Most Americans have reconciled themselves to a federal government of a size that would have once been unimaginable. There are lively social movements—with ecology and feminism at the forefront—that promote an appreciation of connections among people and with nature. Increasing numbers of Americans care more about the quality of their lives than their bank accounts, a "post-material" vision that in some versions works against restlessness. We are more restless than other cultures, less so than our own ancestors—and moving in the right direction. It may be possible to retain the hope that movement offers while reducing some of its more harmful effects.

In the rest of this book, I hope to demonstrate how a cluster of restless beliefs and practices are related to one another. Chapter 1 recounts the dreams that America has embodied throughout its history, the appeal and the ideal, what this country has meant to people even before they came here. Then I turn to their coming. Chapter 2 examines who has come and why, what happened to them, and how they have affected our national images of success. In chapter 3 I address the many ways in which Americans believe in the possibility of starting over and making their lives better, from ubiquitous name changing to reworking the facts of one's life in autobiographies. Immigration and internal migration, in turn, encourage us to view our environment as a resource to exploit, not a place to settle down, as chapter 4 describes. Americans learned very early how to squander their natural wealth. These chapters depend heavily on evidence from the preindustrial period of American history, when so many of our traditions were established.

In later chapters, my emphasis shifts (slightly) to trends and institutions more characteristic of the industrial society that arose in the nineteenth century. In chapter 5, I argue that the belief in starting anew and the resulting boomtown mentality together encourage expectations of upward mobility but also create anxieties and fears about how well we are doing, since we cannot easily overlook or dismiss failures. Most of all, we have a "market vision" of a society composed of individuals. We see markets, chapter 6 shows, more easily than we see the bonds of community. Government, in particular, has had negative connotations ever since it was embodied in the British crown. Organized labor, dominated at crucial moments by immigrants suspicious of government, refused to establish a political party to pursue social justice—a choice that has proven fateful for public policies ever since.

Religion and the arts, evaluated in chapter 7, have rarely provided any relief, encouraging rather than tempering our individualist anxiety and escapism. They typically foster spiritual rather than material seeking. At least the romantic countertradition sometimes values the natural environment as a source of inspiration, even though it retains a suspicion of organized social life. In chapter 8, I examine men's fear of women and family, as demonstrated in our high divorce rates. Children, it turns out, are the biggest victims of restless movement. The conclusion looks to some practical solutions that might alleviate the costs of restlessness while retaining its exciting promise of freedom.

1   *The Land of the Dream*

In happy climes, the seat of innocence,
    Where nature guides and virtue rules,
Where men shall not impose for truth and sense
    The pedantry of courts and schools . . .
Westward the course of empire takes its way;
    The four first Acts already past,
A fifth shall close the Drama with the day;
    Time's noblest offspring is the last.
—*Bishop George Berkeley*

The American writer inhabits a country at once the dream of Europe and a fact of history; he lives on the last horizon of an endlessly retreating vision of innocence.
—*Leslie Fiedler*

When I jog down to the Battery at the southern tip of Manhattan, the Statue of Liberty is barely noticeable across New York harbor. Some mornings she disappears altogether in the fog. From the land, this grand symbol of America appears small and insignificant. But from a boat, for example passing on its way to Ellis Island, she looms quite large. And the myth she represents, before one has ever set foot on American soil, is similarly unbounded, unchecked by realities. For Europeans, America was created as an idea and ideal before it was explored and mapped, and the symbolism of America has continued to outstrip the reality ever since. The image was crafted to match perfectly a dream of freedom and mobility that many Europeans, and in later centuries others, have embraced as the modern world grew out of feudal hierarchies and other caste systems. It has been a peerless blank screen on which to project emotions, aspirations, and in some cases fears. America is an impressive ideal.

Bishop Berkeley, whose fame was due to a philosophy in which ideas were more important than material reality, was articulating in his poem the common understanding of the 1720s: that empires rise and fall in succession, from Greece to Rome, to France and Spain, to Britain, and presumably next to the Americas, which he expected to be the culmination of Western civilization.[1] Berkeley, who lived in the Rhode Island colony for several years, even expressed the reason: natural innocence, in contrast to courtly artificiality, supports virtue. Faith in the westward direction of this movement would blossom within the United States as well as in England, as would belief in America's innocence. For Europeans, and the rest of the world, America has remained a vital symbol, sometimes good, sometimes bad, but always important. In the absence of experience, it is easy to attribute to a distant land every manner of extreme trait. The myth of American opportunity, in particular, has flourished around the world for several centuries, drawing the ambitious from almost every generation to these shores. This is the place you go to start over.

Immigrants know some things about their destination, but not others. Prior immigrants, official policymakers, even poets have varying reasons for distorting the truth. Immigrants' desires shape their perceptions. Especially when the pull of their new country is as strong as the push of their old—about which they know *too* much—their migration is a leap into the ideal in pursuit of a dream that they and others have nurtured. (Because for antimodernists that dream is instead a nightmare, our symbolic position as the most modern of countries has helped earn us the title of Great Satan among Islamic fundamentalists.) So the American fable has been fondly sustained by generations of immigrants and would-be immigrants. We all live by our symbols, and America has represented many things for people around the world. Foremost has been freedom, even though this has been defined quite differently by groups ranging from the Pilgrims in 1620 to the Tiananmen protestors who constructed a monument looking much like the Statue of Liberty in 1989.

This restless ambition, the constant motion in search of better lives, is not exclusively American; it is perhaps the defining trait of the modern world. Vast populations have severed their ties to the land, ties that stretched back into the depths of prehistory. They moved to the cities, enlisted in the new armies of the nation-state, became workers in industrial factories. There is an ability, willingness, and desire to define oneself as an individual, and through one's own choices, rather than being designated entirely as the son of so-and-so, member of this or that

village, and Lord whosit's serf. This is a new image of human identity—
and potential. America's ability to represent this new impulse to people
around the world—and to sustain it when they come here—makes us
the most "modern" of nations.

Movement is a common feature of modern societies, brought on at
the dawn of the modern age by market economies, improved transportation, and the European conquest of most of the world. It was later
reinforced by industrialization, urbanization, and careers based on
movement within far-flung organizations or professions. The first European colonists in North America were simply the far western fringe of
a roiling movement going on all over Europe. But because of the timing
of its settlement, this modern restlessness was given full rein in the
United States, built into our institutions in ways not possible in "Old
World" societies. Or in most other colonial societies, where indigenous
populations better survived the onslaught and retained many of their
own traditions and expectations. North America was emptied of most
of its inhabitants, ready to be filled with Europe's emerging projects and
ambitions.

"In the beginning, all the world was America," wrote another English-
man, John Locke, whose philosophy was opposed to Berkeley's in every
way except for the important role they allotted to America (and their
shared interest in colonizing it). Locke meant that it was a pristine
blank slate, upon which all the problems of European societies had not
yet appeared. Different thinkers and groups saw differing problems in
their own societies, but all believed these were absent in America.
Whatever they disliked, they could escape it in the New World. Whatever culture and civilization eventually did to humans, they had not yet
affected America's inhabitants, old and new. And all America was California, the place that, for Americans themselves, would eventually ab-
sorb the aspirations and connotations that foreigners attributed to the
whole country. Such images grew out of the psychic needs of other peoples, out of their apparent need to believe that, somewhere, perfection
reigned. *The American dream was born in Europe.*

America was the most exciting discovery in an age of exciting discoveries. According to Tzvetan Todorov, it ushered in the modern era: "The
history of the globe is of course made up of conquests and defeats, of
colonizations and discoveries of others; but it is in fact the conquest of
America that heralds and establishes our present identity; even if every
date that permits us to separate any two periods is arbitrary, none is

more suitable, in order to mark the beginning of the modern era, than the year 1492."[2] Europeans knew of the other great land masses, Asia and Africa, but not the Americas. Here was a surprise, a place about which they knew nothing. It inspired awe and wonder, and left everything to their imaginations. As a later Dutch historian wrote, America became the place "onto which all identification and interpretation, all dissatisfaction and desire, all nostalgia and idealism seeking expression could be projected."[3] In the beginning, everyone's understanding of America was imaginative projection.

Even before its discovery, Europeans had a symbolic place ready for America. "Throughout the Middle Ages," says another historian, "Europeans had posited the existence of a place—for a time to the east, but mostly to the west of Europe—without the corruptions and disadvantages of the Old World."[4] This yearning for an earthly paradise, not unlike the Garden of Eden, was no doubt stimulated by wide recognition of Europe's social problems, including poverty, disease, war, and a general sense of disorder. As the term implies, the New World would be the antithesis of the Old. Only twenty-four years after Columbus's first voyage, Thomas More located his *Utopia* in the New World, giving both a name and a likely location for a literary tradition that has continued to this day. Initially, in the utopian genre, native Americans were often thought to be living in a kind of golden age not unlike that of early Greece, but as colonization got under way this impression gave way to the more self-serving view of them as nasty and cowardly barbarians, fit for enslavement. Europeans quickly gave up hope of discovering somewhere among them a perfect social system that could provide "methods of reforming European society," as More put it.[5] Instead they began to see America as a site for their own utopian ventures. At any rate, the natives never interested the Europeans as much as the land itself and what riches it might contain. From the start, their utopian dreams included material abundance.

At first Europeans were enthusiastic about America as a source of treasure, to be settled only if profitability required it. On his first voyage, Christopher Columbus set the tone for his own later voyages, and those of most other European explorers, in his obsession with gold. As he sailed from island to island in the Caribbean, he interrogated—roughly, given the lack of any shared language—all the natives he encountered about where he might find it. On one island he instructed his men not to accept gifts lest the natives realize that he primarily desired their gold. When he saw what he took to be small gold ornaments, the native wearing them "told" him (through hand signals, apparently, fancifully interpreted by Columbus) of a powerful king with large vessels of gold on another island. Columbus immediately set sail. His surviving writings keep up a constant monologue about gold, and in one case he "proved" that gold must be nearby due to the beauty of a certain island, and the way a river came into the sea. Often, he cited the arguments of respected authors rather than direct empirical evidence to the effect that gold must abound in these new lands. Hoping to inspire financing for future voyages (he made four), he assiduously laid out the hope of great profits. But as he brought back no gold, with each voyage he more and more emphasized the promise of *future* wealth. Postponed fulfillment did not dim anyone's hopes and may have even heightened them.

The image of America as the culmination of modern dreams was partly the result of good public relations work like Columbus's, a campaign that began long before the English colonies were founded. Most of the early explorers were Spanish, and a striking monotony pervades their accounts. They shared Columbus's concern with gold and silver, questioning all natives they encountered about where they might find such treasures. Using one or two unfortunate captives as translators, they received predictable answers: We don't have what you want, but they most definitely have entire cities made of gold just a little farther along. In other words, please move on and pester our neighbors and rivals. Fantasies of great wealth made the conquistadores deeply gullible when it came to any tale of gold—as did their need to secure future financing. Indian translators quickly caught on, as they saw others put to death for disappointing news.

Many explorers simply saw what was not there. One, traveling along the Gulf Coast west of Florida in 1520, saw "many rivers carrying fine gold, as the Indians demonstrated by certain samples, and also they wore many gold jewels in their noses and ears and on other parts of their bodies." In Canada in 1534, Frenchman Jacques Cartier saw a "good store of stones, which we esteemed to be Diamonds," as well as "the best iron in the world," and "certain leaves of fine gold as thick as a man's nail."[6] If these men saw anything at all, the diamonds were other rock crystals, the gold a form of pyrite. The English followed suit with Martin Frobisher's three voyages to the Canadian arctic in 1576–78, financed by private investors. Frobisher returned from the first with an Inuit and his kayak, and a black rock. His main investor, after considerable searching, found an assayer willing to declare that the rock was gold ore. This opinion helped finance the other voyages, on which Frobisher hauled back as much as two thousand tons of the black rock (eventually used, in one of history's most expensive construction

By 1595 many were discounting the promise of easy gold, but not Sir Walter Raleigh. He was out of favor with Queen Elizabeth, partly because he had seduced and married one of her maids of honor, Bess Throckmorton. (His unsuccessful Roanoke colony, 1585–87, could not have helped his reputation either.) The Raleighs were broke, living on his Dorset estate, and Sir Walter desperately hoped that a new expedition would return him to favor: an opportunity, as he put it in a poem, "To seeke new worlds, for golde, for prayse, for glory." Bess wisely begged him not to go, but he managed to find backers and was soon tromping around the Orinoco delta in Guiana (present-day Venezuela). He found nothing but hostile Indians and some Spanish to kill. His luck did not improve when he returned, and when James became king in 1603, he put Raleigh in the Tower of London. He was released in 1616 to make another trip to the Orinoco, but this time the penalty for failure was more severe: upon his empty-handed return, he was beheaded (under the original charge of treason). Because of economic and political pressures, Raleigh's American ventures were true dreams of desperation.

projects, to pave roads around Bristol). So strong were European expectations (and investments) that the New World *had* to be filled with treasure. Here was wishful thinking at its most potent.

The only surprise in the history of early exploration is that many fantasies were fulfilled. Large quantities of silver and gold were indeed discovered: gold on Hispaniola almost immediately, a much larger supply of it in Peru in the 1530s, silver in Mexico in the 1540s. The flow of treasure back to Spain helped it become Europe's preeminent power in just a few decades, although the flow of precious metals did not peak until 1600. The Americas were actually living up to their stupendous reputation.

But gold and silver treasures were exceptional, especially in North America, and gradually the smarter or more disillusioned explorers came to see the land itself, rather than what was hidden inside it, as America's greatest wealth. Pedro de Castañeda spent several years in the early 1540s wandering with Coronado through the heart of what is now the United States, penetrating as far north as Kansas, but only later did he come to appreciate the land. In praising it, though, he continued the tradition of gross exaggeration: "The country is so fertile that they do not have to break up the ground the year round, but only have to sow the seed, which is presently covered by the fall of snow, and the ears come up under the snow. In one year they gather enough for seven."[7] And here was a truth about America: When one resource was depleted or proved less abundant than expected, there was always another to replace it as the object of hopes and dreams.

Gold, native slaves, furs, land: all were opportunities waiting for

Europeans to exploit them, a means for individual enrichment—or national, when sovereigns had to be persuaded to finance new expeditions. Monetary gain was the foremost, but not the only, hope pinned on the new land. The New World was a trope that could be put to many purposes, indeed to any purpose a writer might favor. These were not only economic. Evidence for any political argument, for any moral lesson, for any religious inspiration could be located—or imagined—in America.

As it became clear that colonization would be required for the full exploitation of the new lands, the English were not content to leave such riches and possibilities to their Spanish rivals. In 1583 the government commissioned Richard Hakluyt, eager compiler of stories about voyages to the New World, to write a report on the advantages of colonies in North America. His "Discourse Concerning Westerne Planting" enthusiastically listed them. Treasure remained a draw, if a mistaken one when it came to what would be most of the English colonies: "The manifolde testimonies [of explorers] prove infallibly unto us that golde, silver, copper, perles, pretious stones, and turqueses, and emraldes, and many other commodities, have bene by them founde in those regions. To which testimonies I shoulde have added many more if I had not feared to be tedious." Perhaps more important were the opportunities for work, as Hakluyt saw idleness as one of England's great moral problems: "Yea many thousands of idle persons are within this realme, which, havinge no way to be sett on works, be either mutinous and seeke alteration in the state, or at leaste very burdensome to the commonwealthe, and often fall to pilferinge and thevinge and other lewdnes, whereby all the prisons of the lande are daily pestred and stuffed full of them."[8] Migration meant moral improvement as well as economic success, a panacea for all the problems of the Old World.

The first English colonies were founded by private companies with a financial stake in spreading excitement and interest in their ventures. In 1610, only three years after the founding of Jamestown, now teetering on the edge of disaster, the Virginia Company wrote an anonymous pamphlet defending the colony from the rumors reaching England. It went into great detail about the kinds of trees to be found there, the animals and fish, including fur-bearing otters, and insisted that oranges, lemons, and silkworms could thrive there. It asked "why those that were [eye witnesses] of the former supposed miseries, do voluntarily returne with joy and comfort?"[9] The company also sponsored sermons bemoaning England's urban poverty and devastated countryside, recommending

Publicity agents seized on any and all accomplishments of the new colonies. A pamphlet, "New England's First Fruits," was published in London in 1643 to celebrate Harvard College, which had graduated its first nine students the previous year. The curriculum, described in detail, included the more obvious Greek and Latin but also Hebrew, "Syriack," and "Chaldee." Then came evidence that God had "favoured our beginnings." His help included "sweeping away great multitudes of the Natives by the Small Pox, a little before we went thither, that he might make room for us there. . . . And in that Warre which we made against [the Pequits] Gods hand from heaven was so manifested, that a very few of our men in a short time pursued through the Wilderness, slew and took prisoners about 1400 of them, to the great terror and amazement of all Indians to this day." As further proof of God's blessing, the colony had managed to reeducate or banish those holding "erroneous opinions." The brochure then listed fish, furs, minerals, wood products, and many other resources as not only "plentiful" but "farre more faire pleasant and wholesome" than in England. Major elements of American mythology and national character were already here: God's will, economic abundance, the defeat of the natives, and vigilance against those who believed or acted differently

America to those dispossessed by enclosures and unemployment. They knew there were profits to be made from the American dream.

After the charters of the colonial corporations (none of which found the profits it sought) were withdrawn, other private companies benefited from boomtown conditions in the colonies. Thomas Jefferson commented that Virginia planters were simply a form of property attached to the great British merchant houses. The links were based on the elaborate system of credit that British merchants extended to the planters (Jefferson's own debt was notorious), who in turn advanced credit more locally and used their monies to take advantage of local opportunities such as the purchase of land or slaves. Credit and speculation, present from the beginning, depended especially on a continual flow of new arrivals who would drive up land prices and do the actual work of exploiting the continent's riches.

The vastness of the Americas was always part of their draw. Their resources were surely boundless. All the idle persons of the realm, what Hakluyt's cousin (also named Richard Hakluyt) called "waste people," could be swallowed up by the "great waste Woods" there. Many of these waste people were old or lame, but others simply had limited economic prospects in England, including some younger (or illegitimate) sons of the wealthy. The opportunities that abounded were for individuals. Hakluyt barely mentions, as an afterthought, that there might also be religious motives for emigration. To him, this vast land mass was crying out for economic development. Either way, sheer size mattered: America was a wide open territory with room to maneuver, to experiment, to start over, whether one's goal was following God's intentions, establishing a perfect community, or making money. In America, geography and freedom were thought to coincide, and because they were thought to coincide, they often did. It is not America's wealth that has made Americans so optimistic as a people, but their expectations of wealth.

Inspired by new markets and opportunities for enrichment, Europeans cooked up any number of ambitious improvement projects—in agriculture, manufacturing, and transportation—along the fuzzy border between improving society and improving one's bank account. When it came to settling the new colonies in North America, this practical urge was frequently wedded to a desire for social and political stability of the kind that Europe was thought to have lost. In our eyes these seem incompatible impulses, one progressive and the other conservative, but Europeans of the seventeenth century did not yet see any necessary contradiction between material improvement and cultural and political

Newcomers such as the Pilgrims were not especially motivated by material advancement, but by a sincere desire to live holy lives. Others, too, have wanted mostly to live in their own ways, often in order to reject or control worldliness. But the pursuit of religious freedom is not as inimical to economic advancement as the Puritan suspicion of wealth might indicate. Those rejecting the perceived corruption of the Church of England and those hoping to establish themselves as independent farmers were fleeing a government and social system they disliked in favor of a new culture where they could control their own lives. The Old World meant constraints and impurities of many kinds, while the new represented purity and opportunity. The Puritans, like Christian fundamentalists today, wished to go back to a more pristine form of Christianity based on direct reading of the Bible; this is not so different from others who hoped to create a society of individual autonomy and reward for hard work. Both sought freedom to pursue a dream. As Toni Morrison put it in *Playing in the Dark*, "The flight from the Old World to the New is generally thought to be a flight from oppression and limitation to freedom and possibility. Although, in fact, the escape was sometimes an escape from license—from a society perceived to be unacceptably permissive, ungodly, and undisciplined. . . . Whatever the reasons, the attraction was of the 'clean slate' variety, a once-in-a-lifetime opportunity not only to be born again but to be born again in new clothes." Since the idea is to rebuild social life from the ground up, economic and moral motivations are hardly separable. Starting over entails changes in all dimensions of life.

stability. What was common to both urges was a desire to start things over and to get them right this time.

Most of the new colonies were carefully thought out in England as utopian projects. Lord Baltimore hoped to establish in Maryland the neatly hierarchical feudal order that England had once had (or that he believed it had). In the 1660s John Locke himself tried to work out the first principles for the political structure of the Carolina colony, which belonged to a group of investors that included his patron the Earl of Shaftesbury. Soon after, William Penn established his colony to avoid the kind of religious warfare that had devastated England and Europe. As late as the 1730s humanitarian reformers planned Georgia as a more egalitarian, slaveless utopia of small farmers. Even the plans for cities such as Philadelphia (in the 1680s) and Savannah (in the 1730s) carefully placed public buildings and various activities along squarely uniform street grids. In Virginia and Maryland colonists decided to start over, abandoning Jamestown and Saint Mary's to build the new capitals of Williamsburg and Annapolis with wide avenues and squares for the several hundred families who would live in each. Every man with an idea of what society should look like saw an opportunity to fulfill his vision. One prominent historian of the period insists, "Virtually every one of the new English colonies established in America after Virginia represented an effort to create in some part of the infinitely pliable world of America—a world that would perforce yield to English mastery—some specific Old World vision for the recovery of an ideal past in a new and carefully constructed society."[10] Whether they were looking forward or backward, or some of each, America was the place to try to put their schemes into practice.

Not a single one of these colonial utopias worked out as intended. The planners and organizers were too far away to impose their will on the colonists, and conditions were often too rough to allow much concern for social and political order anyway. Outside New England there was little authority of any kind. Individual young men, and occasionally families, came to the colonies for their own reasons and made their own ways, with little regard for anyone else's utopian aspirations. Many were trying to escape, for one reason or another, precisely the kind of authority (usually in the person of aristocrats) that London planners thought crucial to the success of their colonial ventures. If America helped inspire utopian schemes, it was also—as Daniel Boorstin has said—their burial ground. Collective projects continually gave way to individual ones.

Even the modest elites that eventually emerged in the colonies used

In the harsh conditions of the early settlements, there was hardly time for utopian projects. The Virginia Company needed its relentless publicity drives—with successive sales of shares, blizzards of enthusiastic pamphlets, official sermons, even public lotteries—just to keep its Jamestown settlement populated. During its existence from 1606 to 1624, the company sent almost 9,000 people, almost all young men, to Virginia, but at the end of that period only 1,275 had survived the swampy land's diseases. Profitability was not even a remote possibility. Ship after ship was sent with new recruits, livestock, and other supplies, returning with a few furs, some timber, sassafras, and the most promising item, the first crops of tobacco. Fittingly, the colony would survive by pandering to England's new vice, an herb smoked primarily in brothels and taverns. Gone were the intellectuals and sons of nobility who had added spice to the initial group of settlers, replaced, as Bernard Bailyn put it, by "tough, unsentimental, quick-tempered, crudely ambitious men concerned with profits and increased landholding, not the grace of life."

their wealth and political power to pursue their own ends, not the collective good. As historian Bernard Bailyn says of Virginia's embryonic planter class in the seventeenth century, "The private interests of this group, which had assumed control of public office by virtue not of inherited status but of newly achieved and strenuously maintained economic eminence, were pursued with little interference from the traditional restraints imposed on a responsible ruling class."[11] The American dream, even at the top, quickly came to be one of individual advancement, not social engineering. From the start, it was a vision based on maneuvering in economic markets.

Alongside (and eventually displacing) utopian urges there was money to be made off immigrants, appropriately enough, given most immigrants' own economic motives. Any number of employers, developers, and promoters had an interest in maintaining America's image as the land of opportunity. The companies that founded the colonies hired shipping agents to roam the English countryside looking for likely prospects. Others were more general publicists, promoting the image of America as the land of opportunity for all. Shipping companies made increasing profits from the trans-Atlantic voyage, so much so that there were scandals of on-board overcrowding and starvation in the mid-1700s. Eventually the colonies took over their own promotional activities, driven largely by a perpetual shortage of labor that lasted into the nineteenth century.

Even in the seventeenth century the concern for profit had political ramifications. By the middle of that century economic conditions in England were improving, so ambitious dreams were less likely to issue in migration. The pull remained, but not the push. The image of America had to be polished with new enticements. As historian Edmund Morgan puts it, "The courtiers to whom the king granted princely domains in America nevertheless expected to grow rich from the rent and sale of lands to settlers. In order to entice increasingly reluctant emigrants, they had to offer 'concessions and agreements' stipulating generous terms on which they would grant land and a share in government to the people they granted it to."[12] That a say in government was an enticement to potential immigrants shows how much their aspirations differed from those of the nobles, whose utopian dreams were more authoritarian. Wealth and freedom (especially the freedom to pursue wealth) were the draw.

Employers themselves have promoted America and advertised for—*ordered* is perhaps the better word—immigrant workers when they needed them. Sometimes they were quite specific about the skills they needed. As early as 1714, Virginia Governor Alexander Spotswood "rescued a group of about forty-two German ironworkers and their families stranded in London, contracted with them for three years of labor in the ironworks he planned, and established them in a tiny, palisaded, log-cabin settlement he called Germanna, at the edge of Virginia's northern frontier."[13] Both public relations and direct recruitment continued after the new nation was born. Ronald Takaki reports a chilling order for supplies needed by a business as late as 1908, which listed "Filipinos" alphabetically right after "Fertilizer."[14] By 1900, elaborate networks of agents linked Croatian villages, say, with railroad companies in need of workers to repair tracks in Pennsylvania. Factory owners learned they could fill all their job openings simply by encouraging their workers to write to relatives back home; no one worried what would happen to the recruits in the next depression. African slavery was only the extreme form of this continuing attitude toward immigrants as nothing but labor.

Individual employers were not the only ones interested in immigrants. Entrepreneurs and land developers, whether wealthy individuals or state governments, were always in search of settlers to drive up land values, work the mines, and build the railroads. In the late nineteenth century, no fewer than thirty-three states and territories established immigration offices to induce newcomers to move west. Minnesota's pamphlet trumpeted the American myth of newness: "It is well to exchange the tyrannies and thankless toil of the old world for the freedom and independence of the new . . . it is well for the hand of labour to bring forth the rich treasures hid in the bosom of the NEW EARTH." Wisconsin apparently found it easier to disparage Minnesota, so its pamphlet pointed out that Minnesota was farther away, with fewer railroads and more natural disasters.[15]

With inexpensive steamship passage available late in the nineteenth century, migration became even bigger business. The shipping lines sent agents to scour villages throughout Europe, enticing travelers by assuring them their dreams would come true in the United States. On a festival day in 1891, one crew arrived in the village of Orsomarso in southern Italy. "Early in the morning they set up a podium in the town square," the prefect observed. "From there they addressed the people, offering explanations and especially dispelling doubts, whenever peasants approached them and showed interest in departing." As ubiquitous as the red, white, and blue posters they put up, these salesmen, paid by the head, were not likely to understate America's promise.[16]

Profit was not Americans' only motive for exaggerating their favorite images of themselves; virtue could also be used to attract immigrants. In Massachusetts, religious leaders thundered against the sins of their congregations in church but extolled their merits to outsiders. William Bradford set the tone when he described the members of his Plymouth Colony as simple farmers, hiding the origins of most as townspeople and artisans. He was creating a public-relations image of their purity that might attract like-minded sects from England. Yeoman farmers were good, living in some kind of pastoral bliss. In the Massachusetts Bay Colony, leaders tried to control the flow of information back to England. During divisive theological controversies in the 1630s, leaders on both sides joined in appealing to those returning to England to downplay the strife. But the best way to control images was after the fact, and religious leaders were in charge not only of the colony but of writing its history. A veritable swarm of Mathers chronicled Massachusetts history, with Cotton Mather especially industrious at finding parallels to events and figures of the Bible. Religious motivations were all, it would seem from their accounts. Their American dream differed slightly from the usual economic versions, but it was packaged just as carefully for export.

If Europeans projected every manner of hope and fear onto the newly discovered hemisphere in the sixteenth and seventeenth centuries, later generations on all continents had their reasons for continuing the distortions. In her study of Salvadoran immigrants to Long Island in the 1990s, Sarah Mahler shows why immigrants, even those on the very bottom rung, portray their new country as the promised land in the letters and videos they send home. Even in the media-saturated age of the so-called global village, it is possible for potential immigrants to harbor astounding illusions about the United States. Among Mahler's Latin Americans, she says, "virtually all of my informants left their homelands with idealized visions either of the United States itself or of the lives they would lead there, only to realize shortly thereafter that these visions were fantasies." Some still expected to find so much money that one could "sweep it up off the streets."[17] The immigrants themselves, despite remaining at the bottom of American society, are responsible for much of the illusion. Whether showing off or trying to assuage family worries, immigrants tend to insist that they are doing well, often to the extent of posing in front of other people's automobiles (what better symbol of both America and affluence?) for photographs to send home. But their audiences don't like to be told discouraging stories (such as the reality of long hours for little pay in horrid living and working conditions). Everyone, it seems, has an interest in maintaining a vision of the United States as the land of the dream. The need to believe remains strong.

America remained a dream after immigrants had arrived. Not only did they and their descendants continue to believe in opportunity, they also continued to look for special corners of this promised land. If New York did not live up to expectations, perhaps Wisconsin would. If not Wisconsin, surely California. Not only immigrants, but native-born Americans tend to dream about other regions, other states, other lives. Since it is easier to dream about places you have never seen, the American dream was displaced onto the frontier, the West, someplace farther along the trail.

In the beginning, all America was a frontier. For three hundred years, as Frederick Jackson Turner famously proposed in the 1890s, there was always a frontier somewhere on the continent, even as the "civilized" seaboard grew larger and larger. Most of the images Europeans had developed of America were gradually transferred to the western parts of the country. The wide open spaces there were just what the country as a whole represented to the rest of the world. The West was an easily transferrable symbol. Just as "the course of empire" was moving westward to America, it could continue moving west within the continent. The movement was not steady, of course, but came in spurts, the largest of them in the early nineteenth century. In the decades following the Revolution, land mass was added to the young country at a dizzying rate sure to capture the imagination, quadrupling the nation's size by the mid-nineteenth century.

The ultimate western frontier, of course, was California, which, like America, began life as a magical word before Europeans discovered it as a place. It appeared in a Spanish book of fantastic tales written around 1500, described as an island rich in gold near the newly discovered West Indies. The writer, who had not been to the New World, had no particular place in mind, but by mid-century it was being used on maps for various places west of the Caribbean. When the Spanish settled some delightful lands along the Pacific, they naturally called the area California.

Rumors of easy wealth continued to fuel most of the internal migration: tales of land for homesteading, high wages to be had on ranches, lucky strikes in gold or silver mines, plentiful jobs in factories or on railroads. But wealth was only the heart of the dream; it was still surrounded by efforts to start over, to establish a better community, to regain one's health, to escape from constraints and obligations (often in the form of a wife and kids). Just as foreigners could project almost any vision onto America, so the West remained a blank slate for those who lived in the East. In recent years, Alaska, Hawaii, Montana, and other sparsely settled states have served similar functions in keeping the dream alive, as the most restless continue to move.

The promised land is always elsewhere, but any elsewhere will do. For southern blacks, facing considerable personal, political, and economic oppression, the North remained the lodestone into the twentieth century. Just as Frederick Douglass looked northward, albeit with some trepidation, so have other African Americans. Through the nineteenth century few of them could pursue this dream, constrained first by slavery and then by its economic successor, sharecropping. But the migration began in earnest at the beginning of the twentieth century and kept growing until the 1960s. In 1917 Chicago's leading black newspaper, the *Defender*, announced "the Great Northern Drive" to encourage southern blacks to migrate, using slogans based on the biblical stories with which blacks had comforted themselves for generations, especially the flight out of Egypt. Labor agents from northern companies helped stimulate and channel the flow, but blacks' own dreams were the driving force behind their migration.

By the twentieth century, dreams were more likely to fix themselves on cities than the countryside, and African Americans were part of a massive migration away from the farm. Toni Morrison captures the rapturous expectations of Harlem in her novel *Jazz*. The main characters, Joe and Violet, have come as far north as Baltimore, where "their Baltimore dreams were displaced by more powerful ones. Joe knew people living in the City and some who'd been there and come home with tales to make

Baltimore weep. . . . White people literally threw money at you—just for being neighborly: opening a taxi door, picking up a package. And anything you had or made or found you could sell in the streets." On the train their excitement builds as they leave southern states and find that the train is no longer segregated by race. "Her hip bones rubbed his thigh as they stood in the aisle unable to stop smiling. They weren't even there yet and already the City was speaking to them. They were dancing. And like a million others, chests pounding, tracks controlling their feet, they stared out the windows for first sight of the City that danced with them, proving already how much it loved them. Like a million more they could hardly wait to get there and love it back."[18]

With the sources of wealth having been decisively urbanized or suburbanized, the wide open spaces of Montana, Idaho, and other sparsely populated states today draw a different kind of person. These are not areas of great economic opportunity, but places to escape what one dislikes about the rest of the country: big government, cities, immigrants, Jews, blacks, or the reach of the so-called new world order. The survivalists, militia members, and white supremacists who gravitate to remote spots like Ruby Ridge in northern Idaho are all too American. They believe that migration will set them free, that a new abode means a new life. It is a belief they share with all the immigrants, African Americans, and city dwellers whom they are fleeing.

Popular novelist Ross Macdonald once wrote that "democracy is as much a language as it is a place. If a man has suffered under a society of privilege, the American vernacular can serve him as a kind of passport to freedom and equality." Many of our immigrants have come from repressive societies indeed, where economic and political rights were limited. Little wonder that the United States should appear to be the land of freedom. America has entered the world's symbolic repertory with many meanings; it is a heightened emotional trope that allows projection far above and beyond the realities to be found here. Unlike most tropes, however, it can be a destination for international migration. Democracy is a place as much as it is a language.

Explanations of American character make much of our lack of an aristocratic past. But at the founding of the colonies, this was hardly a past for Europe, where every manner of monarchic institution and aristocratic practice still flourished (in fact absolute monarchies were becoming more absolute in most of Europe) and would be dissolved only slowly over several hundred years. Immigrants knew well what they were fleeing. Compared to Europe, America really was a land of freedom, and remained ahead of Europe in this regard until the twentieth century. So the symbolism of America was not arbitrary. Yes, it was partly the creation of self-serving publicists and landowners and partly the result of the psychological dynamics of immigrants themselves. But this only explains the exaggeration surrounding the kernel of truth in the image of America as a land of opportunity.

The American Revolution firmly cemented these images of freedom in most of the world's cultures, as it did so many of our own institutions and symbols. America was already a potent symbol of prosperity and freedom. The Revolution developed out of colonists' pride in these, and further amplified both images. Discussing the enormous prosperity of the average white American citizen, historian Gordon Wood argues, "The experience of that growing prosperity contributed to the unprecedented eighteenth-century sense that people here and now were capable of ordering their own reality." He continues, "The vision of the revolutionary leaders is breathtaking. As hard-headed and practical as they were, they knew that by becoming republicans they were expressing nothing less than a utopian hope for a new moral and social order led by enlightened and virtuous men. . . . They were optimistic, forward-looking, and utterly convinced that they had the future in their own hands."[19] This should be no surprise: this opportunity for starting over and controlling one's destiny is what America stood for before the Revolution, and the example of the founding fathers assured that it would do so for a long time after. Dreamy idealism was also there from the start. As Daniel Webster said, the revolutionaries went to war for a Preamble, and fought seven years for a Declaration.

The new republic decided to establish an entirely new city for its capital, choosing swampy lands along the Potomac River as its site. This was another ambitious utopian vision, with parallel streets set at right angles, intersected by broad diagonal avenues and lots of squares, all of it divided rationally into four quadrants. Built by men who believed that virtue resided on farms, not in cities, Washington, D.C., has remained a city for those who don't like cities, with height limits on buildings that keep population densities low. Only a country of dreams would create its administrative capital from scratch like this (although several other colonial countries would later imitate the pattern). Neither politics nor cities worked out as Washington's planners hoped, although the city has remained a kind of administrative experiment, never attracting much of the economic or cultural activity that marks most major cities.

They identified with Tom Paine's claim in *Common Sense* that America was already "the asylum for the persecuted lovers of civil and religious liberty from every *part* of Europe."[20]

The utopian impulse to remake the world from scratch led Americans to divide up their land according to idealized grids. Most American cities are monotonous right angles of streets laid out in regular blocks. A New Yorker will say, "Meet me at Twenty-Third and Tenth," giving street names; a Chicagoan might say, "I live at 18 west and 47 north," meaning the number of blocks from the center. There is a democracy to such grids, especially when the streets are numbered. How can Fourteenth Street be superior to Eighteenth? (Although culture soon imposes such differences, so that "Fifth Avenue" takes on connotations other avenues lack.) The same abstractly straight lines marched across the country in land grants as well as county and state borders. They were the form that would interfere least with the long, straight roads built across them, the form that allowed the vast land mass to be surveyed and divided up most quickly. Grid triumphed over topography. The whole continent was a blank territory on which planners' fantasies could be enacted—and many were. Railroads could be laid down straight rather than, as in Europe, following existing roads. Land could be divided into neat squares, cities established with neat grids. The vast sameness of it all saves one from attachment to any particular place. One must be prepared to move on to the next square.

The dream has not lacked critics. But artists like F. Scott Fitzgerald have only confirmed its potent hold in exploring its dark side. At the end of *The Great Gatsby*, published in 1925, Fitzgerald seems to place the dream in the past. Narrator Nick Carraway thinks of Long Island as the first Dutch sailors saw it: "Its vanished trees, the trees that had made way for Gatsby's house, had once pandered in whispers to the last and greatest of all human dreams; for a transitory enchanted moment man must have held his breath in the presence of this continent, compelled into an aesthetic contemplation he neither understood nor desired, face to face for the last time in history with something commensurate to his capacity for wonder." But almost immediately Carraway describes the relatively unmodified contemporary version of the same dream, embodied in Gatsby, who embraced the dream even if Fitzgerald did not. "Gatsby believed in the green light, the orgiastic future that year by year recedes before us. It eluded us then, but that's no matter—tomorrow we will run faster, stretch our arms farther. . . . And one fine morning—" Daisy, for whom Gatsby created himself anew, was shallow, insubstantial, even a touch vulgar—no match for his fantasy of her. Even if illusory, Gatsby's ability to dream gave him "an extraordinary gift for hope, a romantic readiness" that one can't help admiring. (It also propelled him to great feats of material accumulation.) His dream was so potent, though, that it finally destroyed him. Dreams can disappoint or turn deadly, but they cannot be dismissed.[21]

Today artists are even more aware of, and cynical about, American myths, but the power of their work still derives from the fact that others still believe in those myths. A good example is Sam Shepherd's play *True West*, about the clash of two brothers, set appropriately in a California bungalow on the edge of the desert near Los Angeles (coyotes howl occasionally in the background). They have dealt with the American dream differently. Lee has been a ne'er-do-well drifter, restlessly roaming around the West, while Austin has been a Hollywood screenwriter making up stories about the West, sustaining the legend. The crux of the tension between them is that Lee sells a "realistic" screenplay about the West to a producer, revealing his brother's well-crafted work as mere fiction. The play questions the idea of "mere" fiction, raising issues about the importance of imagination and fantasy. Dreams are vital and important, even though—or perhaps because—as Austin says, "There's no such thing as the West anymore. It's a dead issue." Dreams nurture us partly *as* dreams, whether or not they accurately reflect reality. And in this case, the drifter has finally found his own lucky strike, fulfilling the essence of the American and western dream. Even postmodern cynicism cannot escape the realities of the American myths.

American writers were not the only ones to reconsider this country's symbolism in the twentieth century. Antimodernists in Europe and elsewhere still exploit the United States as a symbol of modern placelessness. Nazi sympathizer Martin Heidegger crafted an image of America as a desolate place where people do not put down roots and hence have no organic connection to life or history. It is "the site of catastrophe." Recent thinkers, often dubbed postmodern for their rejection of modernity, have taken up the same imagery. A cleverer-than-thou Frenchman named Jean Baudrillard has called America an "anti-utopia," lacking a sense of its own past or any connection to its own territory. Antimodernists view as catastrophe the same flexible mobility that modernists celebrate. Either way, America remains a favorite symbol.

⌐⌐⌐⌐⌐⌐⌐⌐⌐⌐⌐⌐⌐⌐⌐⌐⌐⌐⌐⌐⌐⌐⌐⌐⌐⌐⌐⌐⌐⌐⌐⌐⌐⌐⌐⌐⌐⌐⌐

Ignoring the cynicism of writers and philosophers, especially foreign ones, Americans continue to believe they live in the land of opportunity. Despite nasty conflicts over which version of the American dream is the best, all the factions have used the same geography to paint their own vision. Some flee New York City for Montana; others move just as hopefully in the opposite direction. A few religious groups dream of finding a place to aid their search for religious purity, even if most still pursue the dollar. Yet they all dream.

Only since World War II have there been reasonable surveys of public opinion to show us just how widespread these aspirations are. In 1947, 70 percent of Americans thought that their "opportunities for success" were better than their fathers' had been, a figure that has remained almost as high in the decades since. In many surveys, three times as many Americans as Europeans think that they and their fellow citizens have "a good chance" of improving their standard of living (in fact living standards have improved similarly on the two continents). Americans are also, along similar lines of reasoning, more likely to believe that future generations will be better off than current ones. American optimism was highest in the 1940s and 1950s, but even after declining slightly, it remains far higher than in other countries.

Americans believe in the dream even when they feel it has eluded them. General questions about society's future elicit more optimism than questions about one's own. Only 35 percent see good chances for advancement at their current job, and 40 percent think they are likely to be promoted in the next five years. Even fewer think they are likely to ever become rich. Americans can still believe they live in the land of opportunity, even when they conclude that they themselves are not taking advantage of it.[22]

The reason is that personal dreams become cultural symbols and ideals. I may be too old to make a fortune in the great economic lottery, but I am loyal to the ideal of getting rich. Americans have a sense of being special, of being watched, even of being marked by God. When he and his followers were about to land in Massachusetts, John Winthrop spoke of the colony as "a city upon a hill. The eyes of all people are upon us." The eyes belonged to critics who expected the venture to fail, and who thereby provided an enormous incentive for the Puritans to insist that they were succeeding—whatever they actually believed. Like today's Salvadoran immigrants, they had to put on a good show for the audiences back home. Winthrop thought it was only if the colony failed that "we shall be made a story and a by-word through the world." But America became a byword even more through its success. Again and again, Americans' optimism has proven well grounded.

America was born as a dream and has been maintained as an ideal. As President Woodrow Wilson said, "Sometimes people call me an

American men dream of escape even when they think they could never do it. Richard Ford describes one of them in his story, "The Womanizer": "In the past, when he and Barbara had had a row and he had felt like just getting in the car and driving to Montana or Alaska to work for the forest service—never writing, never calling, though not actually going to the trouble of concealing his identity or whereabouts—he'd found he could never face the moment of actual leaving. His feet simply wouldn't move. And about himself he'd said, feeling quietly proud of the fact, that he was no good at departures." On the other hand, he admits, "it had occurred to him that what he might be was just a cringing, lying coward who didn't have the nerve to face life alone; couldn't fend for himself in a complex world full of his own acts' consequences." It turns out that it does not take much of a push, despite his self-image, for this middle-aged salesman suddenly to flee the Illinois suburbs for Paris. Real men are those who run.

idealist. Well, that is the only way I know I am an American. America is the only idealistic nation in the world." More vapidly, eighty years later, Bill Clinton's Secretary of State (immigrant) Madeleine Albright could use the same language: "If we have to use force, it is because we are America. We are the indispensable nation. We stand tall. We see further into the future." Both vapid and dangerous.

Here is one of the most important conceits of American history. Americans have seen their newness as a moral model not only for them, but for everyone. Their country is important not just because it allows people a good place for starting over; Americans feel it is the best possible society, in general, for anyone. They do not just believe in an American national character, simply different from French, or English, or German character. They believe that Americans, freed from accumulated layers of culture and institutions, are fortunate enough to embody a pure, universal human nature as God created and intended it. They are better than Europeans. What is good for Americans is good for the world: they mistake American institutions for natural institutions. This arrogance has taken dangerous forms, for it suggests that American institutions should be imposed on others, even those who have no interest in them. If native Americans resisted, they had to have markets and related "liberties" imposed on them, by force if necessary. Even today, our foreign policy is rationalized in universal terms, not in terms of American interests; we fight wars in the name of freedom, or against communism (although these two goals often conflict).

Americans expect to have ideals and principles, which are only dreams applied to reality. If America is a symbol of what is natural, pure, and good, then what I like has to be "true" American, and what I dislike has to be un-American. "This is America": every expression of anger, outrage, even hatred may be prefaced with this phrase, meant to set a high standard for what should go on here. "America" becomes a catch-all term of moral worth. Part of the contrast between Old World and New is a contrast between bad and good, an instinct that has guided many of our adventures in foreign policy. Speaking to troops in Saudi Arabia in 1990, James Baker asserted, "I think Americans are at home wherever their principles are." Without any loyalty to places, they carry their ideals with them as they move about.

Americans are not altogether naive, and they are quick to recognize some kinds of lapses from the ideal. When church leaders appear too worldly or politicians too corrupted, we are quick to attack them as un-American, our worst term of abuse. We are cynical about individuals in positions of authority, for they can never match our images of the ideal, whether that refers to the Founding Fathers or the Constitution or some other ideal. Dreams are hard to match in the flesh. Real-life institutions can only disappoint.

Expectations are not always self-fulfilling, but they always have effects. Some theorists of American character have thought that our sheer abundance created our dreamy optimism. Instead, it was our expectations of what we could do with that wealth. It was our anticipation that we would be transformed by it, allowed another chance, a fresh start. People came here who wanted that kind of chance, who were willing to put our natural resources to work in pursuit of it.

The United States is held together as a nation, not by (real or imagined) primordial ties of blood or ancient ties to the land, but by the dream that brought its voluntary immigrants here, ideals that persist today. As Richard Hofstadter said, "It has been our fate as a nation not to have ideologies, but to be one." The ideal construction of the country has effects in many areas of life. Perhaps the only other nation to be constructed around an idea was the Soviet Union, which helps explain why these two nations were destined to hate and battle each other through most of the twentieth century.

Through most of American history, the utopian schemers, those ambitious enough to try starting over, have primarily been men. I don't know whether men dream more than women, but their dreams tend to be different. They fantasize about starting over, founding a new social order. Their dreams are less connected to the family and friends they already have. As a result, they often involve moving to a new place. Until recently, it was mostly men who saw the gold.

At the beginning of the new millennium, the dreams are not untarnished. In recent decades a certain degree of realism, even cynicism, has spread to temper them. Prospective immigrants can learn more about the United States than ever before by using the mass media. Utopian plans, most of all, have a bad reputation today. And since Vietnam, there has been persistent criticism of efforts to impose our dreams on others. But this is a small, if growing, countercurrent against the broader flow of American history.

If nothing else, many Americans recognize that it is hard to create a new life. The literary critic Leo Marx once wrote that American ideals combined two images of nature, a pastoral Garden of Eden and a darker, primitive wilderness. The country is both a land of plenty and a dangerous wasteland to be conquered. "If America seemed to promise everything that men always had wanted, it also threatened to obliterate much of what they already had achieved." If, as he claimed, this is a paradox, it is one easily solved. The American leap into the ideal requires hard work. Immigrants come to America for its dreams, not because the dream is always easy to attain, but because it is possible. Recreating one's life involves rearranging one's surroundings. Too much emphasis on an already-existing garden, and Americans would become complacent, settle down. Too much on the dark challenge, and they would give up trying. Yes, the public-relations hype might exaggerate the ease of attaining wealth here, but the heart of the image remains the challenge of wresting wealth from the land, creating the new from the old. This may be the land of gold, but that gold is not simply handed out upon arrival.

Migration is a leap of faith. Even today, when some potential immigrants can visit first to reconnoiter, immigration to the United States or moving to California is based on an ideal, a symbol, a dream. From the European perspective, this country began as a dream, or as the fulfillment of one. It has flourished as a symbolic ideal ever since, sometimes because of and sometimes despite its realities. The country has been, as the French philosopher Comte Destutt de Tracy said at the time of the American Revolution, "the hope and example of the world." That hope has moved sixty million immigrants into action.

American immigrants have shared one thing in addition to their restlessness: a conscious choice to come here, based on their expectations of what their new home would be like. Few of our immigrants have been refugees, forced to flee their homes. Most had options and chose America as the best of them. They picked this country because of its promise. They dreamed the dream. Riches and other possibilities like those associated with America would make anyone restless. Immigrants are those with the starkest sense of how this country differs from all others, and their very belief in that difference makes it—partly—come true. Like the Spanish explorers who actually discovered the gold they had imagined, Americans have made their country a land of unparalleled wealth. But it begins as a symbol of promise. And no one is more aware of that than immigrant Americans, who feed the symbolic flame generation after generation.

2 *The Most Likely to Succeed*

Your daddy's in America, Little son of mine
But you are just a child now, So hush and go to sleep.
America is for everyone, They say, it's the greatest piece of luck
For Jews, it's a garden of Eden, A rare and precious place.
People there eat challah in the middle of the week.
—*Russian Jewish lullaby from the nineteenth century*

They came largely to get *away*—that most simple of motives. To get
away. Away from what? In the long run, away from themselves.
Away from everything. That's why most people have come to America, and still do come. To get away from everything they are and
have been.
—*D. H. Lawrence*

At the age of twelve, Spyridon Ionnais Demopoulos had never left his
village in the Greek Peloponnesus, and despite the village's name—
Seavista—he had never seen the sea. He would encounter a lot of it on
the steamer to Ellis Island, though, after his village's elders picked him
as the area's most promising youngster, raised the necessary money,
and sent him to America in 1902. He took a ferry directly from Ellis Island up the Hudson to the Erie Lackawanna rail terminal, and from
there a train to Cumberland, a small city in western Maryland where his
American sponsor employed him as a dishwasher. Now named Stephen
Demas, thanks to an immigration clerk as well as his own desire to fit in,
he received twenty-five cents a week, plus food and a cot in the back of
the restaurant. This would prove to be the first of several new starts for
Demas. In the next one he moved the hundred miles to Washington,
D.C., soon saving enough money to buy, along with a partner, several
small lunchrooms. These generated sufficient income for him to bring
two brothers and a sister to America, each of whom worked in what was

becoming the family business. Stephen was drafted in 1917 and served in an engineering corps in the U.S. Army, but returned to find that his brother was a less able entrepreneur than he. They were down to one lunchroom. So Stephen sent his brother off to medical school. He rebuilt his restaurants until, now in his early thirties, he saw an opportunity in a related industry. Demas started a laundry to clean the coats, towels, and aprons of other restaurants, working out of the basement in the house where he lived on Princeton Place (a two-block street mostly filled with European immigrants who ran small businesses). He impressed the owner of another, larger laundry, who offered to take Demas on as a partner. Even though it was the middle of the Depression, he was doing well. By the time Demas died in 1971, this laundry had grown into a flourishing business employing fifty people. Long hours of hard work had paid off for yet another immigrant.

This, at least, is the story that Demas's friends and descendants tell themselves and others. It is one of millions of similar stories about success from humble origins, about how America and Americans got where they are today, the kind of family legend that shapes our deepest sense of who we are and of how the world works. Immigrant stories like this one have profoundly shaped American moral and political character, making it more individualistic, more optimistic, more suspicious of authority, and—in recent years—more conservative. The economic and demographic effects of American immigration have been most studied and debated, but its deepest impact has been cultural and, indirectly, political. The long flow of immigrants like Demas has bolstered American faith that individual hard work leads inevitably to economic success, even in the face of poverty and prejudice. Forty percent of today's Americans have at least one ancestor who passed through Ellis Island after it opened in 1892, meaning a lot of stories like Demas's.

What is missing from this story of one individual's pluck and diligence? Demographic trends, for one thing—like the nearly six hundred thousand other Greeks who came to the United States in the first two decades of the century, most of them after Demas (nearly all the Greeks who ever immigrated to the United States came during these twenty years). Or the closing of immigration in the years after World War I, which allowed earlier arrivals to establish themselves with less competition from below. Missing too are the personal connections in the restaurant industry that got Demas his first job and helped him establish his laundry; a huge proportion of Greek immigrants opened tiny "greasy spoon" restaurants for reasons that have nothing to do with habits or customs in Greece (virtually none had operated restaurants back in

Greece or even served Greek food in their restaurants here). Also missing are the government policies that allowed him to come here, and later to bring three siblings. Most important, perhaps, is the phenomenal growth, not just of the restaurant industry in Washington but of the economy as a whole from 1902 to 1971, a tide of expansion that carried both immigrants and native-born upward along with it. Finally, all the Greek immigrants who returned home (more than half) are outside this picture. The ones who did well here stayed to tell their stories to their grandchildren; many of the failures (and many who could not find a wife) went back. The typical immigrant story ignores broader structures to concentrate on individual virtues, efforts, and rewards.

It's a truism that the United States is a nation of immigrants, the "first universal nation," with members drawn from virtually every other country around the globe. As Herman Melville put it, "Settled by the people of all nations, all nations may claim her for their own. You can not spill a drop of American blood, without spilling the blood of the whole world." *Sixty million people* have immigrated to this country since the beginning of the seventeenth century, the largest such migration in world history. Even more striking is how permanent the stream has been, so that however immigration may affect American society and character, it has done so almost continuously for four hundred years and continues to do so today. Only in the 1930s did more people leave the United States than came to it. Countries such as Australia and Canada were also founded as colonies and nurtured by immigration, but no other nation has had such a large and relatively steady flow as the United States.

As the country of dreams, America has been the star destination for migrants. Of the seventy million people who left Europe during the nineteenth century, fully half came to this one country. Just as immigrants have had a continuing effect on American culture, politics, and economics, so images of the United States—the dreams we examined in the last chapter—have affected many people's decisions to migrate. These are the people who feel that American ideals fit their aspirations.

American immigration has seen some ups and downs, thanks to wars, economic conditions, and government policies. The Seven Years' War stopped the flow in the 1750s, and the combination of the American Revolution and then the Napoleonic Wars caused a longer dry spell until the 1820s. After that, though, the stream grew rapidly until restrictions in the 1920s cut arrivals from a peak of over one million a year just before World War I to an annual average of only fifty thousand in the 1930s. Since

World War II, immigration has expanded again, peaking at 1.8 million in 1991. Today around one million restless people reach the United States each year, almost three thousand a day. This translates into four new arrivals for every thousand people already here—roughly the rate of the early 1770s or 1830s, but barely a third of the levels reached in the early 1850s, the 1880s, and the first decade of the twentieth century.

Left to its natural rhythms, immigration would undoubtedly have crept upward throughout American history. The more the North American land mass was colonized in the seventeenth and eighteenth centuries, the safer it became. Two thousand arrivals a year through most of the seventeenth century doubled to four thousand in the early eighteenth, and grew to six thousand by the 1750s and 1760s. From 1770 to the outbreak of the Revolution, the flood crested at fifteen thousand a year. The more immigrants who came, the easier it was for succeeding ones. Urbanization and industrialization in the nineteenth century also opened up jobs for foreigners, even those who initially spoke no English. Each national group established networks and communities to welcome later arrivals. As the population and the economy grew, so did chances for advancement. For most of its history, America has lived up to its worldwide image as a land of opportunity, and immigrants themselves became the country's biggest boosters, alongside labor agents and corporate publicists.

From the 1850s through the 1930s, immigrants represented more than 10 percent of the country's total population, peaking just before World War I at 15 percent. But even as this figure bottomed out in the late 1960s, it was still almost 5 percent, or one in twenty Americans. Today it is back up to 8 percent and rising. If we add to this the children growing up in the households of their immigrant parents—to get the figure demographers call "foreign stock"—the numbers for all these years would more than double.[1] Today, around one in five residents of the United States is foreign stock. And almost 40 percent of Americans have at least one grandparent who was an immigrant. In other words those close to the immigrant experience have always been numerous enough to have a profound effect on American culture. Immigrants like Steve Demas are pervasive emotional symbols.

Their influence has been especially strong in certain times and places. In 1890, roughly one-third of the American population consisted of immigrants and their children. But in cities, this foreign stock made up fully half of the population, and in the large cities of the Northeast, especially New York, they were two-thirds or more of the inhabitants. New York was the largest Jewish city in the world, as well as the largest Italian one. Even in 1890, during the swift growth of huge cities, most of the "native stock" (native-born with native-born parents) still lived in rural areas. Only 8 percent of native-stock Americans, whether white or black, lived in cities of more than one hundred thousand people. But among the foreign stock, 58 percent lived in cities, one-third in these largest cities.[2] Even today, New York State's population is 16 percent foreign-born, and California's is 22 percent. A *majority* of New York City residents are foreign stock. Their urban concentration has increased immigrants' visibility in American culture, especially in the mutual suspicions between city and country running through American history.

Average statistics about immigrants miss the wide-ranging contributions individuals have made to American culture. Many became captains of commerce, such as John Jacob Astor, Stephen Girard, Andrew Carnegie, and Meyer Guggenheim. Others contributed to economic growth through their inventions and products, like William Steinway, Alexander Graham Bell, Levi Strauss, John Roebling, and Albert Sabin. Would we have nuclear energy without Hans Bethe, Enrico Fermi, Leo Szilard, Edward Teller, or Hyman Rickover? Others found it easier to become rich by becoming famous, from Harry Houdini to Charles Atlas. What would the American theater and film world be without Charlie Chaplin, Mary Pickford, or Stan Laurel; Frank Capra, Billy Wilder, or Elia Kazan; the Warner brothers or the Shubert brothers? Or Rudolph Valentino, Bob Hope, Boris Karloff, Edward G. Robinson, Bela Lugosi, Cary Grant, and Elizabeth Taylor? Painting without John James Audubon, Thomas Cole, Albert Bierstadt, or Willem de Kooning? Architecture without Louis Kahn, Ludwig Mies Van Der Rohe, Walter Gropius, or I. M. Pei? Sculpture without Augustus Saint-Gaudens, Hideyo Noguchi, Louise Nevelson, or Claus Oldenburg? Music without Irving Berlin, Leopold Stokowski, Arthur Rubenstein, George Szell—or Guy Lombardo? Dance without Balanchine or Barishnikov? Sports without Knute Rockne or Mario Andretti? Writing without the Pulitzer Prize? And what would our intellectual life be like without names such as Arendt, Barzun, Bellow, Bettelheim, Boas, Carnap, Dubos, Einstein, Fromm, Lovejoy, Marcuse, Muir, Nabokov, Sapir, and Tillich? What about philosophers, from George Santayana to Ayn Rand? Economists alone include people like Joseph Schumpeter, Arthur Burns, Simon Kuznets, John Kenneth Galbraith, and Wassily Leontief. Not many immigrants have gone into politics, but those who did run the gamut from labor leaders like Joe Hill, Sam Gompers, David Dubinsky, and Harry Bridges to black nationalists Marcus Garvey and Stokely Carmichael to conservatives such as Alexander Hamilton, Henry Kissinger, and Senator H. I. Hayakawa. Finally, just as the most famous political cartoons of the nineteenth century were those of German immigrant Thomas Nast, the dreamy Varga girls whose pinup posters got American GIs through World War II were the creation of Peru-born Alberto Vargas. It would be hard to fathom American culture without people like these.

Their prominence as lightning rods for American hopes and anxieties, we shall see, has been even greater than their numbers would suggest.

Immigrants have had diverse effects on American history. First, their direct labor contributions, especially important in periods of labor shortages. Second, their creative contributions, many of them economic and technological but others artistic, scientific, and intellectual. Third has been their importance as cultural symbols, both of the fulfillment of the American dream and also of poverty and difference. Most go through a long period of rejection before they attain a celebrated status. Immigrants encourage a belief in markets as a way of rewarding the successful but also punishing failures. Overall, they contribute to almost all the trends I shall analyze in the rest of the book as restlessness.

Because immigrants have always come to the United States to work, drawn by their restless dreams, often fed by the public relations programs of potential employers, most immigrants have been—like Stephen Demas—very young men just entering their working years. The early arrivals in colonial Virginia were almost exclusively men, which is not surprising, given the brutal conditions there. But the disproportion continued, partly because men had desired skills and partly because coming to America was an economic decision that would pay off better for them. Using extensive shipping records, Bernard Bailyn studied ten thousand British emigrants to the American colonies just before the Revolution: any who left Scotland or England between December 1773 and March 1776. He found that two-thirds were 15–29 years old, three-fourths were men, and two-thirds were apparently traveling alone. Although the Scottish emigrants were more likely to be traveling as families—accounting for most of the women and children in the records—the typical emigrant was "a young man, [barely] in his early twenties, who appears to be acting individually and who decides as an individual to migrate to America."[3] Most of the others were also young men who happened to bring families with them.

For most of the nineteenth century, men comprised about 60 percent of the immigrants, and roughly two-thirds of the immigrants were 15–39 years old. These proportions even increased, to about 67 percent and about three-quarters, respectively, by the end of the century. Only among the Irish were men outnumbered—and only slightly—by women, then in demand as domestics. At the other extreme were the Chinese, among whom there were twenty-seven men for every woman in 1890. Most young immigrant men were unmarried, although many had left families to come here. These demographics remained at work until the new policies of the 1920s, which restricted immigrants to those with needed skills or with family members already here. Among the latter came more women, who have slightly outnumbered men in the immigration of recent decades. But most of these women also came to the United States to work.

The old pattern persists for many groups. A study of poor Salvadoran immigrants found that 60 percent were men, with a median age of twenty-seven. The upheaval of migration itself screens out many potential immigrants. As author Sarah Mahler says, "Many people are not willing to submit themselves to these terrors and challenges; many would not survive them. Children and the elderly tend to be left behind. Often men travel first and only later send for their wives and, less frequently, their children. For people accustomed to a life that knew no privacy, the separation and isolation from family is overwhelming. Paradoxically, it is precisely in the name of preserving [economically] the family that so many people leave their homelands."[4] Immigrants are those best equipped to take advantage of American economic opportunities, those *most likely to succeed.*

Just as immigrants are unrepresentative in age, with few children or elderly, they are economically skewed as well: immigrants have rarely been very poor or very rich. It takes a certain level of resources, as well as resourcefulness, to get to the port and book passage, or persuade a sea captain that you would fetch a good price as an indentured servant. As late as the 1770s, in Bailyn's sample, almost half the immigrants arrived to be indentured, normally for four years. But not all of these bonded themselves because of poverty; some wished to preserve whatever modest resources they had. Those with some craft skills were most in demand, even as servants. Of those whose occupations were recorded (about two-thirds of the total), half claimed to be in skilled trades or artisanal crafts and 20 percent in agriculture; only 24 percent claimed to be simple labor, including the 11 percent who identified themselves as servants.[5] This was not an impoverished lumpenproletariat or a displaced peasantry.

During the massive migrations of the following 150 years, agricultural occupations remained around one-fifth of the total. The biggest change was an increase in domestic servants (including those Irish women) and in undifferentiated labor, which together grew to 60 percent of immigrants in the last two decades of the nineteenth century. The large "general labor" category may, however, reflect inaccuracies in recording the responses of immigrants who spoke no English. Within the limits of the records, those in trades such as mining, industry, transportation, and commerce fell gradually from 59 percent in the 1820s to 25 percent in the 1910s. The liberal professions remained a small proportion, roughly 1 or 2 percent, throughout the period. Only since World War II, with policies in place to encourage skilled immigrants, have professionals climbed to one-quarter of the total.[6] These changes reflect the diverse educational and economic backgrounds of the different nationalities, but for most of American history those arriving have had a variety of skills that proved especially useful in whatever economic sectors had jobs. In age, sex, and skill, immigrants were well poised to make money.

Although some have noneconomic motives for wishing to start over, virtually all immigrants come to the United States prepared to work. One reason they do well here—the individual as opposed to the structural side of the story—is that so many bring marketable skills with them, and many are actively recruited precisely because of their knowledge. Those without specific job skills usually possess, like twelve-year-old Stephen Demas, considerable raw intelligence easily transformed into whatever skills are needed. Most immigrants are not too poor or unskilled to take advantage of new opportunities; they are not too rich to want a chance at improvement. They have the ability and the incentive to work hard at getting ahead. Not only these skills and resources, but this desire for advancement, even on the part of those who start in lowly jobs, positions immigrants for rapid progress.

Immigrants work hard. So far, this drive has always translated into economic success. In 1980 male immigrants earned about 13 percent less than the median for all males; roughly the same is true for immigrant household incomes.[7] But immigrants who stayed have inevitably caught up—usually in ten to fifteen years—and then even surpassed the native-born in earnings.[8] As for their descendants, the longer any group is here, the more likely its members are to have incomes like everyone else's. No group of voluntary immigrants who have been here more than a couple of generations have offspring with incomes significantly below the average—at least if they are white.

The evidence is not so clear for today's immigrants, arriving at a time when work for the unskilled is paying less and less, in other words, when structural conditions have changed. The new arrivals have a greater range of skin color, as well, subjecting them to forms of discrimination that may hinder their progress. Whatever their eventual achievements, one thing is as true today as ever: the new immigrants are driven to work long hard hours—perhaps even longer hours because the pay is lower. Besides, Americans have *always* thought that new generations of immigrants would not do as well as earlier ones.

Although immigrants eventually do well, American culture exaggerates just how well. The first source of this distortion is that less successful immigrants often return home; this is especially true for groups with a high proportion of single men. Of all the immigrants who arrived in the great migration from the 1880s to the 1920s, as many as one-third may have gone home. At the extreme, 88 percent of the Greek migration consisted of men, and 54 percent eventually returned home. The next highest percentages were for Italians: 75 percent of Italian immigrants were men, and 46 percent returned.[9] Currently, around 30 percent of immigrants eventually return to their countries of origin. These "birds of passage" are no longer here to tell their stories, to start families.[10] We just don't see or hear about them. This is one reason that unsuccessful immigrants seem rare (although a few successful immigrants return too).

Because stereotypes portray new immigrants as hopelessly poor, special attention is paid to those who—with monotonous regularity—break these expectations. Heartwarming stories of success are also more pleasurable than tales of defeat and suffering. No one boasts of having failed to take advantage of the land of opportunity. As we saw, immigrants themselves are often responsible for exaggerating the opportunities that abound in the United States by embellishing their own success. Most immigrants succeed, but we concentrate on those who succeed the most.

Some of their upward mobility is unique to immigrants. Part comes from the fact that they start so low—artificially low. Many come with skills they cannot immediately exploit. They might have been professionals in their old countries, but they take blue-collar jobs here. The reasons include a poor command of English, extensive licensing requirements for many occupations (often having little to do with actual ability to do the job), a lack of social-network connections in their field, discrimination by employers, and a general inexperience at maneuvering in the new culture. Immigrants' initial jobs seldom fit their skill levels, expectations, past job experience, education levels, or even financial resources. With time, especially as they learn English, they often advance rapidly, getting jobs more appropriate to their backgrounds. So they move up the ladder fast.

We can see these initial barriers at work when we look at immigrants' ability to capitalize on their formal education. Several groups, including Indians, Iranians, Koreans, and Filipinos, have a lot more education on average than native-stock Americans, but only slightly better jobs. In other words, they are not getting the same "economic payoff"—what

each additional year of schooling adds to their earnings—from their education. Only the Koreans have higher payoffs than those of native-
born white Americans, while British and Indian immigrants have about
the same returns as the native-born. For women, only the Canadians
match the returns for the native-born.[11] Strikingly, British, Indian, and
Canadian immigrants avoid the language barrier. Koreans are an exception because so many own their own businesses, avoiding many of
the barriers immigrants typically face. Eventually, immigrants crack
barriers like these, and when they do they advance rapidly.

Training is another initial barrier. For several reasons, including
sheer prejudice, employers are often willing to give native-born but not
foreign-born employees the chance to pick up skills on the job. Immigrants more often have to finance their own training, which further de-
presses their initial earnings. Immigrants are more likely to have to pay
for their own schooling, working while they study. Later, once they have
acquired the necessary education and training, their earnings increase
at a faster rate than those of the native-born.

If language difficulties are especially severe, as they are with many
Asian immigrants, the dramatic upward movement of immigrant groups
may be delayed, occurring primarily among their children. Family
economic strategies frequently concentrate on the next generation's
education. Many southeast Asian immigrants who are not doing well
themselves have children with very high rates of educational success;
one group of scholars studying the children of "boat people" found their
educational success to be "truly startling."[12] Other large studies of the
children of immigrants (now one out of five American children) have
determined that they have higher grades and lower dropout rates than
native-stock children.[13] Such accomplishments probably reflect the
immigrant drive of their parents as much as traits of the children
themselves.

If they are lucky, immigrants eventually get jobs "appropriate," by
American standards, to their education and skills. And if they don't,
their children will. In doing this, given their artificially depressed starting points, they will experience considerable upward mobility. Some of
this movement merely compensates for the large downward move they
made when they migrated, but in American eyes it looks entirely like a
reward for hard work despite humble beginnings.

In addition to exaggerating immigrants' economic success, Americans
often mistake its causes, attributing it exclusively to immigrants' own
efforts. Like all mobility, immigrant success comes from a combination

of individual and structural factors. Among the former are education, skills, and restless ambition. These are the much-vaunted character traits. Those who want material success more than anything, enough to travel thousands of miles for a chance at it, are most likely to get it. Even today immigrants are the ones who bend over in hot fields to pick crops or sit in crowded sweatshops for twelve hours a day. Just as Stephen Demas was chosen as Seavista's "most likely to succeed," other immigrants are unusually talented and relentlessly driven.

Less-apparent structural factors are also at work, however, including the state of the economy in which immigrants arrive (the mix of skills needed, growth rates, unemployment levels); government policies (or lack of policies) concerning immigration, employment, and welfare; attitudes and actions of potential employers (who favor some groups over others, and who send recruiting agents abroad); and the size of the immigrant community (which may be too small to provide jobs to its own members, or too large to offer specialized job "niches"). Yet most of these factors are relatively invisible, and most immigrant stories get reduced to individual effort leading to economic success. This is only part of the story. Many immigrants work hard because circumstances force them to.

Let's look at these structural conditions. Immigration itself is heavily affected by government policies, which not only open or close the overall flow but also distinguish among different sources of immigrants. We only think of the immigrants who succeeded in getting to the United States, not those who tried but failed: the Chinese workers barred after the Exclusion Act of 1882, the Jews captured by the Nazis while trying to arrange passage, the laborers passed over in favor of skilled professionals. Government policy also makes it easier or harder for new arrivals to find jobs, learn English, get housing, overcome discrimination, and do many other things that affect their success. State governments once had their own separate immigration policies, but since the 1920s the federal government has tightly controlled immigration flows, affecting who can come and what happens to them once they are here.

The state of the economy also influences what happens to immigrants and would-be immigrants. When conditions are bad, fewer come, and some of those already here return home, disappearing from sight. More directly, economic conditions affect how well immigrants do here. Factory owners actively recruited unskilled immigrants to fill their industrial plants in the late nineteenth century; agribusiness depends on Chicano laborers even today. During most of American history there were real labor shortages, and immigrants filled the gaps. But recession or the decline of manufacturing can push new arrivals into poorly paid service-sector jobs. Real estate markets, too, affect what kind of housing immigrants find, and thus where (and how) they live. Tight markets can hinder integration.

Barriers such as language and discrimination often drive immigrants to start their own businesses. Certain kinds of business are especially open to them. If there are few or no economies of scale, as in babysitting, large corporations usually stay out. They may also avoid markets that are unstable or quickly shifting. Immigrants are more flexible. In other cases immigrants may recognize market demand that no one else has seen, like the middle easterners who have created car services in New York, especially handy for traveling to airports. Through their own creativity many immigrants manage to create jobs for themselves and fellow arrivals. By the time large corporations take over the industry, a number of immigrants will have saved up enough to set themselves on the road to American success. What is common to these small-business opportunities is that they don't require much capital, they are labor-intensive (allowing immigrants to devote long hours of their own and their families' time), and they allow a slow but steady accumulation of wealth. Like all small businesses, immigrant entrepreneurs operate on cash, which allows them to avoid a certain amount of tax, and they are especially touchy about government regulations.

Demography is another structural determinant of immigrant success. Ideally, new arrivals want a network of fellow countryfolk, speaking their language and perhaps offering initial employment. Many immigrants succeed by opening small businesses catering to their own community. In New York, West Indians have created an industry of vans that, for $1.00 (compared to $1.50 for public transportation) take other West Indians from Brooklyn and Queens into Manhattan and then back during morning and evening rush hours. Some ethnic niches exist because a group has special tastes or needs. Supermarket giant Safeway would be hard-pressed to open a Chinatown grocery store stocked with appropriate vegetables, spices, herbal remedies, and smoked duck feet, so openings exist for a certain number of Chinese immigrants. Other immigrant groups have filled market niches catering to the general public: today's Korean grocers, yesterday's Italian barbers or Chinese laundries. The Greek immigrants of one hundred years ago who overwhelmingly went into the restaurant business catered especially to other poor immigrant men who did not know how (or lacked the facilities) to cook for themselves. Today, those Latino immigrants who manage to reach the middle class do so most often through the same route of small businesses. These niches, whether immigrants serve only their own group or reach beyond it, are especially helpful if a nationality is not arriving in large numbers (too many arrivals can overwhelm the niches). Depending on how many of their fellow countrymen have preceded them, immigrants may have special opportunities for economic advancement.

Even when we exhaust the structural factors, however, personal traits still tell us that immigrants are different. They seem to embody individual choice, guts, and determination. Americans can tell themselves, with considerable truth, that these economic adventurers were not forced to move, to travel thousands of miles to come to America. Like all those who are geographically mobile, they appear to be making individual choices and benefiting from the consequences. It is easy to attribute their success (or in some cases failure) to their own choices and actions—and to ignore the broader contexts that also affect how well they do.

Immigration is not a normal action: it is dramatic, unsettling, and costly. Because academic researchers have stressed the "networks" through which immigrants come to the United States, including family ties and ethnic communities, they have downplayed just how traumatic an upheaval immigration can be, even for an energetic teenager. And they have often overlooked the numerous immigrants without special ties to anyone at all in their new country. Even among those with some tenuous connection, or at least a sponsor, as Stephen Demas had, this connection is often monetary rather than familial. At the extreme are illegal arrivals like Mahler's Salvadorans. She says of one, "She has gone from citizen to foreigner, law abider to law-breaker, legal to illegal, independent to dependent, social member to social outcast; and her personhood is degraded. Fragments of her previous self remain, but they lie scattered like shards of broken glass."[14] The sense of embeddedness in a given place that supports one's identity has also disappeared. For illegal immigrants, today mostly from Latin America, the journey itself is usually an ordeal. They typically must entrust illicit travel agencies and guides with money—what is, for them, a fortune, often in the thousands of dollars ($20,000 for a Chinese immigrant)—not to mention their lives. Immigration also abruptly introduces them to a world in which their bonds with others depend on money rather than blood. For many immigrants, these new monetary relationships remain even after they have arrived. Uncles demand repayment of the loans used for migrating, cousins expect rent for sharing their apartments. Immigrants can never forget that they are in a new, more individualized world.

Because most have been voluntary migrants rather than involuntary refugees, immigrants to America have chosen to abandon their communities and cultures in the hope of finding better ones in the United States.

Refugees have a kind of communal solidarity forced on them by their plight, but the restless immigrants leave that kind of solidarity behind. They are unusually autonomous individuals, able to pursue family and individual goals with relative freedom. But their choice to migrate should not make us think the trip was easy. If anything it may be more traumatic because it is voluntary. The psychological stakes are higher.

One reason for immigrant success combines individual and structural forces. Immigrants show unusual creativity in figuring out new ways of doing things and new things to do. Scholars have remarked on the artistic and intellectual creativity of the generation of refugees, especially Jews, who came to the United States in the 1930s to flee Hitler. But far more immigrants, across many generations, have been creative at making money: at figuring out new business practices, perceiving new market needs, and establishing new businesses. Immigrants are not constrained by "traditional" ways of doing business, by ingrained and easy habits, or by the social expectations of neighbors. They can compare American practices with those of the old country and import skills and habits they think might succeed in their new land. They bring fresh and energetic eyes to old challenges. Their position as new arrivals allows them to be creative—exactly what an economy needs to remain healthy.

If nothing else, immigrants are flexible enough to go where the jobs are. They entered agriculture when most Americans farmed, manufacturing when factory jobs were plentiful, and they work in the large service sector today. In today's "knowledge economy" many go into higher education: at American universities, one-third of Ph.D.s granted in the sciences (one-half in engineering) go to foreigners, most of whom remain in this country. Today's immigrants don't come to the United States in search of manufacturing jobs that have gone abroad.

American immigrants have always been extraordinary people. There is a lot of truth in the perception that immigrants and their children flourish because of their own characteristics, for they are driven, flexible workers who often start off in artificially low positions. The major lesson drawn from Americans' immigrant experience, however, that underprivileged backgrounds are no obstacle to anyone willing to work, is exaggerated if not downright mistaken. Yet it is a key component of the symbolism of America, where individuals can remake their lives in pursuit of success.

———————————————————————————————————————

The eventual success of most immigrant groups has not prevented hostility on the part of the native-born, as the impoverished-immigrant stereotype has been popular alongside that of the accomplished success. Today's immigrants are incomparably more diverse than those arriving two hundred years ago, or even one hundred years ago, but the native-born of those periods were as dismayed by the newcomers as any Americans today, perhaps more so. There has been a constant challenge of "assimilation" in American history, as the native-born felt the need to subdue the newcomers. This is paradoxical, of course, for a nation constructed by immigrants. Each generation has feared that the new waves were different from earlier ones, lacking the skills or moral character essential to life in America. Older immigrants have proven themselves, we feel, but the new ones lack the moral fiber to do the same. Every time, we have been proven wrong.

Cultural diversity characterized the colonies from the start. In Jamestown there were friendly Indians, whom the settlers hoped they could put to work. Beginning in 1619 there were also Africans, whom the white settlers did put to work. Both groups posed every sort of cultural challenge to the English, with different languages, habits, and religions. In New York, tensions between English and Dutch inhabitants were high, especially during wars between England and Holland in the mid-1600s. In early New England, religious schisms played a parallel role, providing regular occasions for soul-searching and public discussion of what to do with groups who were "different." The Puritans simply banished dissenters such as Roger Williams and Anne Hutchinson into the woods or back to England. Since the beginning, public debate has raged over what to do with those who are different.

In almost every period immigrants have arrived from new, unfamiliar countries, bringing with them lifestyles that could be stigmatized as un-American and hence immoral. Germans started to appear at the end of the seventeenth century, disembarking primarily in Philadelphia due to Pennsylvania's broad publicity drive and the relative universalism of the Quakers. The earliest arrivals, who founded Germantown in 1683, shared many of the Quakers' beliefs, but after 1715 most German immigrants did not. Benjamin Franklin feared the Germans could never be assimilated: they "are generally the most stupid of their own nation; . . . it is almost impossible to remove any prejudices they entertain."[15] Scots (from both Scotland and Ireland) also arrived early, disembarking like the Germans in Philadelphia but soon pushing beyond them to settle areas along the Appalachian foothills, eventually as far as South Carolina and Georgia. Established landowners were pleased to have the Scots-Irish, with their reputation for rowdy violence, as a western buffer from the Indians. By 1790, when the first census was taken of the new nation, those of English ancestry were only 49 percent of the total population of nearly four million. Africans represented another 19 percent, and the rest were Scots-Irish, German, Irish, Dutch, French, Scandinavian, and others.

The heterogeneity of immigrants has only increased since then. In the 1830s Catholic Germans and Irish began replacing the earlier (and more skilled) Protestants, especially after famine struck Ireland. Vicious cultural conflicts erupted in eastern cities in the 1840s and 1850s over religious instruction and control of schools. In a few short years in the mid-1850s the Know-Nothings exploded from a small, anti-Catholic fraternity into a national political party, controlling state governments in much of New England. They limited naturalization proceedings, eliminated militia units composed of immigrants, imposed English-literacy tests for voting, and banned individual ownership (for example by Catholic bishops) of churches. The Know-Nothings simply articulated common Protestant images of Catholics as lazy, criminal, poor, and altogether immoral. Their condemnation of cities as hotbeds of immigrant sin would survive into the twentieth century.

Except in the 1920s, xenophobia has had little effect on the increasing diversity of American immigration. More than a hundred thousand Chinese arrived in San Francisco before the Chinese Exclusion Act of 1882 closed this flow; they represented a quarter of California's labor force in 1870.[16] Another turning point came in 1896, when immigrants from Eastern and Southern Europe began to outnumber those from Western and Northern Europe. By 1970 immigrants from the Third World were outnumbering those from Europe, aided by the Hart-Cellar Act of 1965, which repealed the restrictive policies of the 1920s. By 1990 there were as many immigrants from Asia in the United States (with the Philippines providing the largest national contingent) as from Europe and Canada combined, and an even larger number had arrived from Latin America and the Caribbean. Each succeeding cohort of immigrants has challenged American cultural predilections about religion, ethnicity, and race. Even while employers were arranging for their passage, native-born Americans were eyeing each new wave of immigrants suspiciously, stigmatizing them as different and inferior.

Hysteria over immigrants has been remarkably consistent over time. It began especially as Protestant hatred for Catholics. In the 1830s newspapers appeared with names such as the *Anti-Romanist*, *Priestcraft Unmasked*, the *Protestant Vindicator*, and *Priestcraft Exposed*. *The Protestant* declared its purpose to be "to inculcate Gospel doctrines against Romish corruptions, to maintain the purity and sufficiency of the Holy Scriptures against Monkish traditions."[17] In 1890 Henry Cabot Lodge, then a Congressman, wrote in alarm that immigration was increasing, especially among "races" that were "most alien to the body of the American people and from the lowest and most illiterate classes among those races." In the biological ethnocentrism of the day, he probably meant bodies, physical traits, quite literally. He later advised that "more important to a country than wealth and population is the quality of the people." The quality of newcomers is always suspect, linked (in popular perceptions only) with crime, ignorance, poverty, and mental illness. Eugenic arguments, once explicit, have merely gone underground since World War II. Again and again, alarmists argue that immigration is increasing and that the new immigrants are different: "The character of our immigration has also changed—instead of the best class of people, we are now getting the refuse of Europe—outcasts from Italy, brutalized Poles and Hungarians, the offscourings of the world," argued the *Philadelphia Inquirer* in 1890.[18]

Since they began in the 1940s, systematic national surveys have reflected these attitudes. In poll after poll, solid majorities would have our government restrict immigration even more. Almost all favor "tighter controls" over our borders. Only 7 percent of Americans, on average, and at no time more than 13 percent, have believed that the number of immigrants permitted to enter the country each year should be increased. Always strong, anti-immigrant sentiment increases during bad economic times, no doubt due to fears of immigrants' voracious appetites for hard work. Even those whose ancestors arrived recently are likely to oppose continued immigration. In 1992, for example, a poll of Americans of Mexican, Puerto Rican, and Cuban descent found that 65 percent believed there were too many immigrants in this country. Americans are apparently quick to conclude that their immigrant ancestors—or they themselves—are wholly superior to current immigrants.[19]

Given America's composition, immigrant bashing has always involved strong distinctions between current and past arrivals. Those who came before—the critics' ancestors—had the advantage of every virtue, and succeeded in the right way. Those who come now have every vice, and lack any chance of success. Indeed, when Americans are asked to assess the overall contribution made by different groups to the United States, their responses show an almost perfect correlation between how long the group has been here and the contribution they are thought to have made, with the English and Irish at the top, and the Vietnamese, Puerto Ricans, Haitians, and Cubans at the bottom.[20]

Part of the process of Americanization has consisted of older waves of immigrants learning to treat newer waves as badly as they were treated themselves. (The process is not unlike the hazing of fraternity pledges.) Only the earliest English settlers, who saw God's hand in the extermination of the natives, escaped this traumatic cultural transition from un-American to American. A recent book by Peter Brimelow, *Alien Nation*, is an arrogant but typical example. The author, himself a two-time immigrant from Britain to Canada and then to the United States, stridently worries that "a culture of a country, exactly like its ecology, turns out to be a living thing, sensitive and even fragile. Neither can easily be intruded upon without consequences." Brimelow does little to explicate this dubious metaphor, other than to bash recent immigrants—different, naturally, from previous waves, despite their including Brimelow himself—for potential criminality and welfare dependence. On slim evidence he insists that today's immigrants are less skilled than those of the past (by which he seems to mean those of the 1950s, not the 1890s), ignoring the possibility that, even if this were true (evidence is mixed), immigrants might compensate for skill deficits through enthusiastic hard work. He takes few pains to disguise his racism, worrying what life will be like for his blond, blue-eyed son in a country whose current immigrants (in contrast to the nation's "white core") are "overwhelmingly visible minorities from the Third World." What's most interesting is that Brimelow's charges are the same ones contemporaries leveled at all those supposedly superior immigrants of the past. It is not surprising that the book became a best-seller—despite being dismissed by every reputable scholar. The best indicator of an immigrant's assimilation is a willingness to attack later arrivals. When the television show *Firing Line* dignified Brimelow's book with a panel discussion of immigration in May of 1995, two of the eight panelists were immigrants—both of whom favored curtailing immigration.

Today the arguments against immigration are all too familiar: the new immigrants have fewer skills; many are coming simply to be reunited with families rather than to work; and at any rate the economy has changed so that fewer jobs are available for them. This Know-Nothing mantra is at least 160 years old. Once again, new arrivals are condemned because they are poor in a society where poverty is a sign of sin or vice. As soon as they succeed, they escape the stigma and become symbols of American opportunity.

Perhaps sensing this, immigrants have been more concerned with economic success than cultural assimilation. Some groups have wanted to look like native-born Americans, but others have been happy to teach their children in their own languages, maintain old traditions, and even establish their own enclaves when possible. If a strong cultural community seems likely to enhance economic success, immigrants usually try to retain it. If it does not, they usually escape it. Most come here for economic rather than cultural reasons and, this being the culture that generations of such immigrants have created, they are ultimately assimilated on economic grounds. At any rate, their main cultural effect on the United States has never been what they wore or what they drank; it has always been to affirm core American beliefs in the autonomy of individual actions, in the possibility of economic success, in the virtues of starting anew.

Immigration is the second piece of the American puzzle we're putting together, to be added to the country's reputation as a dreamy paradise of freedom. Employers' public relations campaigns have kept the ideal of American opportunity alive around the world, and waves of immigrants drawn by this promise have encouraged all of us here to believe in it as well. Because of their bicultural backgrounds, they have a clear image (right or wrong) of what it is to be "American," and how that differs from other nationalities. The new arrivals not only hope for, but confidently expect economic success. Neither rich nor poor, and bringing many useful skills with them, they are well poised to attain their dreams. A contrast with the old countries has continually implied that America was new, better, the home of the future. Because men have dominated immigration through most of our history, they may have been especially free to fantasize and then to tear themselves away from their old cultures in order to start afresh. Few immigrants were political

The patterns I have described still flourish today. In 1997 Sam Dillon, a *New York Times* reporter, visited Alaska, where more than twenty thousand Mexicans have gone in search of work, heading straight for what is left of the American frontier. Among them he found Dr. Martín D'Giesecke García, whose Mexican medical practice had been wrecked by the devaluation of the peso in 1995. D'Giesecke knew nobody in Alaska, but was drawn by help-wanted ads placed by American fishing companies in Mexican magazines. He ended up gutting cod on a trawler working the Bering Sea. America is still the land of opportunity, especially in its frontierlike boomtowns such as those of Alaska; immigration is still inspired and channeled by active publicity, and immigrants still take jobs with less status than those they left. And even working on a fishing trawler, they make money. Dr. D'Giesecke returns to Mexico for half of every year to live in considerable comfort on his American earnings.

refugees, but by fusing political and economic freedoms, we could congratulate ourselves on being the preferred destination of the world's freedom-seekers.

The founding of America and its renewal by generations of immigrants were based on a rejection of other social systems and their governments. Established in the rejection of social institutions, American culture retains a suspicion of all forms of authority. Immigrants do not think they need to rely on the aid of authorities when they have such confidence in themselves (whatever hidden aid government policies provide). Who but the most self-confident, perhaps pushy, people would uproot themselves, leave behind all the certainties and connections they know, in pursuit of their dreams? They are the kind of driven people most likely to attain those dreams. But because they are not bound by family or tradition, they often pioneer new ways of doing things, see new consumer needs to meet, transform production processes, restructure organizations. They bring the fresh perspective of outsiders to our economy.

Just as they reject one government in leaving home, immigrants often avoid the American government after they arrive. For the minority of immigrants who arrive illegally, the U.S. government is more than an inconvenience; it is an active, brutal threat to their staying in their new home. At any moment they may be rounded up by the Immigration and Naturalization Service, held in detention centers for long periods without hearings, and sent home. Even legal immigrants are not always treated well by the INS. A larger number of immigrants, legal and illegal, thrive in the shadow economy outside the purview of the government (whether regulators or tax collectors). Some are here illegally and fear discovery; others are small business entrepreneurs who use cash to hide some of their activities and avoid taxes. Others, providing personal services for rich Americans, from babysitting to waiting tables or housecleaning, prefer to remain off the books. Activities that are already illegal, such as drug sales, are perfect for people who are themselves illegal. From the start, many immigrants discourage full respect and compliance with government. In the United States, this shadow economy accounts for more than one-tenth of our total economic output. For many immigrants, economic freedom means not only working hard, but also avoiding taxes. They believe in America, but not necessarily its government.

If immigrants do not have much faith in government, they do have faith in markets, which embody the individual freedoms and room to maneuver that most of them seek. The majority of America's immigrants (including recent ones) have come here from countries still dominated by agriculture, but that does not mean that most of them were farmers. They were the ones who had detached themselves from the land. They were more likely to have gone to towns and cities, learned trades, and become accustomed to the freedoms of markets—enough to know that they wanted more of that same freedom. They were the most modern, the most restless.

Let me list here the effects—to be documented in subsequent chapters—that I think immigrants have had on American culture. *Economic* effects: a willingness to move in pursuit of opportunities; low wages, because of competition, at the bottom of the hierarchy; long hours throughout the system; an ability to innovate, to see new ways of doing things. *Environmental* effects: a view of our surroundings as resources to exploit in pursuit of wealth, and of our habitats as temporary. *Political* effects: belief in markets; mistrust of government. *Cultural* effects: the ability to see individuals more readily than structures; a belief in fresh starts; xenophobia, panics over those who are "different."

Has immigration made Americans more individualistic? Two of the main eras of collectivist politics in American history—the 1930s and 1960s—came during the only period when immigration was highly curtailed. Immigrants as a percentage of the population fell to a modern low in the late 1960s—perhaps the only period of economic prosperity with an upsurge in radical politics, with its concern for the victims of markets such as poor people. Are these coincidences? Immigration could make us more conservative by encouraging complacent self-congratulation for being the country where so many people wish to live. And it makes us more individualistic by fostering the belief that people have control over their lives: anyone who works hard can rise to the top, and losers have only themselves to blame. Immigration has "normalized" movement, sending Americans the message that radical disruption of their lives in pursuit of economic success is normal, even admirable. The main effect is individualism, not conservatism. This cultural tradition will become a major theme in later chapters.

If immigrants have bolstered our belief in individual economic rights, cultural freedoms are another story. At the same time that they work hard to attain material security, immigrants are abused for their cultural distinctiveness. They often strive to lose this, sometimes becoming the least tolerant Americans of the next generation. Just as they hope to be free from economic and political constraints, they sometimes hope to shed the corruptions of Old World traditions, lifestyles, and accents. To be American, they must be reborn as new people. From immigrants we get the notoriously American idea that history is bunk, for immigrants leave much of their past behind. Yet even as Americans believe in starting over, they are vigilant about the forms this remaking takes. Ironically, Americans' belief in their own purity makes them even more concerned with the culture of others.

Have these trends changed in recent decades, as attitudes toward the dream have changed? Today's cities no longer contain plentiful factory jobs for those with few skills, and the mix of immigrants now contains more college graduates. There are also more professionals, who need to settle down somewhere in order to establish their reputations, and more family members, meaning more women than before. Overall, immigrants are a smaller proportion of the population than in many other periods in American history. And some of them can visit first, to see if America really matches their dreams. Finally, there are more nonwhite immigrants, who face especially tough challenges. Rapid mobility (social and geographic) for immigrants may be a thing of the past. These are small qualifications in massive trends, but they suggest that immigrants may be less restless in the future and may not always be such sure symbols of success as they have been in the past.

Immigrants keep the American dream alive, but they are not the only ones who believe in starting over. Next, we shall see that native-born Americans also think they can get up and move, find a new job, shed existing reputations and responsibilities, and begin their lives again. The great migration to the United States has masked equally large migrations of Americans around this giant land mass, looking for the same opportunities to start over that immigrants seek when they come here. Like immigrants, native-born Americans associate movement with improvement.

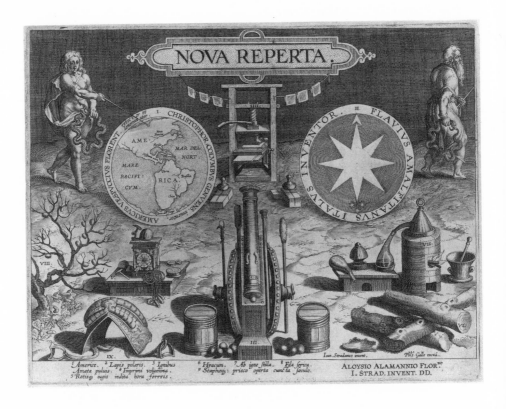

The American dream was born in Europe. This engraving from 1600 is an attempt to sum up the marvelous new discoveries *(nova reperta)* of the Renaissance, the Americas foremost among them. A printing press, cannon, and mechanical clock are also prominent. With no marks on it, the map of the new hemisphere is an exciting blank slate for European dreams, schemes, and ambitions. The figure of a young woman, symbolizing the future, points to the map, while an aging symbol of the past leaves in the upper right. This was the title page of Johanes Stradanus's work *Nova Reperta*, published in Antwerp. Reproduced by permission of the Folger Shakespeare Library, Washington, D.C.

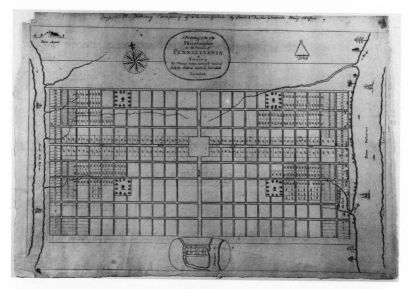

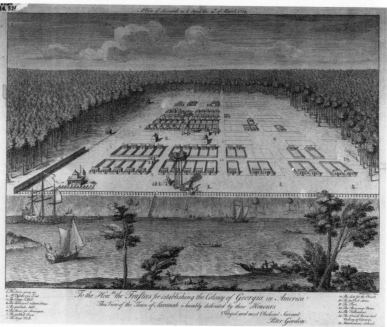

A utopian impulse to start civilization from scratch was present in the detailed plans for early American cities, regular democratic grids dotted with occasional squares for grass and monuments. The blueprint for Philadelphia is laid out in pristine symmetry between the Delaware and Schuylkill rivers by William Penn and his surveyor-general in 1682. In the map of Savannah in 1734 we see the same impulse. This was the place for Europeans to try out all their schemes—whether progressive or reactionary—for creating a new society. The grid form was a striking imposition of European civilization and order on what was perceived as malleable raw wilderness. By the same logic, much of the country would be divided into neat, 160-acre squares for homesteading. View of Philadelphia reproduced by permission of the Library Company of Philadelphia. View of Savannah reproduced by permission of the Ira D. Wallach Division of Art, Prints, and Photographs, the New York Public Library.

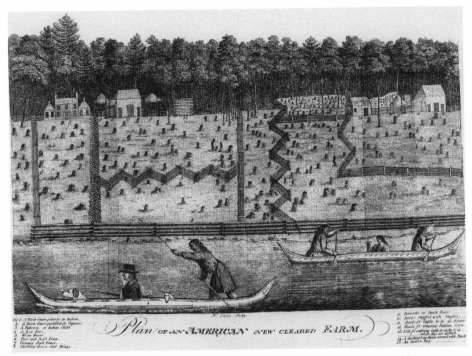

This engraving, published in 1793, shows the American form of the civilizing imperative: remove every tree and put careful fences along every property line. Different kinds of fence are displayed in this work, and stumps are still everywhere. Their land may have been taken, but the Native American Indians remained, in part, apparently, to help settlers negotiate the waterways that operated for a long time as the country's most efficient roadways. Courtesy of the Library Company of Philadelphia.

This advertisement from 1837 recognized that both immigrants (usually called emigrants then) and native-born thirsted for land in upstate New York, just being opened up by the Erie Canal. Of the eight named speculators, or "proprietors," all but one lived in New York City, not near the land, and the bill says nothing about the sale price of the land. There has always been assiduous public-relations work beneath American movement. © Collection of The New-York Historical Society. Reproduced by permission.

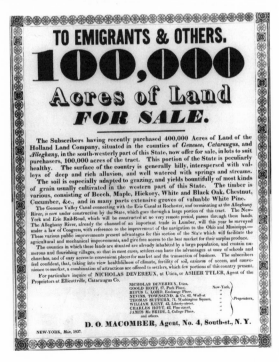

On the Road

Crossing a River

The Second Season

The First Season

EMIGRANTS IN THE NORTHWEST.

Much supposedly objective reporting was disguised boosterism, like these purport-edly realistic scenes from *Harper's Weekly* in 1878. Getting there, clearing the land, and putting up fences is hard work. But in the second season on the homestead (lower left) we already see enormous prosperity, even the leisure for a stroll. This il-lustration accompanied an editorial in favor of continued immigration. The impli-cation: the land of plenty can still accommodate all comers. © Collection of The New-York Historical Society. Reproduced by permission.

The Demopoulos family in the Greek Peloponnese just before eldest son Spyridon, front and center, left for America in 1902. Although he looks to us like a boy, he is wearing men's clothes, perhaps for the first time. His expression seems confident but anxious, different from the sad faces of the brothers who lean against him. His sisters almost look pleased that he is leaving (only the youngest of them, on the left, would join him in the United States, along with two of his brothers). Spyridon, soon to be Stephen, looks as though he is carrying the burden of being the village's most promising youth, fit for success in America. Courtesy of Nick Demas.

Most immigrants have tolerated the intolerable upon first arriving, including cramped conditions and very long hours of work. Samuel Gompers's Cigarmakers' Union could never compete with families working at home, like these immigrants from Bohemia photographed by immigrant Jacob Riis. Using "machines" and a lot of unskilled child labor, they were cheaper and demanded no benefits. Again and again new arrivals have undercut efforts to improve the wages of those at the bottom. © Museum of the City of New York. Reproduced by permission.

The Klondike was the last great gold-rush boomtown. Tens of thousands of young men flocked there from 1897 to 1900. As this group demonstrates, a few months of grime could make anyone look dangerous. There is no obvious path, although this is one of the easiest parts of the Chilkoot Trail. Photo by La Roche (negative no. 10042); reproduced by permission of the Special Collections Division, University of Washington Libraries.

Although the trail led through Alaska, the gold was in Canada; prospectors were thus embroiled in government regulations. For instance, they had to take two hundred pounds of provisions with them, mostly on sleds. Here some wait at the customs station on the border in 1898. Because no one could carry all his provisions at once, he would stack the rest before coming back for them, and many of these caches are visible here. Their own American government rarely intervened in boomtowns, not even to force gold seekers to do sensible things like bring enough provisions to survive the winter. Photo by Hegg (negative no. 3072); reproduced by permission of the Special Collections Division, University of Washington Libraries.

Boomtowners put up with lousy conditions and cramped quarters because they expect them to be temporary. These Klondike miners are checking the local dirt for signs of gold while their mitts dry overhead. They have a can of sourdough for making bread, just about the only healthy food they ate. Photo by Hegg (negative no. 3089); reproduced by permission of the Special Collections Division, University of Washington Libraries.

Some Americans, and more than a few immigrants, have felt that their lives depended on starting over in a healthier climate. Colorado Springs was settled in the 1870s by wealthy, tubercular men who believed their health could be restored through riding, hunting, and sleeping under the stars, partly because they were told this constantly by the town's two promoters, a Civil War general and an English immigrant who first went west as a geologist on a surveying expedition. (So many of his fellow countrymen arrived that the town was soon nicknamed "Little London.") Here we

see that they were still coming in 1916, sleeping in cabins, sitting in the snow, and hoping for rejuvenation at the "Modern Woodmen Sanitorium." One attraction was the promise of getting better without the aid of doctors. Reproduced by permission of the Colorado Springs Pioneers Museum.

Whatever doubts many of them had, most wives went west with their husbands, especially if they had children. These Colorado settlers in the 1880s do not seem especially pleased with their situation. At least the prairies were expansive and the mountains dramatic, compensating for the claustrophobia of living in one small wagon for the months it took to go West. Reproduced by permission of the Colorado Springs Pioneers Museum.

Even in the age of the automobile, traveling has not always been easy. Until well into the twentieth century, roads frequently turned into mud. Here are two families on the road during the Depression in search of work. By today's standards their possessions are extremely modest. Courtesy of the Franklin D. Roosevelt Library, Hyde Park, New York.

We take a lot with us today. The typical American moves every five years, roughly the same rate as throughout American history. Van lines appeared in the 1920s to take advantage of the nation's new system of paved roads, and the older truck, itself an advertisement, dates from the 1930s. The newer behemoth is fifty-three feet long, today's standard size. Relocation has become bigger and bigger business, and companies can expect to pay more than a hundred thousand dollars to relocate a top executive, which today often includes finding a job for a spouse. Photos reproduced by permission of UniGroup, Inc.

3 New Places, Names, and Selves

The youth of America is their oldest tradition. It has been going on now for three hundred years.
—*Oscar Wilde, 1893*

Only a country this young could create a car this cool.
—*1995 ad for Chevy Camaro*

To most Americans, success means moving, over and over again if necessary. Sam Clemens's family was typical. At the beginning of the nineteenth century Sam's grandfather moved his family from Virginia to new land in Kentucky, but he died only two years later, crushed in an accident at a house raising. His son John, Sam's father, unhappy when his own mother remarried, returned to Virginia though still a teenager. He stayed there only a few years before returning to Kentucky, a bit farther west than the area he had left. Within several years he had married and moved his wife to Gainesboro, Tennessee. After two years they moved again to Jamestown, the seat of a newly formed county. In 1831, five years later, they moved their growing family nine miles north to Pall Mall, still in Tennessee, hoping for better farmland. John also practiced law, primarily settling land disputes, and ran a small shop in most of the towns he passed through. Three years later the family moved west, to Florida, Missouri. Despite his land, a new store, and even a judgeship (in those days a perfect opportunity for making money), John Clemens still had trouble getting by. He devoted considerable time to lobbying the state assembly for funds to dredge the Salt River, a tributary to the Mississippi (the town of Florida was poorly situated eighty miles up this shallow river from the great Mississippi). After five years, the Clemenses moved to Hannibal, a prosperous, twenty-year-old town of one thousand people on the Mississippi. Here John Clemens added a hotel to his economic repertory, which at least gave the family a place to live. To no avail. He died in 1847, only forty-eight years old, near bankruptcy. His son Sam was eleven, six years away from starting his own restless motion.

Massive migrations to the United States are not the only movement for which Americans are famous. Once here, immigrants and their descendants—which is to say, almost all of us—continue to move about, associating physical relocation with self-improvement. For most Americans, improvement means economic success, but those with other goals also move in pursuit of them. Religious believers, starting with the Pilgrims but including many other sects since them, have thought it necessary to detach themselves from a sinful society in order to find God. Those from a more romantic tradition, from Walt Whitman to Jack Kerouac, have hoped to touch their deep inner selves through movement. Others, like Huck Finn, are simply fleeing what disturbs them. In all these cases, the assumption is that society is impure, a hindrance, an alien form of pollution that can be avoided through physical flight. Society as it exists in the here and now conflicts with the dream of how it could be somewhere else.

Americans were on the road before there were roads. Even in colonial times, when moving was arduous and there weren't many settlements to move to, both new arrivals and native-born Americans moved. The Puritans had no sooner created villages in Massachusetts than they were pushing out onto new farms, setting a pattern in which community "was dashed by transiency."[1] In late-seventeenth-century Virginia, fewer than half of those appearing on county tax lists in one decade were living in the same county ten years later. There was greater stability in New England, but even one-third of its inhabitants moved in a typical decade.[2] Rates of movement like these would turn out to be remarkably constant throughout American history (turnover rates in Boston were about 50 percent per decade in the middle of the nineteenth century, not too different from today).

By the time of the Revolution, settlers were pouring down the Great Wagon Road that ran eight hundred miles along the Appalachians from Philadelphia to Augusta, Georgia. Families established themselves in clearings in the forests and cut down the trees around them, often at great distances from their nearest "neighbors," if that is the right word for a family a mile down a very rough path. Thousands of applicants would appear whenever a land office opened to allocate parcels in a new area. In the half-century before the Revolution, the population of the southern colonies along the Appalachians was growing explosively, in many areas doubling every decade in spite of high mortality rates. Each year thousands flowed through the Shenandoah Valley heading south, most of them immigrants who had only recently arrived in Pennsylvania. The frontiers of northern New England, upstate New York, and western Pennsylvania were being settled at a similar pace. Not all the native Indians had been subdued by this time, and the Cherokee War of 1760–61 was especially vicious. The grim brutality of the attacks, by both sides, added to the macho "frontier" roughness. But land was an obsession, and people stampeded to claim it. Such activity continued along the frontier as it pushed westward over the next century.

Two hundred years ago migrants traveled at the pace they could walk, along muddy, rock-strewn trails accompanying their wagons—or in some cases crude carts with cross-sections of tree trunks as wheels. Luckier ones moved at the speed they could float or paddle canoes. In the years since, technological improvements have increased our speed, without satisfying our restlessness. They have only made it easier to indulge.

After the Revolution the new federal government, tiny though it was, recognized the importance of opening up new lands through improved transportation. It commissioned a comprehensive survey of roads, published in 1789; a coastal survey followed in 1796, complete with instructions for navigating major ports and harbors. In 1806 Congress appropriated thirty thousand dollars for a Great National Pike, known as the Cumberland Road, to run from Maryland to Ohio; by the time it opened in 1840, it extended all the way to Illinois. State and local governments also enthusiastically promoted infrastructure, first chartering private development companies and then, after the 1820s, frequently bankrolling canals and turnpikes themselves.

The new government's other main expenditures were on land. Territorial expansion held the government's attention from the start, as it fought Indians on the northwest frontier (what is now Ohio) in the 1790s, signing a 1795 treaty in which the British relinquished their claims to the area. An 1819 treaty with Spain, won after an illegal occupation by Andrew Jackson and his army, secured the Florida territory. After violence, the biggest expansion came via the marketplace. Thomas Jefferson, whose main concern as president was to limit the activities of the federal government, had to amend the constitution to allow the purchase of the Louisiana territory in 1803. In his most popular act as president, he more than doubled the size of the United States, igniting into full fury American dreams of land ownership. Forty years later

President James Polk bullied Mexico into war to provide an excuse for capturing the vast lands of the southwest, from Texas to California. The resulting Treaty of Guadalupe Hidalgo, in 1848, increased the size of the republic by another third: just in time for the gold rush, which represented expansionist frenzy at its height. In a single typical lifetime, from 1800 to 1850, the land available for settlement had more than tripled, gold had been discovered at the far end of the continent, and the image of the United States as the land of opportunity was more firmly entrenched than ever.

Water offered this country's first system of roads, for the continent was blessed with enormous stretches of coastline as well as a fantastic system of navigable rivers that proved crucial to opening up its land mass to exploitation. Beginning almost immediately after the Revolution, canals were built in order to perfect the work God had done in making the rivers. No fewer than thirty canal companies were established by 1790. In 1794, a two-mile canal—the nation's first—opened next to the Connecticut River in South Hadley Falls, Massachusetts. During the next half century, these and other companies dug—much of it by hand—almost five thousand miles of canals. Government was also heavily involved, as in New York State's $140-million public-works project that built the 340 miles of the Erie Canal, which opened in 1825 after nine years of construction. Construction like this was not only necessary for moving settlers west but also for transporting their produce east, making their migrations more lucrative.

It was the refinement of steamboat technology, especially in the 1830s, that definitively opened up so much of this land to the restless. Unlike Huck's raft, which only floated downstream with the flow of the Mississippi, steamboats had considerable power to go upstream as well, depositing people in remote areas. Flatboats and keelboats had taken three or four months to go upriver from New Orleans to St. Louis; steamboats took a week. The utility and excitement of steamboats were unmatched anywhere else in the world, for no other country could apply them so extensively. This new invention allowed boomtowns to spring up all along the extensive rivers of the Midwest, and the new country's love affair with transportation technology was in full bloom.

Sam Clemens's Missouri was filled with these towns. For each one that thrived, others failed; all were subject to the vicissitudes of migration and markets. The Clemens family moved to Hannibal at the end of 1839 because their town of Florida was being abandoned as insufficiently profitable. Although Sam's father never managed to benefit from Hannibal's rapid growth, many others did. The town was a regular steamboat stop, and young Sam was exposed to the gambling, prostitution, violence, duels, even murders, of boomtowns filled with restless young men. Because his father landed a job as the justice of the peace, Sam learned about all this firsthand. Most of all, he saw people on the move. He saw people arriving. Missouri had innumerable new towns, many of them founded on utopian principles of one sort or another. The Mormons, for instance, were living only sixty miles upriver in Nauvoo, Illinois. And he saw people leave. Missouri was the gateway to the west, and a significant portion of Hannibal's "permanent" population left for California when gold was discovered. One of Sam's first jobs as a young man, which he liked as much as writing, was that of riverboat pilot, at which he might have continued had the Civil War not stopped traffic on the Mississippi. Like many Americans, Sam Clemens saw this as a dream job: to be constantly on the move, to be paid well for one's work, to be at the forefront of opening up the North American continent. So much did water set the pattern for American transportation that today we still "ship" a package, even when it travels in a large brown truck.

Water travel opened up the great midwest, but it was a cumbersome way to get to the other side of the Continental Divide and the Rockies. It required a passage around Tierra del Fuego that could take six months, or rough portage by canoe over the malarial Panama isthmus. (That did not prevent five hundred ships from leaving Eastern ports for California in 1849, at the height of the gold rush—cramped boxes of stress, disease, and poor nutrition.)

Enter the railroads. Whereas in Europe the new railroads were simply a new means for what Europeans were already doing—bringing coal out of mines, moving from one city to another—in the United States they made all sorts of new activities possible in new areas. They were part of the utopian urge to build a new civilization from the ground up. Rather than being laid alongside existing roads, as in Europe, railroads created new routes to open up the interior of the country. They were used, not to travel between known points, but to discover new ones. They determined where the cities and towns would be. They also generated economic activity, and virtually all the great American fortunes of the century had their roots in the railroads. As the engines for the industrial revolution, trains and steamboats appeared to be creative, opening up new possibilities, rather than destructive, as they did in Europe, where they displaced older roads and ways of life. Americans found heroic new uses for European transportation technologies.

The automobile, too, was first invented in Europe, but the United States was quicker—taking only two generations—to develop a way of life centered on this easy new form of movement. From the start the motorcar promised individual mobility. One of its initial draws was the ability to escape what was perceived as immoral and unhealthy cities for restoratives in the countryside. This took two forms: a house in the suburbs, to which the breadwinner could escape each night to be with his family, and weekend escapes even deeper into the countryside. In the three decades after 1920, two thousand state parks and forty thousand motels and tourist courts were created.[3] American restlessness could be satisfied short of a completely new habitation, although cars also symbolized more permanent escape. The American dream of freedom, flight, and starting over received an enormous technological boost. And of course it was men who most embraced the new machines and what they represented.

As we saw with the success of immigrants, though, what appears to be the result of individual consumer choices depended heavily on economic forces and policy choices. These are most obvious, perhaps, in the purchase by General Motors of many city trolley lines in the 1930s (in order to replace them, most often, with buses of its own manufacture). But federal, state, and local governments have encouraged reliance on automobiles too. There have been enormous federal subsidies of highways, peaking in the great interstate highway construction of the 1950s, itself another kind of utopian vision of remaking the country by laying down upon it this abstract new grid of north-south and east-west expressways. The only opposition came from those who feared expansion of the federal government, not from anyone who doubted the virtues of autos and trucks. There is also the longstanding refusal to tax gasoline more than a token amount, which does not nearly cover the social costs of the pollution that results. Our gasoline costs less than bottled water, and about one-third or one-fourth what it costs in most other countries. By some estimates, the United States gives automobiles more than seven times the public subsidies it offers to more cost-effective public transportation. The most prominent historian of the automobile in the United States says that observers in the 1930s claimed "that the private passenger car had won out over mass transit . . . because travelers preferred the freedom and convenience it gave them. Other evidence, however, suggests that the promotion of highway transportation by special-interest groups and resulting public policy decisions were perhaps more important to the decline of public transit than consumer choice in a free market."[4] In our imagination the automobile won because of the individual freedom it offered; in reality it had more to do with corporate strategy.

Anyone who wonders what cars and trucks mean to Americans should look at the vehicles' names, which still promise escape and adventure. Some sound speedy and dangerous, like Barracudas, Sting-rays, and Tempests, while others refer directly to the frontier: Cimarrons, Mavericks, Mustangs, Thunderbirds, and the notorious exploding Pinto. (European cars, like Mercedes or Volvos, tend to come in sedately numbered series.) Station "wagons" seem descended from the Con-estoga. Nissan recently introduced a Frontier pickup. But none capture American sensibilities better than the recent minivans and "sport utility vehicles," each one of them a small environmental disaster. Some of their names merely allude to movement and escape, such as Voyagers, Quests, Explorers, Navigators, Expeditions, and Ventures. Others have explicit wild-west connotations, like Blazers, Caravans, Pathfinders, Pi-oneers, Tahoes, Trackers, even Rodeos, Wranglers, Cherokees, Navahos, Laredos, Silverados, and Yukons. The newest entry is the Dodge Du-rango. (In Japan, the same vehicles have names like Town Cube, Gravel Express, and Utility Wizard.) And of course there is the Bronco, made notorious by O. J. Simpson when he demonstrated just how deeply he believed in escape. The police could have pursued him in a Ranger. A few push the flight theme beyond the borders of the United States, to places—other regions (Outbacks, Safaris) or outer space (Windstars, Aerostars)—still thought to be frontiers. There is irony in housewives and middle managers driving to the local mall in such vehicles. The one thing the preposterous names never express is what the vehicles are ac-tually used for: you'll never see one called the Commuter, Kid-hauler, Mallstar, or the Middle Manager (although there is a candidly named Suburban).

Car advertisements tap into American fantasies of flight through set-tings on the tops of mesas, the edges of canyons, or empty country roads, inevitably out West. In one, the car travels through someone's purely imaginary landscape, drawn in rough cartoon style. Even wimpy small cars try to get into the act. A recent commercial for the Chevy Mal-ibu boasts, "This is not a country for wimps. We invented the cowboy, the jawbreaker, and the quarterback blitz." The Malibu, too, can be tough and aggressive, since it is the "equivalent of Rocky Balboa." It is almost impossible to find an ad for a sport utility vehicle that is not set in rugged mountains.

Even the counterculture, while rejecting some aspects of American materialism, embraced the supposed freedom of the car culture. Beats were "on the road," usually heading to California, often in a stolen vehi-cle. There was no purpose or destination; the road itself was the point, a place to strip away nonessentials and find one's true self, or perhaps to forget oneself in the cosmic rhythm of the wheels. Ken Kesey's magical bus roamed about, spewing forth diesel pollution as well as psychedelic fantasies, its destination sign merely saying "Furthur." Novel upon novel, movie after movie, has been set on highways, celebrating automobiles and the open road.

Americans' reluctance to wear seat belts seems to confirm that they see their automobiles as small islands of autonomy and freedom. In countries like Canada, Britain, and Germany, virtually all drivers wear their belts, but in the United States barely 60 percent do—with the rest actually breaking the law in forty-nine states. My own father, who used to wear seat belts religiously, declared when his state passed its mandatory seat belt law that he would never wear his belt again. And, perversely, he hasn't. Everyone knows that seat belts save lives. So it must be their symbolic connotations that Americans dislike. They remind each of us of the dangers of driving, and of our own potential mortality. But if this were all, citizens of other countries might also dislike them (although it is possible that an American cult of youth leads us to deny death more fervently). Even more, I suspect, seat belts now symbolize government intervention in our little automotive free spaces, much as gasoline taxes do. Restricting our migratory impulses is un-American.

The enthusiasm with which Americans have deployed new technologies for moving about, while spurred by restless dreams, has had big economic payoffs. Transportation systems (which until the telegraph were also our communication systems) were the dynamo behind American economic development. From canals to railroads to cars, innovations in management and control—from the joint-stock corporation to state regulation—began here before spreading to other sectors. The opening of the continent to restless individuals was also crucial to the industrial revolution. According to one student of the matter, listing organizational innovations, "Ship's husbands, regular traders, scheduled packet lines, turnpike and canal companies, and the freight forwarders all appeared in the first half-century of the American republic and flourished well before the onset of the Industrial Revolution in the 1840s," forming a "necessary precondition" of the latter.[5] In a country this large, transportation technologies did not simply facilitate economic activity, they created it.

Just as transportation preceded other industries in the United States, so roads were laid out before most of the cities and towns that sprang up along them. In most other countries, roads run from one important place to another, then stop. Or they change names with each turn or each historical site, becoming, essentially, different roads or streets. In the United States roads run on, oblivious to their surroundings. Route 1 extends from Key West to Canada, Interstate 80 from New York to San Francisco. Broadway starts at the tip of Manhattan and does not stop until it is out of the city altogether, somewhere in upstate New York. Nothing is allowed to interfere with the flow of traffic. Over most of the country, Americans were on the move first, and stopped to build along the roadsides only when their last mule died or they sensed money to be made (from those coming later, of course).

As each new technology appeared, Americans were quick to drop the old ones. Canals fell into decrepitude after 1850, many after only a decade of use. Their successors, the railroads, would suffer a similar eclipse when cars and trucks appeared. In 1922 passenger miles traveled by automobile were one-quarter those traveled by rail, but only seven years later they were four times as great. More recently, air travel, while it cannot entirely replace the automobile, has flourished to the point that many Americans think nothing of commuting thousands of miles each week. Many Congressional representatives fly from Washington home to their districts in Florida or California each week. Rich college kids fly home for a weekend with family and friends. Even a professor I know, who teaches at U.C.L.A., flies home to his family in New York every Friday. With this kind of convenience, you hardly need to move permanently in order to start a new life; you can come home for the weekend. Yet we still move.

Today, with advanced technological means at our disposal, we change our residence, on average, *once every five years*—more often than any other culture except nomadic tribes, although in line with our ancestors. In an average year, almost one out of five Americans moves. More than a third of these move to a different county. Roughly 3 percent of Americans move to a new state. That may not sound like much, but that's in a single year, and over time these moves add up. Few Americans spend their lives in the same city or town, and almost none stay in the same house, street, or neighborhood. In a typical five-year period, only about half the population (53 percent) is living in the same place at the end as at the beginning. Another 2 percent of the population has moved here from abroad, leaving 45 percent who have moved within the United States. Of these internal migrants, almost half, 21 percent of the total, have stayed in the same metropolitan area: they've moved from Queens to Manhattan, or Manhattan to Westchester. But that still leaves 24 percent of the total who may have moved long distances—in just five years. At least 5 percent—one person in twenty—moved *very* long distances, since this is roughly the number who migrated from one of the four major regions (Northeast, North Central, South, and West) to another.

This is a lot of movement. In a typical year, while 20 percent of Americans move, only 4 percent of Dutch citizens do. Rates are 4 percent in Germany, 8 percent in the United Kingdom, 10 percent in France and Japan. In a less developed country like Thailand, only 12 percent of the population move in a five-year period, barely a quarter of the rate in the United States.[6] Only Canada and Australia, also popular destinations for international migration, have levels of internal migration close to those in the United States.

Not all Americans are equally likely to move. Regions of the United States, for example, vary somewhat: in the Northeast only 38 percent of the population move in those five years, but in the West, 57 percent do (the North Central figure is 45 percent, and for the South, 49 percent.) The restless still look west, as they have throughout American history. They may eye Oregon or Idaho instead of California—or after trying California—but they're still ready to move around until they get it right.

Younger people are more likely to move than older ones. Nearly 40 percent of Americans age 20–24 move in a given year, as do more than 30 percent of those in their late twenties. For internal migration, as for international immigration, moving is associated with *finding work*. For those over 65, fewer than 6 percent move in any given year: many start new lives in Florida or Arizona and then stay put. Blacks and Latinos are a little more mobile than whites, largely because they are somewhat younger overall. Another big but unsurprising difference is between those who rent and those who own their homes: renters are more than three times as likely to move (one-third of them move in a given year). Men are only slightly more likely to move than women (perhaps because so many men and women move together).

The propensity to move is not affected much by family size or income. Young, unmarried people are not the only ones on the move: 18 percent of single-person households move in a given year, but so do 18 percent of households with seven or more people! Wealthier people are only slightly less likely to move in any year: 12 percent of those making over $100,000 a year move, compared to 17 percent of those making under $30,000. Nor does education matter much. (Education makes more of a difference for the kind of move, with college graduates going greater distances.) Everyone, it seems, is on the move. Like immigration, *geographic mobility has been a constant in American history.*[7]

My father's father, Jones Dudley Jasper, grew up on a farm six miles from Manassas, Virginia. He was the eldest child in a family hardened not only by poverty but by an old-fashioned Protestantism which saw children as unruly creatures who needed discipline beaten into them. He grew up fast, learning to read and write in a one-room schoolhouse at Buck Hall, a mile from home. He got straight A's, but at the end of seventh grade, as high as the little school went, he left home. His father told him he could no longer support him and gave him five dollars to start him on his way—a chilling sendoff, but he was happy to go. After all, whenever he earned money working odd jobs for neighbors, his father took every penny of it. Who needed high school? It was the spring of 1916, the United States was moving toward entering World War I, and Jones heard there were construction jobs in nearby Quantico, where the U.S. Marines were expanding their base. Despite his youth, he was soon in charge of a road-building crew. This was the Jim Crow South, where a white child—Huck Finn's age—would naturally be put in charge of a crew of middle-aged black men.

Grandpa began studying surveying through the International Correspondence School, ever a boon to self-starters willing to educate themselves. When the war ended, he moved to Detroit with the same construction company that had rebuilt Quantico. After two years, the company moved him to Washington, D.C., to help build the National Cathedral for the Episcopal Church. Within another couple of years he left to start his own construction company, specializing in the kind of iron fences he had built around the Cathedral. Although today Manassas is a suburb of Washington, the thirty miles that separate them seemed a long distance in 1923. Except for the language, my grandfather's leap from the rural into the industrial age was almost as staggering as the one Steve Demas had made at almost the same age, fifteen years before. Both entered a new world with no contacts, expecting to make their fortunes with nothing more than ingenuity and hard work.

Both were aided by a booming local economy, sustained even in hard times by a federal government growing into a world power. But this was no accident. Demas left Seavista because he knew (or his village elders knew) there would be better jobs in America. Grandpa left home because the future clearly did not lie in hardscrabble farming in the hills near Manassas. Both boys were ambitious, so they followed the jobs. Their ability to work hard and manage others helped them become successful small businessmen. Some do make it.

The sixty million immigrants who have come to the United States from abroad is an impressive number, but it is smaller than the number of Americans who have made the unsettling trip from farm to city over the past two hundred years. In 1800, only thirty-three towns had more than 2,500 people in them (containing only 6 percent of the population), and only six had more than 10,000. The largest, New York, had barely 60,000 inhabitants, but one hundred years later thirty-eight cities had populations greater than 100,000 (three of them topped 1 million). If anything, the move to cities accelerated in the twentieth century. Forty percent of the population lived in towns of more than 2,500 in 1900, but 75 percent do now. Urbanization happened faster in the United States than in Europe, which had already had large cities for hundreds of years and yet today retains more of a rural population than we have. At the beginning of the nineteenth century, when more than three-quarters of Americans still worked in agriculture, barely a third of the English did. Today, hardly 2 percent of Americans work in farming, while 6 percent of Europeans still do. Americans may wax nostalgic about family farms, but no one wants to live on one. When job opportunities shift, Americans are fast to move with them.

The great migration of jobs from country to city began before the creation of jobs on farms had even ended. In the late nineteenth century, would-be farmers were still heading west with hopes of cheap land, especially on the arid high plains, and the number of American farms nearly tripled between 1860 and 1900. Available land was no longer so cheap or so fertile, however, and many of these new farms were abandoned within a few decades. Families that in one generation were part of the farm movement, in the next were headed toward the

Some Americans have moved for reasons of health. Thousands of tuberculosis patients headed back to nature in the late nineteenth century, especially to pursue the vigorous life in the Southwest. They may have accounted for a third of the migration to many states, even more to those cities—Pasadena, Colorado Springs, Denver, Tucson—that actively promoted their healing climates. Poor victims settled for the Adirondacks instead. Tuberculosis was the greatest killer of the century—Ralph Waldo Emerson lost two of his four brothers to it—and its horrid wasting encouraged radical solutions. It is not clear if the outdoor life of hunting, hiking, and camping helped, but as usual people thought so in their letters and published accounts. In *Living in the Shadow of Death,* historian Sheila Rothman notes that "the tone of the narratives, whether published or unpublished, in letters or in books, is almost always confident and hopeful, telling of bodies restored and fortunes made [even consumptives did not give up on that goal]. To be sure, there are occasional references to separation and loss, to the pain of men dying far from home, puzzled at their bad luck. But it is the success stories that dominate the literature." Just as typical was the gender of the health seekers, who were mostly men; women preferred to face their illness at home. Individual men were willing to travel several thousand miles by themselves to be reborn to health.

cities. Most of the famed Okies who fled the Dust Bowl for California during the Depression, for instance, were only a generation from the hill country of the South. While they were trying to find decent land in the late nineteenth century, most immigrants—more adaptable in their striving—were already settling in the cities to pursue the opportunities there. For an Italian or Polish immigrant, New York was as much a frontier to conquer and exploit as Kansas was for a Kentuckian. Stephen Demas saw in Washington the kinds of opportunities others saw in the Klondike, one of the last sites of the gold stampedes, starting in 1896, four years after Demas's arrival. By the early twentieth century, however, the balance in opportunities had taken a decisive urban turn.

Once Americans were firmly planted in cities and suburbs, they began to fret over the disappearance of the small family farm. But the economy and its shifting opportunities had already spoken. The American urban movement looks very much like the immigration movement. People moved because jobs did, because cities looked like the place to go to get ahead. Land began to lose its attraction as a source of wealth in the late nineteenth century, and by the twentieth it looked more like a trap. Unlike the frontier, the city was as likely a destination for daughters as for sons. Until they married, they too needed work, initially as the secretaries and salespeople who proliferated in the late nineteenth century. Whichever direction they chose, westward or city-ward, everyone was ready to start over.

The purpose of moving is self-transformation. We hope to rearrange our inner, "true" selves and of course to make a fortune in the process. As with immigration, moving is influenced by both push and pull factors. We feel constrained by who we are in our hometown, or we can't find work there, or we have had a brush with the law. But we are sure there is work somewhere else—the kind of job that will fulfill or enrich us, or at least keep us out of jail. Just as international immigrants tear themselves away from a considerable amount of cultural tradition, so internal migrants are seeking freedom, the ability to refashion their lives as they wish. Jimmy Gatz, to take F. Scott Fitzgerald's fictional example, remade himself, with the help of Franklinesque schedules and resolutions, into his "Platonic conception of himself," the elegant Jay Gatsby.

One indication of our trust in starting over is the frequency with which Americans change their names, an action still legally difficult in many countries. Immigrants, it is well known, have often shortened

American etiquette books used to offer advice on choosing and announcing new names, the practice was so common. "Try to have your name match your background," Amy Vanderbilt advised in her 1952 guide, *Amy Vanderbilt's Complete Book of Etiquette.* "It should not be too obvious that your name has been changed, if it's to fit you comfortably." To avoid errors, such as adopting an Irish surname if you are German, she recommends consulting a librarian, a genealogist, or an English teacher. She provides alternative wordings for formal announcements. "Simple white cards are engraved with or without plate marking in black script or in any of the restrained English-style types." Unpronounceable names and difficult spellings should of course be changed. But never forget, she says, "It's a serious matter to change one's name, and the procedure should be treated with due dignity."

their names upon arrival, just as Spyridon Ionnais Demopoulos became Steve Demas. This was not the exclusive work of impatient immigration officials; ship registries were often responsible—and immigrants themselves complicit. Conformity is one motivation. First names are "Americanized" when children enroll in school or when impatient teachers need to call roll; many immigrants Americanize their last names not only to fit in, but also to enhance business or social contacts. Some changes used to be routine, as when Israels became Lees (such as immigrant Lee Strasberg) or Feeneys became Fords (like director John Ford). Who but an immigrant could write a song like "God Bless America"—but only after changing his name from Israel Baline to Irving Berlin.

Immigrants are not the only ones to craft new names. Take the writers of the American Renaissance, the first major flowering of American letters, which we will examine later. James Cooper began using his middle name after his father died bankrupt; Ralph Emerson also used his middle name, Waldo; David Henry Thoreau switched the order of his first names; Herman Melvill and Nathaniel Hathorne each added a letter; and Walter Whitman Jr. shortened his first name and dropped the suffix—small changes, perhaps, but all of them self-conscious efforts to craft a new sense of self. Later writers, acutely conscious of the sound of words, have made similar alterations, or greater ones. Nathan Weinstein became Nathanael West; William Falkner added a *u;* Thomas Lanier Williams III called himself Tennessee; immigrant Solomon Bellow decided at age twenty-one that he preferred Saul. William Penn Adair Rogers and Ringgold Wilmer Lardner doubtless improved their prospects as earthy humorists when they dropped their middle names and shortened their first ones.

Writers often create identities for themselves with pen names. The best example is "Mark Twain," Sam Clemens's alter ego and public persona. A recent biographer insists that Sam Clemens and Mark Twain had an "uneasy alliance" that helped Clemens forge a distinctively American form of fame. "Among Clemens's most important contributions was the invention of the modern concept of fame itself, a phenomenon of a world just coming into being. Fame—and the manipulation of personal image that fame implies—has become the defining characteristic of American culture."[8] As a distinct identity evolved for Clemens's pseudonym, he could craft it to fit popular tastes—always in the hope that it would make money for him. To shape that image, he spent years working on an autobiography, and he was delighted to use new technologies when possible—especially photography. Says another biographer, "Mark Twain painstakingly molded a self-image as product, forged in part from the proliferation of his photographic image."[9] Clemens used other names in his early writings, starting at the age of sixteen with "W. Epaminondas Adrastus Blab," and later in his life he adopted the more distinguished "S. L. Clemens" as something of a persona. But only "Mark Twain"—a reassuring riverboat term meaning two fathoms, about twelve feet, deep enough water for any boat to pass safely—developed into a fairly full and consciously crafted persona of its own (as well as being a legally protected trademark). Clemens paid a cost for his fresh starts, as a sympathetic biographer finds a "hollowness" at the core of this "underdeveloped boy-man."[10] We seek new identities that fit us better, but they often prove rather shallow.

Actors, whose careers are also based on carefully constructed personas, often select compelling new names. In many cases they are fleeing an ethnic or immigrant identity. Think of Betty Joan Perske, Anna Maria Italiano, Anthony Benedetto, Dino Crocetti, Margarita Casino, Bernard Schwarz, Doris von Kappelhoff, and Melvyn Hesselberg. They became, respectively, Lauren Bacall, Ann Bancroft, Tony Bennett, Dean Martin, Rita Hayworth, Tony Curtis, Doris Day, and Mel Douglas. Virtually every Jewish entertainer from the 1920s through the 1950s adopted a blandly American name, from Peter Lorre and Paulette Goddard, through Kirk Douglas, Dyan Cannon, and Danny Kaye, to Woody Allen and Bea Arthur. Of the Hollywood Ten who refused to cooperate with the House Un-American Activities Committee in 1947, seven of them were name changers—a fact the anti-Semitic committee found suspicious but which was extremely American. At the opposite extreme, rather than enhancing assimilation, names could become part of the act. Samuel Joel Mostel spiced up his comedy routine by calling himself

Zero. And what mother would name her sons Chico, Harpo, Groucho, Gummo, and Zeppo?

Jewish name-changing has been especially frequent, as well as the source of jokes, in part because most Jewish families of northern and eastern Europe had carried surnames for a relatively short time. Most dated to the early nineteenth century, when new state bureaucracies insisted on them as a replacement for traditional naming practices of the form Isaac ben (son of) Abraham. In 1898 the *New York Tribune* interviewed an "East Side patriarch," who said, "We honor our fathers just as much, even if we drop their names. Nothing good ever came to us while we bore them; possibly we'll have more luck with the new names."[11] New names of one's own choosing are especially attractive replacements for names forced on one's family by hated governments.

Other entertainers and public figures adopt new names too, since their identities are part of their publicity package. Immigrant Mary Pickford was Gladys Smith until she got the anonymous role of the Biograph Girl and fans began calling her Little Mary or the Girl with the Golden Hair. Names like Pola Negri, Rudolph Valentino, Theda Bara, and later Rock Hudson and Marilyn Monroe were designed to conjure romance and sexuality. Joan Crawford sounds better than Lucille Le Sueur. You don't have to be an entertainer to change your name, although you may not have an agent to help you think up a new one. Other Americans have changed their names too. Gary Hart is hardly the only politician to do so. That prince of authenticity, Bob Dylan, shed the name Robert Allen Zimmerman. More recently, the pop musician Prince, partly for legal reasons having to do with recording contracts, began to record as "The Artist Formerly Known As [Prince]." This would seem the ultimate dead-end of name changing, but in the late nineties he began identifying himself with a symbol rather than words.

African Americans have always had special reasons for changing their names. Many slaves considered themselves to have surnames, which they never revealed to their masters. On both sides, surnames were seen to lend dignity, and so owners rarely gave their slaves more than a first name, often a simple, goofy, or ironic one such as Cato. After emancipation, former slaves could openly proclaim their names or adopt entirely new ones as part of creating new lives. They had legal as well as personal incentives to have surnames, as the Freedmen's Bureaus required them for enrollment. Many ex-slaves, fearing that their freedom might be taken away, believed new names might make it harder for their former owners to find them. Some adopted their owners' names, less out of respect than out of a concern for maintaining ties to their own families. Those who had been raised elsewhere frequently took the previous owners' names, again in an effort to recognize connections to earlier generations of their own families. A few took names of national leaders. One boy, called Jeff Davis by his former owner, adopted the name Thomas Grant. "Rather than reveal a sordid past," says historian Leon Litwack, "the names assumed or revealed after emancipation reflected a new beginning—an essential step toward achieving the self-respect, the personal dignity, and the independence which slavery had compromised."[12]

Frederick Douglass had been named Frederick Augustus Washington Bailey by his mother, but he dropped the two middle names as a young teenager. In his illegal flight he had good reason to change his last name, first to Stanley and then to Johnson. When he arrived to settle in New Bedford, Massachusetts, he decided there were too many Johnsons there already and so became Douglass. When an immigrant slave named Isabella was freed in 1827, she adopted the last name Van Wagenen, after the family who had helped free her. Five years later she joined a religious cult that gave her a new identity; eleven years after that, when she herself decided to become an itinerant preacher, she finally settled on a name that stuck, Sojourner Truth. Booker T. Washington and others too had the opportunity to select names, or portions of names, that they felt best reflected who they were. Like so many Jewish immigrants, black Americans had few historical loyalties to their names.

African Americans have continued to use names as a source of identification with group, culture, and religion: hence Elijah Muhammed, Mohammad Ali, Kareem Abdul-Jabbar, and Amiri Baraka, to name just a few. H. Rap Brown was transformed into Jamil Abdullah Al-Amin, and Stokely Carmichael (an immigrant from Trinidad) into Kwame Ture. Sometimes the names become simpler, as when Chloe Anthony Wofford became Toni Morrison, or Gloria Jean Watkins remade herself into bell hooks (the lowercase letters themselves making a statement, even though the name came from hooks' maternal great-grandmother). Malcolm Little took the surname X upon entering the Nation of Islam, and El-Hajj Malik El-Shabazz after exiting; before that he had been known as "Detroit Red," dubbed that by his friend "Shorty" to distinguish him from "St. Louis Red" and from "Chicago Red," who later became the comedian Redd Foxx! Having faced systematic efforts to strip their identities from them, many black Americans see names as a way to regain control over that identity for themselves. As the aptly named Ralph Waldo Ellison put it, "It is through our names that we first place ourselves in the world. Our names, being the gift of others, must be made our own. . . . They must become our masks and our shields and the containers of all those values and traditions which we learn and/or imagine as being the meaning of our familial past."[13] A large part of personal identity is wrapped up in one's name, which is not changed or constructed lightly.

For African Americans, new names have often been a way to rebuild a sense of family and identity of which they felt robbed. For whites, name changing has more often been a way to escape from undesired families—or from the law. I was happy to learn that Jeff Gillooly, troubled partner of Tonya Harding, changed his name to Stone upon exiting prison, following a long line of American men who have changed their names to escape notoriety. Whatever the motive, names are signs of a new beginning.

Traditionally, women have changed their names when they married, one way—not always the best—for them to start over. Recently, this has become one option among others, and they must decide what kind of statement to make about continuity or discontinuity in their lives. Taking a new husband's last name may represent either a new start or a lack of individualist assertion. Most women follow tradition. More than 95 percent of women without college degrees change their names upon marriage. But even among those with postgraduate degrees (those most likely to have professional identities based on their maiden names), almost 80 percent still adopt their husbands' surnames. In all likelihood, men adopt new surnames as a way to disconnect from their pasts, women as a way to connect with their new husbands—even when that means losing some ties to their own pasts.

Nicknames are another way to change identity. They cut across the American grain of self-creation, since one's friends or coworkers inevitably create the nickname, but they follow an American tradition of new personas for new settings. They also reflect a kind of egalitarian camaraderie, in which your family name, like the rest of your background, counts for little. Athletes, gangsters, and the young men who populate boomtowns are perfect examples. H. L. Mencken found nicknames a deep part of American culture, especially, he thought, among "the evangelical tribesmen of the South and Southwest."[14] In certain periods of our history, this rough familiarity has been a political advantage, with nicknamed candidates—Old Hickory, Honest Abe—faring well in elections. In others, acronyms like FDR, JFK, and LBJ have served equally well.

The creativity that goes into renaming oneself even more frequently goes into naming children, who bear the burden of parents' social aspirations, poetic fancies, and political allegiances. Not only do parents water down the ethnicity of their children's names, as they do to their own, but they frequently choose names that sound vaguely middle- or upper-class, such as Tiffany or Ashley, Ryan or Michael. Your given name may say more about your parents than about you. One prominent scholar of American history, Sacvan Bercovitch, bears his father's radical politics and sympathy for Sacco and Vanzetti. "One can read in American naming patterns and practices the same strains of restlessness, envy, striving, confidence, and overconfidence to be found in other indices of middle-class behavior: the accrual of possessions, for example, or clothing, leisure activities, political groupings. If the brand of beer you guzzle and the way you spend your Sunday afternoons say something piquant about you, so does your name."[15] The same restlessness that keeps them moving encourages Americans to shed old names and adopt new ones.

Names are only one marker of personal identity. Another way to start over, and one of the easiest, it to make up a new story about your past. Some people simply make up details about their histories. I once had a colleague who, we eventually discovered, played unusually loose with the facts of his childhood. He had one cluster of stories that emphasized his family's poverty, and even on occasion seemed to include life in a Chicago housing project. Another set of stories presented a more august lineage. Although it is conceivable—barely—that both stories were true, they gave very different impressions of who the teller was. This man was unusually schizoid in retaining two seemingly opposed "lives" for himself, but plenty of other Americans change their stories at some point, creating new lives for themselves just by fiddling with the details of their memories. Many come to believe the new story, not the old.

With some talent you may be able to publish your new story as an autobiography, giving the authority of the printed word to your new history. This is probably the most convincing way to change your life after the fact. Frederick Douglass wrote three autobiographies about "how a slave became a man"—largely through flight. Samuel Clemens, too, worked sporadically on an autobiography that he never published. A whopping twelve thousand self-identified autobiographies have been published in the United States—doubtless only a small portion of those that have been written. Everyone has a story to tell and, quite often, some profit to make in telling it.

If restless people write autobiographies to remake themselves, I guess the most restless dictate autobiographies, as Malcolm X did with Alex Haley. Malcolm's story is a lot like Frederick Douglass's. There is a dizzying list of places and a blur of travel: Philadelphia, Omaha, Milwaukee, Lansing, East Lansing, Boston, New York, Mecca. His wife Betty receives a few brief pages in the middle of four hundred pages; Malcolm no sooner introduces her then he stops to describe his busy Muslim schedule. Most of all, the center of his story is the remaking of a man into someone new, in Malcolm's case through religious conversion (and moving), which have the same effect as Douglass's fight and flight for freedom. It is a most American story of remaking oneself to pursue one's dreams. The critical edge is directed at the man Malcolm used to be as well as the society that put so many obstacles in his path to a new self. Like Franklin or Douglass, he was obsessed with the person he had become.

Of all American autobiographies, however, Ben Franklin's has been read so often as to set the tone for most others. Early on, he gives a dramatic example of a fresh start, when he skips town on his own brother, to whom he was legally indentured as an apprentice. Ben, the youngest of ten children, admits that he was perhaps "too saucy and provoking," but he deeply resented his brother's occasional beatings, even though this seems to have been normal treatment for apprentices. In Ben it led to an "aversion to arbitrary power that has stuck to me through my whole life," and led him as soon as possible to book secret passage on a ship leaving Boston for New York. The "respectable" excuse for his passage, told to the ship's captain, was that he had gotten a girl pregnant and would be forced to marry her, which today hardly seems a better rationale for escape. Ben's love of freedom—from the demands of an employer as well as the obligations of starting a family—was reinforced by his inability, thanks to his brother, to find work with any of Boston's other printers. In other words he needed a job. Franklin was all of seventeen.[16]

When published after his death, Franklin's *Autobiography* established personal transformation through migration as a key piece of American mythology. Written as the colonies were becoming a nation, by one of the key men who made them into one, the book was the most effective piece of propaganda for the new country, helping to define a distinctive American character. Franklin began his *Autobiography* in England in 1771, put it aside, took it up again in France in 1784, and finished it in Philadelphia from 1788 to 1790, the last two years of his long life. The son of an immigrant and well-traveled himself, Franklin knew better than anyone else how Europeans pictured America, and he worked hard to embody the common sense and simple style they expected. He meant his work to be read by European statesmen and potential immigrants as well as by young men trying to make their way in the world. His shrewd awareness of his potential audiences helped make this the most popular autobiography in history. He understood the dream.

Foremost, Franklin crafted his own life story to exemplify the imagined virtues of America. Near the beginning of the *Autobiography*, several pages describe how, at the age of twelve, Ben and his father worked out what occupation he would enter. He disliked his father's trade of candlemaking and soap boiling, so his father took him around to see other trades: joiners, bricklayers, turners, braziers, and cutlers. They finally settled on printing, less because than despite the fact that one of Ben's older brothers worked at it. Even at the age of twelve, Franklin showed, men make choices over their own fates in the New World. From the start, he portrayed a society of considerable personal movement and opportunity based on individual achievements. Franklin was a new kind of literary hero, celebrated for his utility to society rather than warriorly exploits or hierarchic rank. Human excellence could be found in pragmatic accomplishments, not just in aristocratic lifestyle or military conquest—dubious virtues that most immigrants to America hoped to escape. Nor was religious piety a prominent virtue in Franklin's world, just as it was failing, by the late eighteenth century, to attract many immigrants to the New World.

At the time he wrote his life story, Franklin was one of the most famous men in America or Europe, less for any particular accomplishments than for being an American. His reputation served him well in diplomacy, especially during the Revolution, for his persona implied that Americans were sensible, witty, and straightforward. His book would be read as an allegory of the rise of the United States. It was a world—possibly the first such world portrayed in literature—free from hereditary restrictions, religious authorities, or aristocratic dominance. It was a modern world, in which individuals mattered and made choices for themselves, a world of possibilities and new beginnings. Franklin's homely diction, lessons for the common man, and anecdotes about groups of citizens organizing for education and the public good all pointed to the virtues of the "new" democratic society, implicitly contrasted with the aristocratic societies of Europe.

The *Autobiography* is not a simple story of "the way to wealth," the title of another of Franklin's essays. It shows Franklin moving from one role to another throughout his life, that of the astute businessman accumulating wealth being only one of them. But he was as driven to make fresh starts as any immigrant. He remade himself again and again, not least in his *Autobiography* itself, which he kept revising until his death.

Autobiography, which William Dean Howells called the "most democratic province of literature," has affinities with American character. According to the authoritative *Columbia History of the American Novel*, almost all literary critics "agree that while autobiography is not unique to this country, the form embodies peculiar American characteristics. . . . In its valorization of individualism and its focus on the success story, [it] has always been eminently suited to the dominant American temperament."[17] Autobiographies celebrate individual striving and success much as immigrant stories do.

Even critics of the American tendency to remake one's identity have been hard pressed to fight against it with any alternative. Herman Melville wrote an astounding novel, *The Confidence Man*, whose eponymous character goes through a dizzying sequence of identities that would put Alec Guinness to shame. Even the reader doesn't always know who the confidence man is, because virtually all the characters in the novel are perpetrating some scam of self-presentation. The novel's action unfolds on a Mississippi steamboat ironically named the *Fidèle*, a microcosm of the West's confident self-promotion, with everyone looking for the main chance. The confidence man, and the novel, deflate all the beloved stances of the age, from liberal theology to Emersonian individualism. The novel is usually read as a critique of the self-made man of market society, whose self-presentation is more important than any abiding inner identity. After demonstrating the ease and treachery of rapid changes in one's identity, though, by the end of the novel Melville turns to mock the corrosive disbelief of the skeptics. Market societies, he seems to be saying, require considerable faith in other people's self-creations. If we refuse to take people at face value, what is left?

There are many ways to remake oneself. Americans are notoriously fond of "self-help," sometimes in the form of books, sometimes groups. Americans feel they can learn how to do anything and—even more—to be anyone. Most self-help groups are about becoming a new person: one freed from substance abuse, one in touch with the spirits of ancient warriors, one in control of codependence. Like a cheap form of psychotherapy, improvement through teaching oneself is very much in the American spirit of starting over.

You start over in order to become someone new: a better Christian, an autonomous individual, a more successful entrepreneur. And the best way, though not the only way, to encourage others to honor the new identity you desire is to move somewhere new. As Melville (or Melvill) saw, in a new place people have little choice but to accept you as you present yourself to them. As one of the South-to-North migrants in Morrison's *Jazz* boasts, "Before I met her I'd changed into new seven times. The first time was when I named my own self, since nobody did it for me, since nobody knew what it could or should have been."[18] Considerable reconstruction of the self—although it ultimately needs confirmation from others—is possible through individual migration. Another possibility is to belong to a group collectively intent on some kind of transformation.

Americans don't always start over as individuals, or even as families. They also form groups and communities that promise them a fresh start, often moving long distances and establishing new towns—Plymouth, Boonesboro, Salt Lake City, Jonestown—in the process. Most of these groups have been religious, a few have been political, and some have been based solely on shared lifestyles, but all are efforts to start over with a pure culture, in defiance of, contrast to, or flight from a corrupt world. Like individuals who try to start over, these groups believe in the possibility of stepping outside one's culture in order to improve upon it, almost inevitably by moving somewhere new.

Chapter 1 showed that America was seen as a place for fresh starts as early as the sixteenth century: most North American colonies were founded as utopian schemes for creating perfect societies, impulses often combined with a desire to turn a profit. The Massachusetts Bay Colony was the most famous of these "cities on a hill," but Lord Baltimore, William Penn, the Earl of Shaftesbury, and others had similar utopian aspirations of beginning again, away from the corruption of the Old World. Only the Massachusetts Bay experiment lasted more than a generation; none were ever fully implemented. Early utopian motives were disappointed as quickly as the founding corporations' hopes for instant profits.

Religious and quasi-religious sects have continued to crop up throughout American history, yet few of the endless list of names—even of the more famous—are familiar today: Millerites, Shakers, Perfectionists, Finneyites, Fourierists, Owenites, Adventists, Dorrilites, Koreshanites (not to be confused with the later Branch Davidians); colonies like Oneida, Amana, the Harmony Society, Zoar, the Order of Enoch, the Iowa Pioneer Phalanx, Llano, or the Northampton Association for

Education and Industry. Most simultaneously looked back to an original, often preindustrial, purity as well as ahead to a perfect future. The archetype was millenarian Christians, who expected a sweeping revolution at Christ's return. Traditionally millenarians had believed that the situation on earth would get worse and worse before the Second Coming, but in the nineteenth century a more optimistic interpretation spread, in which conditions would improve as the moment approached. This view encouraged human efforts to improve worldly affairs; if enough Americans lived righteously, they could entice Christ back for the Second Coming. The belief in perfectibility, even when not explicitly millenarian, inspired communal efforts to achieve it.

One of the earliest of these communities was the Shakers. "Mother Ann" Lee immigrated from England with nine followers in 1794, already full of the ideas that would define her cult. Some of these had to do with the equality of men and women, based on a theology that featured God as both female and male. Others concerned the evil of sex, perhaps the legacy of Lee's own bad marriage and difficulties in childbirth. Because a new age of resurrection had arrived, the Shakers had to live like angels, abstaining from all sexual contact. This wait turned out to be longer than expected. Neither the postponement of the resurrection nor the celibacy in the meantime dissuaded followers, thousands of whom joined the group in the 1830s and 1840s. Over the past two hundred years as many as twenty thousand Americans have belonged to Shaker communities at some point in their lives. Today all that survives is their furniture and simple aesthetic—and a handful of elderly members on Sabbathday Lake, Maine.

The decade of the 1840s was the high point in the United States for the founding of new communities, which often had spiritual impulses even when they were not explicit religions. Many were inspired by the utopian ideas of philosophers such as Robert Owen and Charles Fourier, who hoped to reengineer society from the ground up. Most of the founding ideas of these groups came from Europe but fell on especially fertile soil in North America. One historian of Fourierism, for instance, argues that "it was in the United States, not Europe, that Fourier's theory had its greatest practical impact." Forty Fourierist communities (known as phalanxes) were founded in the 1840s, from Massachusetts to Iowa, with as many as one hundred thousand supporters either living in them or active in other ways. Like the initial schemes cooked up by colonists, most communes were short-lived. After only a decade, by the mid-1850s, just one phalanx survived.[19]

Religious or secular, immigrant or home-grown, these nineteenth-century utopian communities had a lot in common. Each felt that

Two utopian groups give the flavor of many of the rest. Frenchman Etienne Cabet, after his own government denied him permission to start an experimental workers' community, left with his five hundred "Pioneers for Humanity" for Texas in 1848. Despite some wavering when revolution broke out in France later that year, Cabet and his followers decided that America, not France, represented humanity's future. Texas apparently did not, however, for the group soon left for Nauvoo, Illinois, which the Mormons had recently abandoned. Cabet's Icarians, as they were more commonly known, lasted eleven years in Nauvoo, before moving on to Missouri, then Iowa, and eventually California. One of the leaders was explicit about the purpose of their journey: "Our pioneers were not rich, but they inhaled the air of pure freedom. Uncle Sam left them perfectly free to try their experiment. I doubt if the president of the United States at that time ever noticed their presence on this continent. . . . They had nothing to struggle against but human nature, their own human nature. They had the will power, the skill as mechanics, a new and rich country, and complete freedom" (quoted in Robert S. Fogarty, *All Things New*). A new, rich, and free country, where the central government hardly noticed what its citizens did, was what these Europeans (and the Americans who joined them) cherished. The Icarians used those freedoms first to oust Cabet as their leader, then to start smaller splinter colonies, and finally to abandon the group altogether and start over as individuals and families. The centrifugal habit of rejecting authority is hard to give up.

Another group of immigrant utopians needed American freedom in order to reject modern freedoms. A German Catholic priest, Father Ambrose Oschwald, derived a prophecy from the Book of Revelation that saw Christ returning to earth some time before 1900. Soon after he published his theory in 1848, his archbishop relieved him of his parish, and Oschwald began a new community (modeled on the first Christians) in the Black Forest. An economic depression in the 1850s pushed him and his flock to migrate to the United States, where they bought 3,800 acres of cheap farmland in a German-speaking area of Wisconsin. The St. Nazianz colony had several hundred members, who lived like a cross between German peasants and a monastic order as they awaited the Second Coming. They waited twenty years, longer than most communities lasted, before going their separate ways as individuals. Unbelievably, they were but one of many German immigrant communities (including Zoar, Ephrata, and Amana) inspired by the Book of Revelation.

society, as it existed, threatened or prevented the realization of some important value. In the United States, especially in the western states that were just being settled, new communities could constitute themselves along proper lines. Government would not interfere, they believed, and cheap land would sustain them economically. From Ohio to California, most utopian efforts pushed westward where land—and freedoms—were thought to be plentiful. But like the original colonial attempts to establish well-planned communities on this continent, those same lands and freedoms constantly undermined communal efforts. The lure of land forever pulled these communities apart. According to Ralph Waldo Emerson, material concerns were often there from the start, corroding the utopian vision. Of the communes he saw springing up around him, he said, "This fatal fault in the logic of our friends still appears: Their whole doctrine is spiritual, but they always end with saying, Give us much land and money."[20] The restless seeking that attracted converts rarely ceased once the commune was built. Anyone who was unhappy could move on—and did.

Movement was the glue that held these communities together, as well as what quickly pulled them apart. Says one historian of the trend, "If there is a single idea that holds these disparate utopians together, it is the notion of journeying. . . . They believed that it was possible to redeem oneself by undertaking a journey, that migration in both a physical and a psychological sense could create community. . . . By the simple act of journeying, they gave their enterprise a new significance. They embarked on a hegira, usually to what became a holy place, one that they could invest with new meaning. They did not have to call it Zion, or New Jerusalem, or New Odessa, although some did; such a move signified new beginnings, new hope, and a rejection of the past."[21] The defining importance of the journey, the hopes of starting over, and even the unexpected centrifugal results are all reminiscent of the success-minded immigrants we met in the last chapter.

Other communities have been established in the decades since—for example, the communes of the 1960s, which numbered in the thousands. Such efforts are both *a refuge and a hope:* their members escape from the corruptions of their society in order to try to create something new and better. Alongside the importance of the journey, perfectibility is their driving belief: individuals are essentially good, but their social environment corrupts them. Left to their own devices, they would flourish peacefully. (Although some have believed their members needed discipline and surveillance to achieve this goodness.)

Frances Fitzgerald has found this same tendency to create new communities in contemporary America. Studying the San Francisco gay community, a Florida retirement community, Jerry Falwell's Baptist church, and Oregon's Rajneeshpuram, she was struck by their common willingness to remake themselves, often as a prelude to transforming the rest of society. (Since Americans can expect to live fifteen or twenty years after they retire, why not start over as a new person in a new community? It is never too late.) Fitzgerald traces this remaking impulse to evangelical Protestantism, with its considerable equality within the group, hope for a sudden change in one's consciousness (being "born again"), and an emphasis on direct experience rather than abstract intellectual theories. The therapeutic language of countercultural communes of the 1960s, then, has much in common with conservative Protestant fundamentalism.[22] Both dream of escaping from the decadence of society in order to be reborn, fresh and whole. And for most, that requires migration.

No one has more incentive to start over than people at the bottom of American society. They more frequently start over with new jobs than with new abodes, although they do plenty of moving as well. Poor people often have different reasons for starting over, such as legal difficulties, credit problems, unemployment, evictions, and convictions. Young men (and a few women) in trouble with the law found it convenient to go west in the nineteenth century. Jumping bail is always a temptation. Money borrowed from friends or loan sharks is another push. Between the Civil War and the Great Depression, the South was the main source of migrant labor. Landless farm workers moved around the South despite restrictions and were finally cut loose in large numbers in the 1920s and 1930s after the collapse of the cotton industry. Tenants could be turned out of their homes for any number of reasons, including temporary inability to work, disputes over wages, or simple redundancy. Southern blacks and Appalachian whites both set out en masse to find industrial jobs in the North and West. Even though push is often stronger than pull for them, the poor still move in the hope of finding a better job, a better place to live, a better self.

Those forced to flee the Dust Bowl in the 1930s were often tenants pushed by landowners rather than farmers devastated by debt and drought. One-third of Oklahoma's farm population, even in 1938 after most of the migration to California had already occurred, had lived on their current farms for less than a year. Beginning in the rural South, these poor whites had been tenants on one farm or another for generations, resisting trends toward mechanization and consolidation of holdings. They were simply following the jobs, which soon led them out of agriculture altogether.

If the bottom of society has its special push factors, African Americans have faced them more continuously than any other group. After Emancipation, many slaves moved just to get a taste of freedom, to

In the late 1980s journalist Nicholas Lemann interviewed an elderly black woman, Ruby, living in Chicago public housing, and told her story in *The Promised Land*. She had been poor since her birth in rural Mississippi. Her story is one of movement. Growing up, she moved because her family was evicted. She moved because her parents tried to find new work on a different plantation. She moved because she and her mother were living with her grandparents, who separated. She moved because her mother sent her to live with a long series of relatives. She moved to Chicago to start a better life. She moved back to Mississippi to be with a man she loved. When he abandoned her, in 1948, she moved back to Chicago. By this time, she was only thirty and had moved at least two dozen times. Economics was one factor; the unreliability of men (who seem to find it easier than women to leave in the middle of the night to make a fresh start elsewhere) was another. Either way, for Ruby, there was always hope of a better life. There had to be.

show that they *could* move. They realized that, in America, freedom meant movement, and they wanted it. Most slaves left their ex-masters' plantations, often without even saying goodbye—at least to the whites. "If they were truly free," says Leon Litwack, "they could walk off the plantation where they had labored as slaves and never return. Whatever else they did, that remained the surest, the quickest way to demonstrate to themselves that their old masters and mistresses no longer owned or controlled them, that they were now free to make their own decisions." As a black preacher more colorfully put it, "You ain't, none o' you, gwinter feel rale free till you shakes de dus' ob de Ole Plantashun offen yore feet an' goes ter a new place whey you kin live out o' sight o' de gret house. . . . You mus' all move—you mus' move clar away from de ole places what you knows, ter de new places what you don't know, whey you kin raise up yore head douten no fear o' Marse Dis ur Marse Tudder."[23] Just as they felt they had to change their names, former slaves knew they had to move somewhere new in order to start over again as free men and women.

After 1865, African Americans joined mainstream America: setting out, fleeing tyranny, and trying to better their lot in life. Movement remained the heart of that quest. Some of the more daring, especially the men, moved west. Some became cowboys. But most blacks moved north. The northward migration remained small in the nineteenth century, increasing from 70,000 in the 1870s to 170,000 in the 1890s. In the second decade of the twentieth century more than half a million blacks moved north. The main push factor was the boll weevil, which devastated cotton crops and cut demand for labor. The main pull factor was exactly what it had been for so many immigrants: enthusiastic recruitment by employers, who faced a simultaneous cutoff of foreign immigrants and increase in industrial demand after World War I began in 1914. New black migrants from the South, unaware of local conditions and excluded by racist unions, proved useful strikebreakers. The migration continued to increase through the 1950s and 1960s, a twenty-year period when nearly three million blacks left the South. From World War I to the 1960s, the African Americans who migrated north and west were more numerous than the immigrants who arrived from abroad. Black Americans have their dreams too, we saw, and places like Chicago and Harlem looked like the promised land.

Those at the bottom of the economic hierarchy tend to have a long series of frequent fresh starts forced on them, as they find only temporary jobs or are pushed out of work during recessions. About one-third of those who move do so reluctantly, more "pushed" than pulled. Even today hundreds of thousands work as migratory agricultural workers, moving with the crops and seasons. (Much of this grinding work is done by recent immigrants.) The poor dream as much as anyone, even if they have fewer cultural and economic resources with which to maneuver.

Structured incentives underlie all this starting over. The sheer size of their country and the decentralization that goes with it have a lot to do with Americans' willingness to move. More than half of the fifty million Americans who move each year do so *to take or find a new job*, and many of the rest are accompanying a family member after a job. In a recent Harris poll, a little more than half of employed Americans expected to leave their jobs voluntarily within the next five years, an astounding level of disloyalty. Americans still expect to follow the jobs. If you want to work in the film industry, you go to Los Angeles; in computers, to Silicon Valley or Seattle, just as, fifty years ago, automobile assembly jobs were concentrated in Michigan. A rapidly growing industry is likely to be in a different region from a stagnant one, so even relatively unskilled jobs migrate. Companies constantly relocate and take their jobs with them, sometimes to places that are less densely settled, like parts of the West (even professional sports teams are shockingly mobile). Corporate executives make decisions that have much the same effect as the drought that forced Steinbeck's fictional Joads to pack up their pickup and their 1925 Dodge and leave Oklahoma for California. The migration of jobs feels like an act of God or nature that encourages everyone to think about moving.

Some occupations require movement, since job markets are national in scope. If you want a job teaching late medieval French history, you had best be willing to move to whatever college or university in the country wants someone in that area. If you are a radiologist specializing in a single piece of machinery, a certain amount of flexibility will help you get a job. Moreover, professions like these exhibit a kind of status hierarchy: the higher up you want to go, the more you must be willing to move. A fresh Ph.D. in history may be able to find a job at a nearby community college or small four-year college. But if she wants a "power" career in which she spends most of her time writing or training the next generation of scholars, in which her profession grants her high prestige, she will restrict her job search to a few dozen top departments around the country, only a handful of which may be hiring in any given year. She must be ready to move.

Like the professionals who operate in national job markets and look down their noses at colleagues who do not move, surveys show that corporate executives are especially likely to value moving and to attribute their own success to the moves they have made. One scholar (who must not know many Americans despite being one herself) had expected people who moved to be unwilling victims of corporate policies, but instead she found most of them to be rational calculators trying to benefit from new opportunities. Restlessness is often subsidized, especially for corporate managers whose companies pay to relocate them. Executives can hire consultants to help calculate the cost of living in a new town, manage all aspects of relocating, or help their spouses find a job. Add to that the costs of buying a new home and selling the old, hotels and meals during the transition, and house-hunting trips, and the costs of moving an employee reach into the tens of thousands of dollars. A corporation can expect to pay more than a hundred thousand dollars to move a top manager.[24]

This hierarchy of prestige linked to movement begins earlier, though. High-status colleges brag about their geographic diversity: how many different states are represented among their students, how many different foreign countries. This distinguishes them from public colleges and universities, which draw primarily from their own states—not to mention junior colleges, which draw from their own city or county. Those who have only attended high school, namely, the poor and working class, frequently have greater place loyalties than elites do. The higher one goes in the class system, the greater the expectations of movement: one must be a "cosmopolitan" to succeed in many professions.

There are different ways to leave home. Working-class kids are likely to do it when they get married and have children. Lucky children of the professional middle class leave home to attend college, then leave college to attend graduate school, then move again for their first job—all before they actually have to make their economic lives as adults. We train them early in restlessness. And the more prestigious their work, the more likely it is to require movement. Americans with college degrees are only 10 percent more likely than others to move in a given year, but they are 50 percent more likely to move to a new state, and twice as likely to move to an entirely new region of the country. At the bottom, Americans are still pushed, sometimes reluctantly, into movement; at the top they are more likely to be pulled by a greater wealth of available opportunities.

The connection between social and geographic mobility partly reflects the size of the United States as well as the history of its settlement. Compare the American system with that of France, where all educational and occupational hierarchies reach their summits in Paris. It is the political center, the educational center, the economic center, the cultural center—honors which fall to different cities in the United States. As you move up in your profession in France, you move toward Paris. Or, if you are lucky enough to get into a top school to start with, you may stay in Paris, or perhaps return to it after a token stint elsewhere. When French railroads were set up in the nineteenth century, all the major lines led to Paris, where they did not even meet but terminated in distinct stations in different parts of town. One was simply not expected to travel among other French cities. One was expected to come to Paris and stay. The successful, certainly, did.

European countries were put together as one line of princes or dukes conquered neighboring kingdoms; the winners naturally centralized their control around their own capital city, whether Paris or Madrid. Each American colony had its own capital, and when the colonies united as one nation, they were careful not to let any single one gain the upper hand. The country's choice to build an entirely new city as its capital was an effort to avoid centralization of the European kind. It worked well. Washington, D.C. has never attained much in the way of wealth, education, or culture, which remain distributed among other American cities. Decentralization of this kind encourages the reshuffling of people.

A number of hidden government policies also encourage movement. Americans can deduct the cost of relocating to take a new job. The biggest tax break for most of them is their mortgage interest deduction, which—with a standard thirty-year mortgage—decreases in value the longer one remains in the same house. Now, if they sell their home for a profit, a couple can avoid taxes on half a million dollars of those gains—something they can do again and again, as often as every two years. In

Since the Fourteenth Amendment in 1868, Americans have had a constitutional right to relocate. The original intent was to prevent state governments from discriminating against people who had moved in from other states. At the time, this primarily meant southern blacks and white "carpetbaggers" from the North. Although it proved ineffective against antivagrancy laws of the late nineteenth century (largely attempts by agricultural employers to prevent the inevitable migration to cities), the amendment has been used in recent decades to prevent states from offering lower welfare benefits to newcomers. In a 1999 decision, *Saenz v. Roe*, the U.S. Supreme Court struck down a California law aimed at newcomers who applied for welfare before living in California for a year, giving them only the benefits they would have received in their state of origin. This plan interfered, according to the court, with Americans' right to move, any time, any place.

fact, the taxes due above that amount are a strong incentive for the wealthy (the only ones likely to reap that kind of capital gain) to move. By relocating to certain states—including Florida and Nevada—when they quit work, retirees can avoid a number of taxes, especially income and certain estate taxes. Movement is encouraged by the system of incentives that Americans have constructed for themselves.

At the same time, there are punishments for those unwilling to move in search of jobs. The safety net for those out of work in the United States has never been strong. Unemployment benefits usually last six or twelve months; welfare for the impoverished barely exists. Americans favor retraining programs, but the jobs requiring those new skills are often elsewhere. People must move or suffer some serious consequences.

Immigration sets our culture in motion, but other forces keep it there. As Oscar Wilde and others have commented, America is about newness, freshness, youth, and starting over. People come here to begin again, and all are encouraged, sometimes forced, to remake themselves. They adopt new names and rework their identities, but most of all they move. Finding a new "place" is what matters.

Generations of immigrants, migrants, and utopians have frequently been scorned as un-American, but in their restless efforts to start their lives anew, they are quintessentially American. Material success has driven most, especially those who have started over as individuals or families. But there have been other reasons. In an age when such things mattered, illegitimate children (including Alexander Hamilton and

John James Audubon) had their own peculiar reason for starting over. Cultural autonomy, religious belief, or political experimentation has motivated others, especially participants in collective, utopian efforts. But Americans rarely distinguish economic, political, and cultural autonomy, clinging to a naive image of a freedom that fuses these, an ideal that suggests we can live better outside the normal, existing institutions of society. "Protest" meant something slightly different to the early Protestants, but today's meaning is also appropriate. Flight to a new land in order to start over was based on protest against the old order. In the seventeenth century especially, this order was a fusion of the religious, economic, and political: European sovereigns were also heads of churches, granters of economic privileges, and so on. Coming to America has often been an act of protest against one's former government, a rejection of many things at once. Starting over through migration or name changing is also a rejection of the status quo.

The association of migration with improvement has also been accepted in many of the places American immigrants left, whose inhabitants felt that their lives too would be improved by the migration of troublemakers. This was Britain's idea in sending convicts to Georgia and the poor to America more generally. Even in the colonies, migration was a good option. The Massachusetts Bay Colony explicitly thought that banishing unruly members was necessary for the perfection of the community. They sent many members back to England and others into the woods. For those who stayed as well as those who moved, the vast land mass offered opportunities for trying again whenever things were not going right.

Such confidence in freedom for individuals and their families (or family substitutes) can only rest on a belief in the perfectibility of humans. If we were tainted indelibly by original sin, as earlier Christians believed, setting us free could come to no good. Yet this optimism about the future is often driven by anxiety, despair, and rejection of the present. Americans believe in their ideals and define themselves and their country by them, even if that means judging the present harshly. Americans live for what they can be rather than what they are. This is still the land of the Dream.

As with other aspects of American character, most of those examined in this chapter have moderated—somewhat—in recent decades. Rates of geographic mobility have gone down ever so slightly in the 1990s. One reason may be that the great migration from country to city (and suburb) has mostly run its course. Another is the continuing expansion of professional occupations where local reputations are important, as for lawyers and doctors. And as we'll see later, the flourishing of communications technologies may make the movement of people less necessary. Further, in an age of professed multicultural celebration, immigrants seem less likely to change their names when they arrive. And since the 1960s, the creation of utopian communities has slowed. What has not slowed is the writing of autobiographies, reflecting a continued faith in the ability of individuals to make themselves the kind of people they wish to be.

Americans need a place to construct their dreams, and since their dreams usually involve material wealth, it helps if the place has plentiful resources. The land and its wealth have served this purpose well through most of American history, at least until the decisive urbanization of the twentieth century. But the dream is more important than the place, which is only a means for realizing the dream. The young men who have been the primary migrants—internationally and domestically—have seen their surroundings as a way to get rich, not as a habitat with any value of its own. The trees are there to be burned or sawed down, the gold or oil to be extracted, the soil to be plowed up. Americans do not expect to stay long in any one place, so it is important to take what you can as fast as you can. After all, America is a big boomtown, and no one wants to stay very long in a boomtown.

4 Boom Land

> Capitalism came in the first ships.
> —*Carl Degler*

> Land in New England became for the colonists a form of capital, a
> thing consumed for the express purpose of creating augmented
> wealth.
> —*William Cronon*

One of the first American revolts against authority, pitting two ambitious immigrants against each other, was Nathaniel Bacon's curious conflict with Virginia Governor William Berkeley in 1676. Bacon attracted a force of rowdy young men who eventually numbered around six hundred, including—in an example of cross-racial cooperation that especially disturbed Virginia's frail elite—seventy Africans. This motley group, most of them neither poor nor rich, set out to make war on Indians on the frontier northwest of Jamestown, failing to discriminate between friendly and hostile tribes. Indeed, friendly Indians were easier to find, lure into enclosures, and then slaughter. Conveniently, a small amount of such activity quickly turned all the local tribes into enemies. The perception that all Indians were hostile, common to most of the young men who populated the American frontier throughout its existence, was predictably self-fulfilling.

Berkeley's response to this lawless violence transformed Bacon's band into enemies of the colonial government as well. The governor refused to grant Bacon an official military commission, which would have legitimated the massacres, and he further declared Bacon's followers to be rebels. Their hostility, so far focused on Indians, now turned against the governor and his Council, which consisted of the colony's largest landowners. Berkeley, hoping to defuse the potential rebellion, immediately held elections to the Assembly, although he was surprised when, by his own calculations, a majority of those elected proved sympathetic to Bacon. Bacon himself was elected from Henrico. Despite Bacon's arrival in Jamestown on 6 June with fifty armed men, Berkeley captured him, forced him to confess to criminal charges, and presented him to the Assembly on his knees. After this humiliation, though, Berkeley pardoned Bacon, promised him the commission he wanted, and appointed him a member of the Council (thereby making him ineligible to serve in the Assembly). Then he sent Bacon home.

The Assembly immediately passed a series of measures designed to reduce the colony's notorious corruption, or at least to spread its spoils more evenly. Then it turned its attention to the Indians. It first formulated a broad definition of hostile Indians as any who left their towns without English permission, the penalty being forfeiture of lands and belongings (and their lives, no doubt, the nature of enforcement being what it was). One thousand troops were to be raised to fight the Indians, to be paid not only in tobacco but in any plunder they could take from their opponents, including the enslavement of captured Indians. This unanimous agreement on a racial scapegoat not only offered the prospect of new land but deflected attention away from discontent with the colony's governing clique. A series of new laws reducing Africans to chattel, mostly put into effect during the years following Bacon's Rebellion, had the same effect of splitting their interests from those of landless white servants and settlers.

Two weeks after leaving Jamestown, Bacon returned with several hundred followers, who surrounded the statehouse. After some theatrics on both sides, Berkeley gave Bacon the promised but delayed commission. After Bacon, and more especially his troops, had marched north, Berkeley declared the commission invalid and marched after them, hoping to raise volunteers along the way. He found few willing to fight Bacon, who soon chased Berkeley across the Chesapeake to the Eastern Shore. Although Bacon spent the next several months searching for and destroying Indians, many of his followers spent their time looting the estates of landowners thought loyal to Berkeley.

Feeling the need to justify his mutiny only after Berkeley fled, Bacon wrote a document that pioneered a characteristically American fusion of grievances. The first complaint against the government in his "Declaracon of the People" was, "For haveing upon specious pretences of publiqe works raised great unjust taxes upon the Comonality for the advancement of private favorites and other sinister ends." Given the corrupt standards of colonial Virginia's government, these were no doubt accurate charges. The fourth allegation was, "For haveing protected, favoured, and Imboldned the Indians against his Majesties loy-all subjects, never contriveing, requireing, or appointing any due or proper meanes of sattisfaction for theire many Invasions, robberies, and murthers comitted upon us."[1] This was as untrue as the first was true. Together, though, they form a model for later American complaints against taxes, used to enrich the wrong people and directed toward bad purposes, and against an evil minority group thought to be actively threatening normal citizens. On the frontier, any government at all was likely to interfere with young men's restless pursuit of wealth, except when government was itself a means for enrichment.

The contest between Bacon and Berkeley was also the first American example of the escalation of false campaign pledges. Each promised to those who would follow him the plunder from the properties of their foes, and each appealed to white and black servants by promising them freedom in exchange for loyalty. Bacon, perhaps because his anti-Indian credentials were more recent (although Berkeley had himself gained fame as an Indian fighter), was persuasive to more people, and he managed to control the colony until his sudden death in October. The rebellion then fizzled, its fate sealed by the arrival of several military ships from England.

Back in control, Berkeley and his allies turned enthusiastically to plundering those who had joined the rebellion (this included, at one time or another, almost all freemen in the colony, a fact conveniently overlooked by his current cronies). The more unfortunate were also hanged. The King himself attempted to curb this vendetta, sending a small investigatory commission and offering pardons to those rebels who surrendered—a policy Berkeley simply ignored. Political office continued to be a means of personal enrichment and little else, just as Bacon had decried. One of Berkeley's friends used the troops under his command to clear his land and erect fences on his properties. The blatant corruption of American government at all levels, throughout much of our history, helped create a tradition of cynicism about politics.

The Bacon episode tells us a lot about human motivation in the Virginia colony and, by extension, in later frontier boomtowns. From the governor and the richest landowners on down, everyone was concerned with making money. First and foremost, Bacon's followers wanted land, even if they had to take it from the Indians. The King himself intervened primarily out of concern that the colonists were paying inadequate attention to the tobacco from which he profited. The emerging elite viewed political offices as they viewed the lands they owned, as a means for their own enrichment—naturally enough in a culture obsessed with economic advancement. Colonies established by companies intent on profits recruited the same kind of ambitious immigrants who would appear on American shores ever after.

The rebellion also reveals a great deal about the demographics of the colonies and later frontiers. These border areas have always been populated by young, single men—the ones able to do the hard physical work, the ones on the make, trying to better themselves. They are similar to those who have immigrated, and many of them were immigrants. Wherever men like this have gathered, they have created the same type of culture: with drinking and gambling as their main leisure activities and few respectable women around to shame them into civility, they easily lapse into aggression and violence. Slights to honor are taken seriously, but official authority is not. The rowdy young men who joined Nathaniel Bacon are similar to those who rushed to California after 1848 and to some of the roughnecks who work new oil strikes today.

The Virginia colony was a typical boomtown, with a matching boomtown culture. Beginning after 1615, as tobacco prices skyrocketed, every colonist spent as much time as possible planting tobacco, ignoring necessities such as edible crops and protection against Indian raids. Historian Edmund Morgan has described the frenzy: "Women were scarcer than corn or liquor in Virginia and fetched a higher price, . . . but the numbers were not large enough to alter the atmosphere of transience that pervaded the boom country. The lonely men who pressed aboard every ship in the James to drown their cares in drink looked on Virginia 'not as a place of Habitacion but onely of a short sojournage.' They would marry and settle down later, somewhere else."[2] Natural resources, in this case land, were plentiful, but men to work the land were not; those who became rich were those with the cash to buy indentured servants—if, that is, they managed to avoid the killer diseases for which the colony was notorious. Everyone comes to a boomtown hoping to strike it rich, but few do. For most, reality falls short of the dream.

Boomtowns are communities with a sudden and temporary surge of jobs, and hence of population, usually based on land settlement, a large construction project, or the extraction of raw materials from nature. Whether it's a gold strike, offshore oil rig, or the construction of a nuclear power plant, the idea is for workers to make good wages and owners to turn big profits in a short time. Often the draw is some natural resource that will be quickly depleted, such as a new vein of coal, gold, or oil. Workers tolerate conditions they would never accept if they expected them to be permanent: tiny, cramped quarters, life in small huts or trailers, with little to do for amusement except gamble, drink, and fight (the first two usually leading to the third). The dominant mood, as Morgan says, is one of transience, because soon the construction project will be finished, the mine closed, or the land depleted. When the music stops, not everyone will be rich—far from it—but everyone will move on to the next boomtown. This is a microcosm of America: the land of opportunity for all, attracting those who want to improve themselves but are always happy to move on to the next lucky strike.

Inevitably, those who get rich are the ones who own the oil rig, sell the miners their equipment, or operate the brothels and saloons. Single young men making good wages are big spenders, especially on what Americans have frequently viewed as sins. Although they want money, they are not good savers. As long as they are young enough to do the backbreaking work, they will be available for the next boomtown.

For most of our history, the United States has looked like one large boomtown to the rest of the world, attracting the same young men who go to boomtowns in the hope of wealth. Until the late nineteenth century, the settling of lands was the main boom activity. There were always lands farther west to be taken from the Indians, and agriculture was still the main occupation of most Americans. Even today, a large part of American culture portrays the environment as an opportunity for getting rich quick, a set of resources to be used up in improving one's own life. With the right attitude, even cities can be treated as boomtowns. In the boom mentality your surroundings become a temporary opportunity for self-advancement, not a place to live. Many boomtowns are literally based on the rapid exploitation of natural resources; others only feel that way. But they are the perfect place for starting over.

By the early 1600s images of plentiful gold, there to be picked up, had faded (only to be revived from time to time later), but other forms of natural wealth had taken their place in the North American version of the dream. Land, of course, was the most plentiful resource in the English colonies, and it immediately became an obsession for all who arrived. If America meant opportunity, opportunity meant land. Although most immigrants—even the earliest—had practiced trades, not agriculture, in their old countries, out of necessity most became farmers here. Being immigrants, they were quick to adapt.

Simple, self-sufficient farming was not the goal of most immigrants, who often spent more time settling new land than farming old. Settling land involves different incentives, activities, and rewards than stable farming over many generations. In 1600 the eastern part of North

America was mostly covered with forests, and clearing the enormous trees immediately increased the value of the land. Converting forest to farmland is a temporary boom activity, while farming itself is not. Governor Berkeley and his fellow landowners were interested in farming, for example, while Bacon and his followers were interested in settling new lands. The rebellion's main purpose was to free up additional areas for settlement, creating opportunities for newcomers and small landowners to make quick money. Real frontiersmen were more interested in acquiring new land than in tending it once obtained.

Speculation in land became a mania; with everyone hoping to make money as lands were cleared, Indians disappeared, and additional newcomers arrived looking for farmland. In Virginia's scheme to attract labor, a "headright" to fifty acres of land was issued for each immigrant, but a market immediately developed so that headrights were bought and sold independently of those (mostly indentured servants) in whose name they were issued. Headrights could be exercised even for deceased arrivals. By 1676 a handful of wealthier colonists (the members of Berkeley's council) had amassed holdings of thousands of acres, sometimes secured by nothing more than the felling of a few trees and the construction of a crude hut. Their only challenge was finding men to clear the land and grow tobacco on it for them. New Englanders too were obsessed with land speculation, forever hauling each other into court to contest property lines or the division of estates of the deceased. Throughout the colonies, individuals and families were not shy about pursuing their material interests.

Even though the whole of colonial America looked like a boomtown in land, there were other raw materials to be exploited, and this allowed the development of boomtowns in a stricter sense. Over two hundred ironworks dotted the colonies, especially in Maryland, Pennsylvania, and New Jersey. Huge amounts of timber had to be made into charcoal fuel; iron ore and limestone had to be mined in open-face operations and hauled to the furnaces. Both activities required not just raw materials but large numbers of strong men. So did the forges and foundries themselves, which required hard work in hot, smoky, loud, and dangerous conditions. As in most isolated boomtowns, work was the central activity, with heavy drinking and brutal fights, once again, as the main relief. A similar roughness would pervade the Western frontier towns of the nineteenth century, with the added thrill of plentiful firearms.

Colonists adapted quickly to the scarcity of both capital and labor: they compensated by using even more of their natural resources, which in contrast seemed inexhaustible. This was a rational response to their economic situation, but it had to be reinforced by cultural attitudes that gave priority to market incentives. These attitudes had to be distilled from more complex images of land that prevailed not only among the Indians but in England and the rest of Europe. The boomtowners had to see the world around them as a means to an end and land as a *marketable commodity.* This was a new and unusual way to view the world.

The colonists' treatment of the land contrasted most starkly with that of the Indians. The English colonists lacked a sense of permanence, and hence any concern for ecological preservation of the kind the Indians had practiced, albeit mostly unintentionally. The Indians had lived on the same lands for generations and expected to remain for generations to come, even though they moved around with the seasons and switched fields every few years to maintain the land's fertility. It was the white settlers who were more likely, after improving a plot of land, to move on in search of new opportunities, hoping to turn a profit on the land they sold. Yet dubious boomtown "improvements" marked the whites as serious and civilized, despite their temporary commitment to the land they owned. Indians migrated regularly so they could inhabit the same territory permanently; white settlers moved through once but took much of the land's fertility with them when they left.

At issue were different conceptions of ownership. Like most hunter-gatherers around the globe, the North American natives had seen the land, and themselves, and the animals on the land, as a single system. They lived in one place in the summer, another in the winter, and others in between. Other groups could move through when they were not there. They of course transformed the land: they cleared fields, grew crops, built villages. They had no conception that individuals rather than groups could own land, that one could own land itself rather than rights to use it for specific purposes, or that one could deprive one's descendants of the land by selling it. But the English settlers saw land as a spiritually neutral resource to be used in producing food and clothing, something to profit from, which could be bought and sold like any other commodity. It could even be used up in production, abused and destroyed, if the owner wanted to do that. This "modern" form of ownership was destined to spread throughout most of the world, but its first and fullest application was in the North American colonies. This was the first triumph of market society, in which almost everything could be bought and sold.

This idea of exclusive ownership differed not only from Indian attitudes, but also from practices in England, where elaborate laws and traditions regulated the use, sale, and inheritance of land. In fact the Indians' loyalty to the land as their permanent habitat was not unlike European aristocrats' sense of connection to their lands. Of the various legal forms of English land ownership, the least onerous—"in free and common Socage"—was used in the grant to the Massachusetts Bay Company, requiring no feudal service and allowing easy future sale. All the crown asked was one-fifth of the gold and silver found, which as it turned out was a low rent indeed. The easy terms were meant to encourage immigration, but they also acknowledged the limitations of governing a colony from a distance of three thousand miles, a voyage of a couple of months.

Throughout the rest of the world, land was an intimate strand in the social order. Especially for the English, landed estates were displays of power, wealth, and hospitality. Hunts were carefully orchestrated to show off one's land as well as to entertain guests. Walls, ditches, and gardens were thoughtfully arranged to demonstrate that the owner's power and taste extended to the natural world. The names of leading families were connected with the places they owned as a means of demonstrating the permanence of their rule. Laws governing the inheritance of land were designed to sustain the same patterns across generations, overcoming the possible greed of individual aristocrats. Peasants' lives were equally entwined with the land. "The peasant did not regard his farm as a means of production which could be disposed of when it was no longer profitable," says one historian. "For him, the farm was above all the basis of his existence."[3] The peasant was tied to the land, legally and emotionally. It was where he and his descendants would live—a view he shared with Indians and his own aristocratic lords. Markets in land, even though they eventually appeared, were widely contested as a threat to the social order. Even today European governments regulate land use to a degree inconceivable in America, from banning swimming pools in the Tuscan hillsides to preserving farmland around German cities.

Those who first came to America, commoners and a handful of landless younger sons of the aristocracy, saw the land as property, not patrimony. Even when they wanted to, the first colonists found themselves unable to establish or enforce England's inheritance laws, especially primogeniture, because of the availability of so much easy land. The new colonists had much awe but little reverence for the land and its impressive bounty. In the eyes of more religious arrivals, nature was at best a neutral stage on which the important spiritual action occurred, at worst an evil hindrance to Christian aims. To the less religious majority of immigrants, it was a pot of treasure. More an intuition than an argument, these attitudes had roots in Christian theology and Enlightenment philosophy.

In Judeo-Christian traditions, the physical world has typically been neutral or even negative in value; it's only a stage for the real spiritual action in Christianity. Even though it is God's creation, this is a fallen, corrupted world, incomparably inferior to heaven. God is outside of nature, not dwelling within it, so the natural world is morally and spiritually neutral, open to human modification. The transformation of nature is also supported by the idea of progress. Because history has a beginning and will have an end, change is both inevitable and usually good: there is a sense of advancement through history, which has often been thought to consist especially of technological advancement. At the very least, economic growth and technological change have frequently been taken as signs of spiritual progress. Wresting bright fields from dark forests reflects the development of the soul. As Lynn White put it, "To a Christian, a tree can be no more than a physical fact. The whole concept of the sacred grove is alien to Christianity and to the ethos of the West. For nearly two millennia Christian missionaries have been chopping down sacred groves, which are idolatrous because they assume spirit in nature."[4] White oversimplifies a bit but captures a central truth about Christianity, especially in the fundamentalist form transported to early New England.

The Puritans considered it their mission to subdue this wasteland in God's name. They knew they were God's chosen people, so they *had* to triumph in the end. Although they represented a decreasing proportion of the population after their original migration from 1630 to 1643, hard-core Puritans were the political leaders, preachers, and historians of colonial New England, who interpreted their experiences for everyone else. They continually searched for biblical parallels, stories that could help explain what was happening to them. In the allegories of Massachusetts Governor John Winthrop, North America was a land of dark and evil, which the Puritans, after considerable trials, would conquer. In the same period that Cromwell's armies were fighting the King's forces in England, American Puritans deployed explicitly military language and imagery about conquest. They were not shy about using violent force, since they believed they were doing God's will. This included killing off the Indians when necessary for the land's improvement.

Religious rationales for taking the land away from the Indians were reinforced by philosophical ones, especially the conviction that the land was there to be "improved"—an idea with roots in both Christianity and the Enlightenment. The seventeenth and eighteenth centuries saw the rise of a new form of individualism, an economic individualism in which humans came to be defined more and more by what they owned and how much money they made. This worldview is individualistic in that each human has autonomy and desires prior to his or her connections to others, and it is economic in the centrality of *material* actions and desires, the kind pursued and satisfied through markets, the kind to which monetary values can be attached. We are so familiar with this idea that it is hard to believe there was a time before economic value was the primary way to categorize people. Economic individualism suggests that people should be free to accumulate what they can by trading with each other in markets. This new market sensibility was inflaming the imaginations of Europeans just as they began to settle America, where the new ideas could be given free reign without alternative traditions and laws to constrain them.

The most influential proponent of this image of human nature was John Locke, whose labor theory of property summed up much of the fashionable individualism of the late seventeenth century. Locke addressed the problem of "private property": how an individual could come to own anything exclusively, since God was thought to have given the world to all humankind in common. How could anyone slice off a part of this world and keep others out? This was a lively political issue at a time when progressive aristocrats were enclosing what had been common lands, creating migrant poor out of many of England's peasants. Locke's famous answer was that one needed to survive, and so was justified in taking what was necessary for this. "As much land as a man tills, plants, improves, cultivates, and can use the product of, so much is his property. He by his labor does, as it were, inclose it from the common."[5] By mixing one's labor with the raw materials, in other words, by improving the land and its bounty, one gained a right to whatever one took. This might be nothing more than gathering acorns that have fallen from an oak, in Locke's example, but it might also include domesticating animals or—most relevant for the American colonists—clearing and cultivating fields. The colonists were understandably keen on the idea of permanent improvements as proof of ownership. If the Indians didn't fence in their property, or leave marks on it that were obvious to the (purposely blind) settlers, then they didn't really own it, as the colonists did when they killed off all the trees. Destruction was a mark of ownership.

Locke's "labor theory of value," locating the source of value in labor rather than land, was radical and egalitarian for its time, perfectly suited to colonies in which labor was especially scarce and valuable. This affinity has led scholars such as Louis Hartz to claim that Locke's views are *the* philosophy of the United States. Land and labor had to be subject to market forces to maximize the opportunity for movement.

To contemporary ears Locke has a peculiar idea of who owns his or her own labor. He notoriously argues at one point, "Thus the grass my horse has bit; the turfs my servant has cut; and the ore I have digg'd in any place where I have a right to them in common with others, become my property without the assignation or consent of anybody. The labor that was mine, removing them out of the common state they were in, has fixed my property in them."[6] How could I own turf that I have never touched? Why does this belong to me and not to the servant who actually cut it? Locke's labor theory involved two potentially contradictory sides. One emphasized the literal *work* that went into a product. This attractive idea was that you owned what you had made, what you had mixed your sweat and labor in. The other side emphasized the subsequent *possession* of what you had made. Here was the idea that you had to fence it in, keep it, possess it exclusively. Whatever you fenced in belonged to you alone, to do with whatever you wanted. And money allowed you to store wealth in an easy form. This is a modern, economic idea of property: you don't want it for the pleasures you directly get from it; you want it because it will help you make more money, accumulate more property. I own what my servant makes because I own the land my servant works. I just pay him a wage to work my land for me.

These are two very different rationales for owning property. The Native Americans certainly mixed their labor with the land; they grew crops and set fires to control underbrush. But they didn't fence in the land; they didn't feel they could possess the land, but only use it for certain periods. They had the first idea of property, as something linked with their labor. But the English settlers took these lands away on the grounds of the second definition, that the Indians didn't clearly possess it, exclusively, with well-marked boundaries. Never mind that the colonists' "improvements" had detrimental effects on the land, or that the Indians had indeed managed and reshaped the land in various ways. The Indians' ecologically harmless transformations were invisible to the colonists. The only improvements that counted in their eyes were killing trees and erecting fences, establishing boundaries that could be legally enforced. The Indians gathered acorns; the colonists chopped down the oak trees.

Only one of Locke's definitions was compatible with a full market in land. Only when an individual had complete, exclusive, and permanent possession of the land could he then turn around and sell it. Even English nobles did not have the property rights the colonists did. But such rights were necessary for the largest possible profits to be made in the shortest possible time.

In the end, though, colonists were happy to drop all these rationales when they needed to. Nathaniel Bacon and his crew formulated an excuse for disobeying the governor, not for killing Indians and taking their land. Many of the wealthiest colonists did less to improve their huge land grants than the Indians. Roger Williams, in a dispute with John Winthrop, pointed this out: the Indians did at least as much work on their lands as the King of England did to improve *his* deer parks and royal forests. But fancy rationales mattered little in the face of the universal greed for land.

The colonists had to invent new systems of deeds and surveys appropriate to their unprecedented market in land. Plots could no longer be defined by custom or through the activities that took place on the land. Titles no longer referred to the uses of land or even its topography, such as creeks and hills, all of which became subject to abstractly straight property lines running arbitrarily up and down the landscape. Surveys replaced customary local knowledge, eventually allowing the western United States to be cut up into 160-acre parcels for homesteading—the fastest way to divide up so much land. The laying down of boundaries and roads is one of the few areas where the utopian vision of the first colonial planners, the image of this new land as a clean slate, was implemented successfully.

The boom mentality is not just to make money, but to make it fast. Even improvements sure to enhance property values are rejected if they take too long. Historian Samuel Hays describes the boomland mentality as a barrier to irrigation projects in the western states at the end of the nineteenth century, since "the planning and stability essential for such a program were difficult to foster in a frontier area of rising land values, quick profits, and rapid change." Federal land sales were a special boon to speculators, and many homesteaders quickly initiated a series of resales. In many cases none of the sequential owners desired to improve the land, much less work it thereafter, but only to sell it at a higher price as soon as possible. "Men of small means," Hays comments, "speculated just as frequently as did men of large means," disputing a common impression that corporations were the main speculators, profiting at the expense of individual settlers. He documents a number of irrigation companies that went broke because they could not get landowners to sign on, even though irrigation would enhance land prices. Most speculators were too restless to wait that long; they viewed land as they did other resources that could be quickly exploited or sold as soon as prices rose. Those who can afford costly improvements may benefit more, but, for most Americans, life is too short for that. They want to get rich fast.[7]

Developers' efforts to make money from their investments explain American patterns of settlement. This was true of the promotional efforts of the early colonies. It remained true as the western states were settled in the nineteenth century, with landowners scurrying to profit from their holdings. It is still true today. Large cities are buffeted by the politics of real estate, as "growth coalitions" of developers and politicians pursue rapid profits in expansion with little concern for long-term public amenities or planning. Valleys are irrigated, new towns appear, and inner cities are revitalized because someone finds a way to make money from it. As trains replaced water routes, patterns of development had less and less to do with the natural topography of the land and everything to do with markets and money. Who stays long enough to worry about anything else?

Boomtowns are violent. Again and again, observers of these cultures say the same things, whether talking about Jamestown, Bacon's frontier, the wild West, or the Gold Rush. Men work hard all week, at rough and risky tasks, and let loose on their day off (if they are lucky enough to have one). They willingly face death in both work and leisure, developing a fatalistic belief that, when their time is up, all they need to worry about is dying honorably. They drink enormous amounts of hard alcohol, perceive threats to their honor in the smallest inadvertent comment, and defend that honor in fights. Because the men in these settings almost all carry knives or guns, these fights are frequently fatal. With this culture of honor so pervasive, and the results so frequently fatal, there is little the law can do. Most men are paid weekly in cash, sums that seem to them quite large, and they are ready to defend their earnings.

They are also ready to spend them, especially on gambling and whoring—two activities that are rarely legal, so that their pursuit—and men pursue them regardless—further undermines respect for the law, whose representatives are at any rate often quite distant. The ready cash and fondness for vice in turn attract those who are adept at getting the cash away from the young men. Some are card sharks and thieves, who exacerbate the lawlessness of these cultures. Others are businessmen ready to offer whatever the rowdy young men want to buy. These are the ones who get rich in boomtowns: those who own the saloon or brothel; who sell the horses, knives, and guns; who bring in the foodstuffs, clothing, pots, and pans.

Another common aspect of boomtown culture is a twist on American habits of adopting new names. Miners, cowboys, and the like have a propensity for nicknames. These often replace not only first names, but last names as well, which few bother or need to use among their buddies. In this way, new arrivals are "born again" into the egalitarian circles of boomtown companions. Not using a surname is a way of denying family background, good or bad. It is also a way of eluding legal difficulties or wives left behind. Nowhere in America is one's background less important. Personal honor, loyalty to one's fellows, and ability to do the job are all that matter.

The first backwoods frontier along the Appalachians, just west of the first areas of colonization, was violent from the start. And not just because of warfare with displaced Indians. Its settlers were primarily Scottish, although coming from Northern Ireland and Northern England as well as from Scotland itself. Historian David Hackett Fischer has described the violent culture that dominated the border between Scotland and England. The inhabitants were accustomed to wars, had little regard for legal institutions, and robbed and rustled for a living. In the late seventeenth century, as wars between the two countries subsided, the British government began a long process of imposing peace on the region, executing or exiling the worst offenders, often entire families. As Fischer says, "The so-called Scotch-Irish who came to America thus included a double-distilled selection of some of the most disorderly inhabitants of a deeply disordered land."[8] They were joined in the eighteenth century by convicted criminals, as Britain began a policy of "transporting" most offenders abroad. Between 1718 and 1776, fifty thousand of them, almost all men in their twenties, were sent to the American colonies.[9] Most were thieves, and none had much respect for government authority. Following in Bacon's footsteps, these were the people defining the colonies' relations with the Indian tribes on the frontier.

Little changed on the frontier for two hundred years after Bacon, except the position of the frontier. A historian of California contrasts the frontiersmen who worked their way through Indian territory to get there with those who came by ship: "Most hunters and trappers who arrived overland were Southern or Border State men who had been at least one generation on the frontier. They had less formal education than their maritime counterparts, and they were a lot tougher." In the last two decades of Mexican rule, these men frequently plotted the takeover of California, exacerbating tensions between newly arrived Americans and the governing Mexicans and probably precluding a peaceful accommodation. Those arrivals who were less violent still left something to be desired: "California was filling up with the worst sort of American speculator, piker, and cardsharp."[10]

Even immigrants who considered themselves the finest product of European civilization adapted with distressing ease to the conditions of frontier boomtowns. William Dunbar, son of a Scottish aristocrat, was well trained in mathematics and science and made scholarly contributions to these and other fields, yet he used slaves to transform part of Mississippi's wilderness into a plantation. His was another life of fresh starts. He arrived in Philadelphia in 1771 at the age of twenty-two and soon moved to Fort Pitt on the frontier; after two years he staked a claim in what is now Mississippi. The setting took its toll, as Bernard Bailyn explains in *Voyagers to the West:* "But 4,000 miles from the sources of culture, alone on the far periphery of British civilization where physical survival was a daily struggle, where ruthless exploitation was a way of life, and where disorder, violence, and human degradation were commonplace, he had triumphed by successful adaptation. Endlessly enterprising and resourceful, his finer sensibilities dulled by the abrasions of frontier life, and feeling within himself a sense of authority and autonomy he had not known before, a force that flowed from his absolute control over the lives of others, he emerged a distinctive new man, a borderland gentleman, a man of property in a raw, half-savage world." Despite his success with this plantation, he gave it up after the peace of 1783 left him on the Spanish side of the new border, and proceeded to build an entirely new one on the American side.

Boomtown culture and indigenous natives are a sad combination. The young men who populate boomtowns are prone to violence even among themselves; given an external target, their destructive impulses have few limits. This is the tragic dynamic of frontiers: the rough, brutal, often racist young men who rush to populate them would be the last to deal fairly or sensitively with the native peoples being displaced. Instead they ignite tensions, then wars, which in turn justify full-scale, organized intervention by those with political and military power. Bacon's treatment of Virginia's Indians would be repeated in later dealings with the Mexican government of California in the 1830s and 1840s, and with native Indians almost everywhere along the way, as Europeans pushed the frontier across the continent separating those two states.

The most famous boomtowns in American history were created by the gold rushes of the nineteenth century, which intensified the usual pathologies because young men arrived in greater numbers, were more heavily armed, and (sometimes) made greater amounts of money. While elites in the East were working hard to "civilize" the lower classes, conditions out west were as primitive—*barbaric* was a word commonly used by reporters—as in the early colonies. At the time of its forced purchase from Mexico in 1848, California had fewer than 20,000 inhabitants, but in the following two years 175,000 young men (and a few women) arrived from the East seeking gold. The most common route was around the Horn, a passage of five months or longer made in dark and stinking cabins, under crowded conditions, with exceedingly foul food. Passengers on one ship accused the cook of making their food with used bath water. The overland route took even longer, with wagons moving ten or twelve miles a day. Here illness and accident took a heavy toll, the latter especially in the mountains. Wagons got loose on steep grades and killed those behind them; men went off to find water holes and never returned. One commented, "Any man who makes a trip by land to California deserves to find a fortune."[11]

But few did. Those who survived the trip faced even greater hazards in gold country. Here were the worst boomtowns, full of cholera, dysentery, and other diseases carried by rodents or contaminated water. Heavy drinking and exhaustion from work weakened resistance, and a diet of salted meat, lard, flour, coffee, and alcohol encouraged scurvy. If nature took its toll, human activity did too. Mining is one of the most accident-prone occupations, never more so than when everyone is rushing to get as much out of the ground as fast as they can. Murders, suicides, and lynchings seemed almost as common as the nightly knife and fist fights. California place names like Hangtown and Helltown, colorful today, were more literal at the time. No one expected to remain more than a few years, and none did. They were lucky to survive intact.

Almost all the newcomers were young, but not all were single. Some had simply abandoned their families and changed their names, disappearing into the West. Others remained "loyal" to their families back east even as they tore themselves away, drawn by a dream of riches. Like those who left their families behind to claim new lands out west, forty-niners wanted something better for themselves and their children; unlike the would-be farmers, they hoped for more immediate wealth. Neither group fared well, but at least most homesteaders, if they survived the journey, could hope to become self-sufficient. They, at least, might eventually send for their families.

Many of those who arrived in California looking for gold stayed even after they gave up their initial quest. Some were joined by wives or managed to find other women to marry, and for them the state became a home. Yet in the 1860s, more than half of the (comparatively) settled population of San Francisco still consisted of young men under thirty. Most boomtowners simply moved on to the next strike. As one historian says, "Most noticeably in the areas of hydraulic mining, logging, the destruction of wildlife, and the depletion of the soil, Americans continued

Adolph Heinrich Joseph Sutro was one of the lucky ones. A Prussian immigrant with little formal education (he despised the "drudgery of student life"), he came to San Francisco at the height of the gold rush, in 1850, when he was twenty years old, a typical arrival. But rather than setting out for the hills to pan for gold, he stayed in the city and sold tobacco and dry goods to those who did. In little more than a decade he had made a modest fortune, but he was ready to start anew when news of the big Comstock Lode came from Nevada. Here he made a second fortune by building an ore-reducing mill for processing the miners' silver and later digging an elaborate tunnel that went deeper into the rock than any other. After enriching himself in two big boomtowns, he was ready to move back to San Francisco and make even more money in real-estate speculation, an activity aided by his stint as mayor in the mid-1890s. His combination of politics and speculation would have made him a fitting crony of Governor Berkeley.

to rifle California all through the nineteenth century."[12] In other words, they treated this state like every other. California set the pattern for later gold and silver strikes in places like Pikes Peak, the Black Hills, the Yukon, and a number of other western sites.

We can return to Clemens's *Adventures of Huckleberry Finn* for a scathing portrait of the mob violence of boomtowns. In one scene, based on an incident Clemens observed as a child in Hannibal, a merchant named Colonel Sherburn shoots and kills a drunk who has been insulting him—after giving him fair warning, of course. A mob forms and decides to march to Sherburn's house. Huck describes them: "They swarmed up the street towards Sherburn's house, a-whooping and yelling and raging like Injuns, and everything had to clear the way or get run over and tromped to mush, and it was awful to see." They get as far as tearing down his front fence and filling his yard before Sherburn appears with a shotgun and contemptuously chases them off, dismissing them as "cowards."[13] Yet Sherburn admits that lynch mobs usually succeed—when they come in the dark with masks. Individual violence and mob justice are both part of boomtown restlessness.

Some boomtown violence was organized by the government, with armies attracting those fond of guns and violence. Much of the drama of the frontier has come from wars with Indians, an experience that shapes the identity of the U.S. Army even today. (One of the Army's top bases was built illegally in Indian territory by a headstrong young colonel named Henry Leavenworth; when the top brass found out, they had little choice but to accept and defend the colonel's action.) Buffalo Bill Cody, traveling the country during the late nineteenth century with his

Wild West show and portraying fights between vicious Indians and brave scouts, did much to establish the basic plot that potboilers and Hollywood westerns later followed. They only partly overcame the image of noble savages that James Fenimore Cooper had created, so that there is both savagery and nobility found in these stories. The test of battle was the best way to prove one's manhood, even better than the slaughter of other species in the hunt.

Frontier wars also provided interior battles with one's soul, so important to Americans. Andrew Jackson, who had already "remade" himself once by accumulating a small fortune through land speculation, remade himself again fighting the Creek Indians in 1813 and 1814. As Ronald Takaki puts it, "As Jackson marched against the Indians, he also waged a private battle against his own body. . . . Most importantly, in the war, Jackson had purified the republican self: He was no longer a high-living lawyer and shady land speculator. In the wilderness, he had disciplined and chastened himself, and triumphed over 'indolence,' 'sloth,' pain, and Indians."[14] Like the Puritans, Jackson saw the frontier as an opportunity to test and remake himself. In the process, the same vices that have habitually frightened Americans were used to stigmatize the Indians as subhuman: they were indolent, given to animal desires and passions, incapable of "improving" themselves and their lands. They had all the problems Americans saw in new immigrants.

The purpose of the Indian wars was simple: to open up new lands for white settlement. Indians were assumed, as part of their moral makeup, to be incapable of successful land development. This assumption was self-reinforcing, as Indians were actively swindled, sometimes losing their land through deception, sometimes through the active intervention of the government. For example, state governments would impose taxes on Indians, who lacked cash to pay them. Sure that Indians would fail in white society, and blaming them when they did, Jackson and other politicians forced them into exile farther west. Jackson, in true American form, linked even forced migration with progress: "Doubtless it will be painful to leave the graves of their fathers. But what do they more than our ancestors did or than our children are now doing? To better their condition in an unknown land our forefathers left all that was dear in earthly objects. Our children by thousands yearly leave the land of their birth to seek new homes in distant regions." This movement had allowed Americans to develop the "power and faculties of man in their highest perfection."[15] White Americans are not shy about imposing their own restless movement on others.

Beginning with migratory boom-towns and frontier warfare, the United States as a whole has had an inordinate amount of violence in its history. American cities in 1849 were Hell-towns too, full of young men organized into gangs who regularly battled one another and the police. In New York, many of the fights pitted Irish immigrants, like the Dead Rabbit gang, against those who hated them, such as the Bowery Boys. For many immigrants, cities were real frontiers.

Why are Americans so violent? Until the mid-twentieth century the United States had more men than women, quite an anomaly in the industrial world, where, elsewhere, women inevitably outnumber men. Fed by new immigrants, this male population was young. In the eighteenth century, the median age of the colonial population was around sixteen. As late as 1900 it was only twenty-three. Almost all the individuals described in this book set out to make their mark on the world when they were teenagers. Only since World War II has the gender ratio changed, as women began to outnumber men among immigrants and in the population as a whole. In the same period, the median age of the American population has risen and currently stands at the mid-thirties. As a historian of this phenomenon puts it, "Insofar as young, single men are any society's most troublesome and unruly citizens, America had a built-in tendency toward violence and disorder."[16]

The result, quite simply, has been violence. Americans are heavily armed: an astounding half of all homes contain at least one gun. This is the main reason that our murder rate is twice as high as that of any other industrial nation (although it has dropped in recent years). According to one study, the American homicide rate among young men is more than four times that of the next most murderous of the advanced industrial nations (Scotland, source of so many of our immigrant frontiersmen), and roughly ten times the average rate.[17] It is not American

Many boomtowners learned their violent ways first in cities. Take the case of Michael Henry McCarty, born to an Irish immigrant on the Lower East Side of Manhattan in 1859. He fell in with the kind of youthful gangs typical of nineteenth-century cities, and in 1876 he killed another man in a knife fight (or rather, McCarty had a knife, much to the other man's regret). He fled to New Mexico, taking the name William Bonney. But he became best known on the frontier as Billy the Kid before being killed himself in 1881. Just as improved policing had driven the most lawless residents of the Scottish border region to America, many criminals in the Eastern states found it prudent to start over in the West, taking their violent habits with them.

crime rates overall that are especially high, but the violence that accompanies them. In 1992, for instance, New York City had fewer burglaries and robberies than London. But only seven people died in those crimes in London, while 378 died in New York, thanks to the fact that both criminals and their victims were more likely to be armed. Guns are not the whole story, however, since Americans are also more likely to die in incidents where guns are not present. The rest of the story seems to involve a kind of honor culture, prone to violence, that many believe characterizes the inner city today just as much as the frontier of yesterday. At its heart are young men.

Violence against people merely echoes the central purpose of boomtowns: violence against nature. People come to boomtowns to make money by transforming the physical world, and that is their primary relationship to nature. When the environment is seen chiefly as a way to get rich, there is inevitable waste. Early colonists cleared land by "girdling" trees: killing them by stripping off bark in a circle around their trunks. The trees were left standing as they decayed, and the lack of leaves allowed enough light through to grow Indian corn and other hardy crops among them. Large trees rotting in the air were a bit hazardous, since they dropped large branches and themselves eventually toppled over, yet this method at least had the advantage of returning some nutrients to the soil. Girdling was gradually replaced by an even more wasteful method, in which trees would be felled one summer, then burned where they lay the following spring. Rich humus, deposited over centuries, was consumed in the fire, although its nutrients were partly replaced by the ash—unless the settler gathered up and sold the ashes for use in gunpowder and soapmaking. But the replacement was temporary, allowing only a few good crop seasons. The clearing of trees also fostered erosion, so that soil further lost its fertility. As historian William Cronon says, "Destroying the forest thus became an end in itself, and clearing techniques designed to extract quick profits from forest resources encouraged movement onto new lands."[18] Restlessness became a vicious circle.

Although most of New England's trees were simply destroyed, many of those that could be transported to the coast, especially by floating them down rivers, were sold on the market. The growing maritime industry, as well as the Royal Navy, came to depend on American pitch pines for pitch and turpentine, on white oak for planking and barrel staves, on white pines—remarkably straight and up to two hundred feet tall—for masts. Under boomtown thinking, the best woods disappeared first and fast. Again and again, European visitors were appalled by colonists' wasteful habits of using the finest woods for trivial purposes such as shingles and firewood. Naturally the forests vanished, and in many developed areas even firewood became scarce. New Englanders used prodigious amounts of fuel. By seventeenth-century standards they kept their homes very warm, with fires going all winter in most or all rooms. They used large, open fireplaces that consumed four or five times the wood required by cast-iron stoves, so that the average household required the cutting of more than *an acre of woodland every winter.* Luckily for them, the coal that eventually replaced wood as the country's main heating source was even more plentiful.

Even when they stayed put and farmed their land over some years, Americans indulged in wasteful practices with little regard for long-run sustainability. They rarely rotated crops, a method already known to maintain a field's fertility. They did not save animal manure to spread on fields, in part because they often neglected to fence in their animals, allowing them to forage for themselves in woods and meadows. In the earliest years, fields could simply be abandoned when their soil was depleted. Weeds appeared everywhere. To European eyes, American farms were a mess.

Americans could get away with such waste because they inhabited the world's most richly endowed land. Extremely fertile, arable land with abundant rainfall was the first important resource. Even today, with less than 3 percent of its population working the land, the United States is—by far—the world's largest agricultural producer. But rich land was not the only resource to be found here. The supply of lumber—nine hundred million acres of it when white settlers arrived, covering half the land mass—was unprecedented in the "known" world. The United States also had more coal reserves than all of Europe combined, more oil and natural gas than all but a handful of nations, as well as abundant potential for hydroelectric power. Plentiful iron ore allowed this country to produce half the world's steel at one time, right after World War II. According to one recent estimate, the United States still leads the world in deposits of copper, coal, and natural gas, is second in lead, third in iron and petroleum, fourth in silver.[19] It has large amounts of aluminum, zinc, and magnesium, not to mention the clay, limestone, and gypsum needed for cement. With the invention of nuclear fission, the United States benefited from the world's largest uranium deposits. All these resources could be exploited easily, as geography also favored American transportation, providing a huge network of navigable rivers (roughly eighteen thousand miles in all), and a coastline well dotted with safe harbors and bays. Those rivers, we saw in chapter 3, proved crucial to opening up this land to exploitation.

Even after the frontier was closed, which only meant that land became cheap instead of free, the great expanses of the West still held other resources to exploit, and their exploitation drew the same kind of rough young men. Not only the obvious cowboys who herded and drove cattle, but the men who felled timber, mined for silver, gold, tin, and copper, trapped fur-bearing animals, and hauled out what others produced. Even construction jobs frequently offered boomtown conditions and wages. The railroads, in particular, required hard work under grim conditions, and each end-of-the-line construction depot was filled with the usual trio of gambling, drinking, and violence. Workers were often young immigrants recruited expressly to work on the railroads. There are similar boomtowns today, mining towns or oil fields, although the young men in them are a tiny proportion of our population, and better policed than they used to be.

Americans continue to use almost all natural resources, especially energy and water, at rates far above those in any other country. Per person, our energy consumption is fully one hundred times that of sub-Saharan Africa. With seventy-five thousand dams on our rivers, we use more than twice as much water per capita as any other country (except Canada, which has ten times the water and one-tenth the population and still uses only 80 percent of what we do per capita).[20] Our clothes washers use four times as much water as European models. Personal use alone amounts to one hundred gallons a day per head. But the vast majority of our water is used to make money—by industry, electric utilities, and agriculture. Our wasteful agricultural methods, in which more water evaporates than gets to the crops, are directly descended from colonists' practices. In many parts of the West, water depletion is already a severe problem—and the subject of lawsuits—which will only increase in coming decades.

Today's federal government encourages overexploitation of resources by selling them at extremely low prices. It provides water almost free to California agribusiness, for instance. In 1994 it sold land in northern Nevada to a mining company for ten thousand dollars, even though that land contained minerals worth billions of dollars. Ranchers can graze their beef and sheep on federal land for one-tenth the amount they would pay on the open market. The timber in national forests is sold for less than it costs the government to help get it out; logging roads in the national forests are eight times as extensive as the interstate highway system. Clear-cut logging, in which entire mountains are denuded, is still allowed. Such irrational practices are partly due to laws established in the late nineteenth century, when the government wanted to encourage rapid boomtown exploitation and settlement.

Pollution is the flip side of profligate resource consumption. With about 5 percent of the world's population, the United States produces almost a quarter of its carbon dioxide emissions, the biggest contributor to global pollution and warming. We generate 18 tons of the gas per person each year, more than twice as much as in Europe. Although in 1992 our government was willing to join thirty-four other industrial nations in signing an agreement in Rio de Janeiro to cut greenhouse emissions, the United States has been the worst at keeping its promise, forcing its representatives to fight against most pollution controls in the 1997 round of negotiations. The automobile culture is a dirty culture. The costs of cars and trucks are legion, and all too familiar, from the trees killed and water polluted by road salt to the 250 million rubber tires discarded every year. And that is on top of the more obvious fatalities and injuries, as well as the pollutants, which are measured in the hundreds of millions of tons each year.

Automobiles are only one aspect of Americans' boomtown willingness to destroy their environment to make money. Many industrial processes, such as the production of plastics, create hazardous compounds that slowly leach into the ground. Open-pit mines, especially for copper, fill with water and then spread toxic elements such as arsenic, mercury, and lead into the groundwater. Thousands of other hazardous substances are buried underground or dumped into rivers and along back roads each year. Every once in a while, they come back up.

Government policy both reflects and reinforces our polluting habits. A company that subsidizes its employees' commuting expenses gets a tax break of up to $175 a month for the ones who drive, but only $65 for those who take public transportation. Americans love sport utility vehicles not only because they symbolize freedom but also because numerous government incentives favor them. They are exempt from the federal tax penalizing "gas-guzzler" automobiles, and most get an appalling fifteen miles to the gallon. People who use them for their work, whether or not their work requires such large vehicles, can claim larger tax deductions than for normal autos. Many sport utility vehicles are also exempt from the "luxury tax" on vehicles costing over $36,000. They are also allowed to emit 175 percent more nitrogen oxide (which causes smog) than automobiles. As always, hidden structures shape our choices.

It is partly sheer luck that we have not run out of key resources. New technologies, based on different natural resources, have come along, so coal replaced wood and oil replaced coal—partly. Nuclear and solar energy may yet replace fossil fuels. Americans believe firmly in their own inventive ingenuity, driven in part by the immense creativity of immigrants. The second reason we have not run out is the stunning amounts we have of so many different resources. Wood, coal, oil, uranium, natural gas, even sunlight, abound. Then, too, having used our environment to become the world's most powerful nation, we have been able to begin extracting resources from other countries. This is often a combination of bribes and bullying, with outright military force—as in Operation Desert Storm—always available if nothing else works.

For four hundred years, Americans have been able to produce whatever world markets demanded: fur, tobacco, lumber, indigo, fish, wheat, cotton, iron, uranium, grains, vegetable oils. We are still the dominant producer of many natural resources. But we have found ways to fill the demand for other products, too, whether for sophisticated weaponry, computers, or action movies. An immigrant culture is always flexible enough to find new ways to make money, starting with the exploitation of our natural resources but eventually going way beyond them.

Our bountiful resources, at every stage in American history, have reinforced our get-rich-quick willingness to exploit our habitat. The immigrant's sense of the environment as an opportunity to get rich was easily transferred to the frontier and so to the entire country. How could we ever run out of an entire continent's wealth? One corollary of a boom attitude is that there should be no limit on how much land a person can own; people can own far more than they actually need to live, since they can use it to make money. At the same time, no one has an interest in preserving the land, since that would interfere with profits. Cronon concludes his study of colonial New England with a comment that applies to every region: "Ecological abundance and economic prodigality went hand in hand: the people of plenty were a people of waste."[21] Another historian comments on the plowing up of the sod in the arid Great Plains, blaming the Dust Bowl of the 1930s on "tenancy, the moving itch, violence toward nature as well as other men, disregard for the land as a permanent home."[22] The United States became the world's wealthiest country through a willingness to use up its own natural resources combined with hard (especially immigrant) labor.

Americans' sense of abundance is based on two intertwining notions: that this land is inexhaustibly massive and unimaginably rich. Michel-Guillaume Saint-Jean de Crèvecoeur, an immigrant who changed

Even today, Americans' sense of their country's vast size colors their vision, right down to official plans for evacuating people in case of a nuclear attack. Officials from the Federal Emergency Management Agency, trying to explain why the resulting devastation might not be as bad as most expect, argue, "Defense Department studies show that even under the heaviest possible attack, less than 5 percent of our entire land area would be affected by blast and heat from nuclear weapons. . . . The other 95 percent of our land would escape untouched, except possibly by radioactive fallout" (Lee Clarke, *Mission Improbable*). Lots of places to hide out in those hills.

his name to J. Hector St. John, boasted in his *Letters from an American Farmer* that "many ages will not see the shores of our great lakes replenished with inland nations, nor the unknown bounds of North America entirely peopled. Who can tell how far it extends? Who can tell the millions of men whom it will feed and contain? For no European has as yet travelled half the extent of this mighty continent!"[23] Geography matters. For restlessness to flourish, there must be room to maneuver and relocate. Moving from one region to another feels like migrating to a new country. The country's great expanse even reverberates in the wide arm gestures for which Americans are known, and the way they stand with legs far apart (that is how Europeans recognize us). But geography is not destiny. Moving must be seen positively, as having a payoff, and other conditions must be present: materialism, anxiety about success, resources to exploit, and so on. Wide open spaces are a cultural creation as much as a physical given.

Despite occasional challenges (see chapters 7 and 8), the boomtown attitude toward nature is alive and well. A more environmentalist orientation has flourished in settled, urban areas and among cultural elites, but those living in the wide open spaces still view them as raw materials. This is especially the attitude of many big landowners out west. James Watt, the born-again Christian from Lusk, Wyoming, whom Ronald Reagan appointed secretary of the interior in 1981, was point man for the "sagebrush rebellion" of many westerners against federal efforts to protect the environment. Central to this vision was the insistence that public lands—vast in many western states—"represented freedom to the American people. It was freedom to explore new land, to tap its resources, to settle on it, that brought most of the settlers West. The large public land area of the West still represents freedom."²⁴ Land is still something to conquer, a means for self-enrichment; something to settle, not to use wisely (despite the deceptively named "wise-use movement," a front for promoters of untrammeled exploitation). Most of the West's resources, once tapped, are gone. The gold vanishes, topsoil is eroded, water tables fall, overgrazing turns prairie into desert. "Public" lands are perceived as belonging not to the government but to the people. The federal government, even though it purchased the lands, opened them up, subsidized the railroads, irrigated deserts, guaranteed bank loans, and paid armies to massacre the natives, has always been seen as an unwanted, unnecessary intruder. Large numbers of westerners see the federal government as an eastern imposition, meant to prevent them from taking full advantage of "their" natural resources. Even with the real frontier long gone, there are echoes of the same attitudes. Survivalists, for instance, seek out unpopulated areas in which they feel free from corrupting institutions, especially government. Conquest of the land and a pugnacious militarism still go hand in hand.

During the savings and loan scandals of the late 1980s, Americans heard a number of stories about other men who were "creatures of the boomtown Rockies," or the "boomtown West." Those responsible for undermining dozens of apparently staid institutions avidly pursued penny-stock schemes, dubious oil or mining investments, goofy speculation like the Bre-X gold mine, and other tricks for quick wealth. Like their younger boomtown fellows, they all seemed to gamble and spend money—other people's money, it turned out. The quickest way up the ladder has always been to use other people's money, and throughout American history, being a bank officer or trustee has been an opportunity to do that. One of them, a decade ahead of his time, fled a 1973 prison sentence by driving off in his lawyer's Pontiac LeMans convertible, managing to move around the West and avoid capture for twenty years. During that time his lawyer moved as well, to Washington, becoming sagebrush rebel Senator Orrin Hatch. To such men, the world is a lottery which they know how to manipulate.

The frontier, wherever it was at any given time, has been central to Americans' self-understanding ever since the Puritans battled the forces of darkness. Frederick Jackson Turner, famous for his 1893 lecture, "The Significance of the Frontier in American History," was explicit about this. The frontier's effect on American character, he argued, included a sense of abundance, a weakening of civilized standards and traditional institutions, and a resulting stress on the importance of the individual.

Although Turner exaggerated the democratic impulse that supposedly resulted, he captured much of American culture—except that the restless individualism was not limited to the frontier. David Potter argued that the key to American character was our abundance; in the self-congratulatory genre of 1950s national-character studies, he gave primary credit to our technological ingenuity rather than to raw resources. The flip side of our ability to exploit nature, though, is our willingness to do it. Americans' ruthless attitude toward the physical world had few of Europe's traditions or laws to constrain it; markets were allowed free rein. There was little ingenuity, and certainly no wisdom, in destroying the forests of New England for firewood, or shooting down clouds of pigeons for fun.

When the ore is gone or the land depleted, people leave boomtowns. Sometimes everyone disappears, leaving an empty ghost town like those that still dot many western states. Even more poignantly, a few people usually stay behind, no longer young or ambitious enough to move on to the next strike. These towns also feel like ghost towns, only they are populated by flesh-and-blood people. With the great migration to cities and suburbs, much of rural America has undergone this depopulation, another form of waste. New Hampshire's famous stone walls run through woods that used to be fields and orchards, and it is still possible to find an old well or foundation; farms painfully carved out of northern New England almost two hundred years ago were abandoned a few generations later, as opportunities shifted westward and then to the cities. The same reversion to forest is found in a number of regions— Appalachia, the northern prairie—that proved inhospitable to the techniques of agribusiness (in more fertile regions, the people left, but the machines and a few operators stayed). When a place is no longer profitable, we abandon it.

Even some of our homes reflect boomtown thinking. Farm journals and immigrant handbooks cautioned midwestern homesteaders against building homes that were idiosyncratic, lest they be difficult to sell when the family moved on; mass-produced houses like those sold by Sears or later built in Levittown could be built quickly and sold easily. Americans even perfected the form of housing most suitable to boomtowns, the trailer, which provides temporary housing in many of them. Cheap and mobile, trailers house between ten and twenty million Americans today, mostly young, blue-collar families. They are not intended to last long, and most look shabby almost immediately. Some are moved from place to place, although others remain right where they are first planted.

Permanent carports, sheds, and extra rooms often grow up around them. But no matter how long they last, they still have the transient feel of boomtown housing.

═══

The Americas were colonized at a time when European attitudes toward land were changing, with customary restrictions giving way to increasingly free markets. In North America a few fruitless efforts were made to impose constraints, especially on inheritance, but the availability of so much land made them difficult to enforce. Instead, thoroughly "modern" markets were established that made it easy to buy and sell land and placed almost no limits on what owners could do with their property. Just when profits were taking hold as an acceptable human motivation, this large land mass was made subject to laws that gave free rein to their pursuit.

The frontier meant conquest—of nature and natives equally. Nothing in our wars of extermination against the Indians allows self-congratulation; they only help explain the brutality and violence that set the tone for the settling of the West, as well as the parallel attitude toward physical nature. It was there to be fought, used up, conquered, and then abandoned. Rowdy young men, unafraid of death, were just the people to do this. Here was testosterone culture at its most macho.

The economic importance of land, though not its symbolism, began to ebb in the late nineteenth century, and long before the closing of the frontier, American cities were booming. The subsequent migration of people into them—most of them fresh immigrants—eventually dwarfed the movement of people to the frontier. Strikingly, though, these cities still felt like boomtowns, where the environment was available for swift exploitation and quick fortunes. The same masculine drive that went into mining for gold could go into making money by buying, selling, and producing commodities. The cities were almost as violent and just as aggressive. Of course the frontier has been important in American history, especially in the nineteenth century. More important, though, Americans have treated their entire country as if it were the frontier.

Immigration and the frontier have been two favorite explanations for American national character, but they have rarely been perceived as parts of the same phenomenon. By the late nineteenth century, those pushing back the frontier were only partly immigrants, who mostly preferred the cities. But the two migrations, one arriving in the East and the other pushing West, are part of the same faith: that the center of civilization moves westward, drawing the ambitious from the Old World just as it decimates uncivilized savages. This was a central tenet in Americans' self-image, and there was truth in the ambition and direction, if not in the portrayal of the "savages" being pushed out. More pragmatically, western and eastern ambitions shared the boomtown need for rapid turnover and enrichment. Why people come to America and what they do once here, even if separated by several generations, are similar. If the United States represents unlimited opportunity to those elsewhere, the West has symbolized that to those already here. California is to New Yorkers what America is to Europeans.

The economic ambitions of immigrants fit well with boomtown attitudes. The real action is the remaking of one's self and the enrichment of one's family. The environment is only a set of resources for doing this, or at best the stage on which the real action takes place. It has no moral worth of its own, nor does it command any respect as our permanent habitat. Immigrants and boomtowners tolerate bad conditions in the hope of putting a little extra aside, of taking a step toward financial stability. They have to move fast and work hard, though, because in boomtowns nothing is permanent. Most immigrants manage to save some; most boomtowners spend their wages on "sins." Whether we congratulate them for success or condemn them for wasting their earnings on vice, it is tempting to see both kinds of seekers as responsible for their own fates, as autonomous individuals, even down to protecting their own earnings with guns. As in stories of immigration, government and other social institutions do not loom large in boomtown tales, and it is easy to overlook them altogether.

Government policies and economic structures underlie boomtowns, however, as surely as they underlie immigration. Men come to boomtowns because companies and local governments publicize the riches to be found there, igniting a general hysteria about the possibility of great wealth. They come via railroads erected on government land, highways built with tax dollars.

Some of our boomtown attitudes have softened. Cities were the new frontiers of the twentieth century, attracting fortune-seekers both native and foreign. The boomtown attitude toward one's surroundings as an opportunity for advancement is still there, but its consequences are less destructive. Cities lack the physical resources to extract; more subtle means are necessary for making urban fortunes. Boomtown aggression has also subsided as Americans have aged. The literal frontier is gone, and today there are more jobs for computer geeks than burly roughnecks. The testosterone culture that dominated so much of American history has largely been civilized.

For most immigrants and boomtowners, the excitement of the dream does not lie in the quiet accumulation of savings year in and year out, which might add up to something over a generation or two; it comes from the possibility of big money, quickly gained. For many immigrants, as for most boomtowners, the economic dream looks like a lottery, in which everyone has a chance to strike it rich. This may still require virtue or hustle, but sudden fortunes can spark the imagination in a way that slow accumulation cannot.

Migration encourages a boomtown mentality, and the two share a central goal: to do whatever it takes to make one's way in society. This may simply involve finding one's proper place in the social order (this is the preindustrial version), or it may mean economic advancement (this is the industrial version). With the closing of the frontier, the focus has shifted to mobility within the economic hierarchy, finding a new place in our status system. The next chapter examines the expectations and the realities of markets and social mobility. Boomtowns and immigration both suggest that dreams are about to be fulfilled, the game is about to be won. Because of them, America has all the excitement of a great lottery.

5 *The Great Lottery*

Let me tell you about the very rich. They are different from
you and me.
—*F. Scott Fitzgerald*

Yes, they have more money.
—*Ernest Hemingway*

Most wandering people evolve a culture of tents and saddles and migratory herds, but here [is] a wandering people with a passion for gi-
gantic bedsteads and massive refrigerators.
—*John Cheever*

Harry Houdini, self-proclaimed "King of Handcuffs," was born Ehrich
Weisz in Budapest in 1874. His family altered their name to Weiss when
they came to the United States four years later. His father, a rabbi, was
fired after only two years of service to his Appleton, Wisconsin, congre-
gation and subsequently had difficulty finding steady work. He tried his
hand at a private school and other endeavors, eventually working in the
garment industry and dragging his family to Milwaukee and then to
New York. In both cities they had to turn to religious charities for occasional aid. Ehrich had the drive his father lacked. He ran away from
home first at the age of twelve (he spent the summer on a farm, claiming to be an orphaned shoeshine boy—his first effort at self-creation),
worked a number of odd jobs throughout his teen years, and competed
constantly in athletic competitions. He won a number of medals for
footraces, although—already fabricating a new identity for himself—
he supplemented these with others he purchased.

Ehrich Weiss was only sixteen when he began performing magic
tricks, adopting the mysterious-sounding stage name "Houdini," added
to Harry, an Americanization of his nickname, "Ehrie." For eight years
he inhabited the bizarre world of medicine shows and dime museums,

performing melodrama, burlesque, puppetry, comedy, acrobatics, magic, escape tricks, hypnotism, even seances. He worked alongside jugglers, contortionists, performing monkeys, freaks, and, for a while, "Oklahoma Bill, the Scout, and his prairie wife." There were sprinting contests for fat ladies, and an armless man who played the violin with his toes. (The milieu contained more talented versions of the King and the Duke, the con artists lampooned in *Huckleberry Finn*.) Typographical errors had Houdini as Houdin, Hunyadi, Hondini, Robert Houdini, Harry Houdine, and Professor Houdinis, and he himself went by Harry Raynohr, Cardo, Professor Murat, Projea, the Wizard of Shackles, and other titles. He invested in one traveling group, which left him with heavy debts when it went bust. Like so many immigrants, he was willing to try anything.

Houdini was on the verge of leaving show business when, in 1899, his big break came. He impressed Martin Beck, a German immigrant who ran the Orpheum Circuit, which booked vaudeville shows throughout the western United States. At Orpheum theaters Houdini did card tricks and swallowed needles (which would reappear, neatly threaded, after he had also swallowed the thread), but his escapes were his best act. He would let audience members provide handcuffs and locks, and local manufacturers furnished packing crates or other devices (guaranteeing plenty of publicity for everyone). He would appear at local police stations and offer to escape, often nude, from their best jail cells. He could get out of straightjackets, sealed milk cans, glass boxes, coffins, even an iron boiler riveted shut. He would do anything for money or fame (the two being intimately related for a performer like him), and he made sure that the news media covered every antic. As a friend put it, "Houdini would murder his grandmother for publicity." He succeeded by tapping into the deepest fantasies of American men, coming to symbolize man alone, able to escape all constraints, ever struggling for freedom—and ever on the road.

Houdini's act was based on illusion, appropriately enough. Strong coffins might have a hundred long nails ostentatiously hammered to seal their lids—but only a couple in one of the other panels, so that Houdini could push it out once the curtain was raised up around him. Long screws in one panel might be replaced by short ones right before the show, but after Houdini escaped (yet before dropping the curtain), he would put them back for the benefit of the committees always present to examine his materials. Houdini often spent more than an hour in his escapes, letting the tension build in the audience, distracted only by the orchestra. He might have spent most of this time reading the newspaper behind the curtain if, as many believe, he used hidden keys to escape the most demanding locks. In several of his most difficult escapes, he asked for a glass of water after struggling for some time, which his wife and stage partner Bess would provide—almost certainly slipping him additional keys in the process. But his act and his image were only partly illusion and publicity management, for his skill and strength also set him apart from hundreds of other magicians and escape artists.

The other side of Houdini's restless ambition was his aggressive and petulant bickering over every aspect of his career: fees, advertising campaigns, the position of his name in the bill. He never forgot slights. He quarreled and broke with Beck after only a year, paying five hundred dollars to be released from his contracts. After this, Houdini began to remove Beck, the man who had made him famous, from his life story. He later wrote: "In magical history generally the manager had a great deal to do with a performer's rise to fame. Am not complaining, but have had to be my own manager."[1] In rewriting the history of his life, he also began to deny being an immigrant, claiming to have been born in Wisconsin; he downplayed his family's poverty. Houdini was also notoriously competitive, sometimes appearing at the shows of rivals to taunt them, and frequently exposing others' tricks. "Do others or they will do you," he once told a reporter. Even his testy encounters with challengers and doubters were turned into publicity.

Like Sam Clemens, thought to be the first major American writer to use a typewriter or a dictaphone, Houdini anxiously exploited new technologies for his own self-promotion, whether autos, airplanes, or movies (he went into the motion picture business for a while). But he remained, in many ways, a late-Victorian amalgam of the spiritualism of middle-class parlors and the muscular strenuousness of Teddy Roosevelt. A man's man for whom physical vigor and material success were closely connected.

With the creativity of an immigrant, Houdini was a consummate American: constantly reinventing and promoting himself, seeking success in any number of arenas, denying and rejecting his own origins and circumstances. He was ambivalent about being Jewish and longed for acceptance by WASP elites. "I am an American," he said, "and am more proud of that fact than anything else."[2] Throughout his energetic activities, in true American style, ran a concern with money. He had promised his dying father that he would take care of his mother, and he succeeded in that. He was in constant imbroglios over money, and after he tried his hand at motion pictures in the 1920s, he was both plaintiff and defendant in a number of lawsuits over money and rights. He was not especially astute in business, and continually invested in schemes that most often failed. He worried about ending up impoverished, like his father. Fortunately, his endless drive prevented that. He died at the age of fifty-two, from injuries he got during a bit of macho violence worthy of a boomtown, when he let a strapping young man punch him several times as hard as he could in the stomach. No immigrant could have hoped for greater success or greater adaptation to America.

His career was American in other ways. The adage about a woman behind every great man holds especially for Houdini, whose invisible wife and helper saved his act on many occasions, even though she received no credit. Part of Houdini's illusion—in his life and his act—was that he did everything by himself. Early in their careers, they got equal billing as a team, but as he grew famous, Bess disappeared from advertisements. Houdini was willing to acquire any skill that might please people and earn money, and he learned his trade on the road, moving from town to town with different troupes, absorbing what he could from everyone he encountered. He launched into his career as a teenager and was famous a decade later, but he never rested on that fame. An aggressive obsession with money and success, even when this harmed those around him, kept him forever willing to move and to start over.

Houdini followed in a direct line from Ben Franklin and Sam Clemens. Money was not the only goal for any of them—fame was equally important—but money always came first. It was never far from the thoughts of any of the three. When Clemens was made a river pilot after a relatively short apprenticeship, his biographer writes, "Besting the once-superior younger pilots gratified Sam's competitive rage. In a single coup, he had surpassed his brother and exceeded his father's greatest accomplishment. Still, his father's and brother's uneasy relationship with the commercial world kept Sam apprehensive about his fortunes; his own feelings of unworthiness, drawn more sharply by [his brother] Henry's death, made him doubt the justice of receiving the very money he craved. Money appeared to be an objective measure of a man's worth, but Sam's current affluence did little to assuage his doubt about himself." There is never enough money or fame, which explains why Clemens continued to invest in moneymaking schemes like a mysterious food supplement called "plasmon." In addition, it is important not to appear to be seeking money; wealth should be a by-product of talent and virtue. Clemens "never wanted to appear to care about it, but getting rich and staying that way became the dominant motivation in his life."[3] No wonder Clemens and Houdini came to be ranked among the most famous "Americans" of the late nineteenth and early twentieth centuries—and they were famous *as* Americans. Like Ben Franklin, they fit the mold well.

Fresh starts are fraught with anxiety, even in a culture that favors them, even when they have succeeded. People continue to rewrite their lives around the new starts they have made, sometimes exaggerating and other times diminishing how far they have come. Movement up or down is filled with moral implications for the kind of person you are. Houdini, Clemens, and Franklin were aware of this, and tried hard to rework their life stories around this theme. For them, as for most Americans, the clearest marker of their success was how much money they were making. These men were always anxious about money, and all three were always scheming to make more, speculating in dubious technologies and get-rich-quick schemes, and of course worrying.

Americans don't just move around; they move up. At least they expect to, and among their main reasons for moving around are to get a better job, buy a bigger house, ascend the corporate ladder, or in other cases merely to find a job at all, to avoid slipping into poverty. Boomtown-style restlessness means that a lot of people are looking for their big chance to get rich, hopefully quickly and without too much pain. They are willing to work hard if they have to, but they also buy lottery tickets and bring lawsuits in the hopes of sudden fortune. When other routes don't work, a few even turn to crime, robbing strangers or embezzling money for a new home in Florida. Judging from Hollywood movies, Americans even admire con men. The point is to get ahead, by almost any means. If America is the land of the dream, that dream has usually centered on material success.

And since the nineteenth century, material success has meant a large fortune. Americans play the lottery in order to have a chance at winning big. They don't play in order to accumulate a little money each week, in the hopes it will eventually add up to something. Slow, steady accumulation is for "chumps," and most American men turn to it when they have no other options for getting rich. For Americans, with their enormous optimism, economic life is like a great lottery, in which they vastly overestimate their own chances of winning. Young men move from boomtown to boomtown in the hopes that, next time, they will be among the winners. Even as we come to suspect we will never win big, and settle instead into a lifetime of hard work, the real excitement of the American dream, today more than ever, is the fantasy of being rich, not comfortable. We may complain about the rich, but we need them for our reveries. Why else would Ben Franklin speculate in western lands, Houdini in motion pictures, Sam Clemens in every hair-brained scheme that came his way? As Hemingway said, the rich are no different from other Americans, except that they have won the great lottery. That could be us. We identify with those above us.

We identify with the rich because we believe in markets. Everyone who enters a lottery is supposed to have an equal chance of winning. As long as you can raise the money to play the game, you have as good a chance as Bill Gates does. And you play as an individual. There are no political alliances with others (unless a group buys a ticket together, rather like the communes who preferred to start over together rather than as individuals). There are no structured chances of winning affected by race, or class, or sex. There are just unconnected individuals, only a few of whom will be favored with big winnings, but any of whom *could* be. Vastly unequal outcomes are accepted, since there must be lots of losers in order to have a big pot for the winner. This, we'll see, is pretty much how Americans view the economy, as a fair competition with unequal results. We trust markets to allocate rewards fairly, not equally.

Yet Americans refuse to see life as a pure game of chance. They believe that individuals can increase their odds of winning, and they think that if you just keep playing you are likely to win eventually. Those who work hard, in particular, and are "virtuous" in other ways—avoiding drink and drugs, willing to move in pursuit of opportunities, and maintaining a clean appearance—have a better shot. Those who lack virtue simply cannot enter the competition. Those who are virtuous keep playing until they win; their willingness to keep playing is one of their key virtues. Lotteries are based on luck, but since Americans do not like to attribute economic success to luck, we insist (with considerable contradiction) that virtue and hard work lie behind the luck of the draw. The lottery is a good metaphor for our society, because, of all the effects of restlessness, none is more pervasive than the individualism that comes from our faith in markets. We tend to see the world as consisting of isolated, disconnected individuals. We explain what happens by means of individual traits and choices, not structural factors. We have a hard time thinking about the connections between people, the loyalties and affection they feel for each other. We may grow nostalgic about the idea of community, mostly because we have so little of it ourselves. Except for the male bonding of boomtowns and rafts, which ends as soon as circumstances change, American men have few ways of thinking about people in groups, or about factors that affect people as groups.

Success in the lottery has always been important to Americans, even as their idea of what that means has changed, especially as opportunities migrated from the frontier to the city. Daniel Boone and the cowboys were self-sufficient because they could live off the land and thus needed few possessions. Immigrant Andrew Carnegie, on the other hand, was rich, filthy rich (a term that hides our admiration only a little). Both kinds of hero were self-made, though, and both were autonomous individuals. Industrial fortunes were important primarily because they offered the same self-sufficiency that Boone derived from his musket. The knowledge which Carnegie had of the urban jungles of industrial capitalism paralleled Boone's understanding of game, weather, and Indians. Their skills allowed them room to move and maneuver, free from formal institutions, especially government. But it was important that, just as Boone shot his own game or crafted his own arrows when need arose, the commercial heroes had to make their own fortunes. Carnegie presented himself as a model American, and was widely accepted as one, because he had indeed been penniless as a child. If we admire lottery winners, we admire them most when they have leapt from the bottom of the heap.

We saw how Benjamin Franklin's famous autobiography set the tone for the very American story of the self-made man. Such works have often taken the form of advice to young men, just as Franklin's early sections were written as letters to his son. Ben's father was an immigrant dedicated to hard work, who kept "close to his trade," as Ben put it. From his first bid for autonomy at the age of seventeen, when he illegally fled Boston, Ben also used his surroundings opportunistically in profitable ways. In his case, his own self-aggrandizement eventually took the form of public projects like fire companies and public libraries, but only after he had amassed a fair amount of wealth himself. (Often through ruthless means: he drove several competitors out of business and used his position as Deputy Postmaster General to his own advantage as a printer. And he never gave up his interest in wealth, speculating in land throughout his life.)

The full myth of the self-made man blossomed soon after, in the Jacksonian period, even as realities diverged further from the ideal. In the 1830s the egalitarian fervor nurtured by the Revolution encountered the development of big factories, national markets, and renewed immigration, and many felt that the newly wealthy were stealing economic control from the people. The dream of self-creation became even more important, especially as a critique of industrialization for threatening that mobility (it was indeed creating a distinct working class, out of

The "log cabin myth" of humble origins has proven useful to presidential candidates, even though one historian of presidential careers, Edward Pessen, could find only two presidents who qualify as true rags-to-riches stories (Millard Fillmore and Andrew Johnson). Rather, he concludes in *The Log Cabin Myth*, "Most of the presidents were born to families at or near the top of the American social and economic order. And abetted by their youthful advantages, they forged successful prepresidential careers and made good marriages that further widened the gulf between the leaders and the led in America." Yet the image of being a "common" man, just like the voters except somehow risen to lofty heights, has remained, in one form or another, an asset for presidential candidates all the way down to Bill Clinton. We like to think of our presidents as normal guys who have won an electoral lottery.

which it became harder and harder to climb). As soon as Andrew Jackson was elected president in 1828, he was celebrated as the first man from middling background to reach such heights, a culmination of the opening up of suffrage to all white males in the early decades of the Republic. This myth, based on the fact that Jackson's father had died before he was born, seriously distorts his early circumstances. (He was raised by his uncle, a wealthy merchant and landowner, and was schooled in a private academy.) Yet during the next two decades it proved important to emphasize his self-creation, as a way first of criticizing but ultimately of justifying the rapid and obvious increases in inequality that would characterize the mercantile and industrial revolutions. Inequality would prove palatable as long as it was accompanied by opportunity. A lottery was all right if everyone (or everyone who mattered in those days) could play.

Nineteenth-century writers like William McGuffey and Horatio Alger, both former ministers, insisted that the solid Protestant virtues were still the path to success, even as the economy looked more and more like an arbitrary lottery. One of their lessons was that you had to be virtuous even to enter the game: the elderly stranger you help across the street may turn out to be wealthy—and without an heir (these authors surreptitiously acknowledged inheritance to be the surest road to wealth). Another lesson was that vices undermined self-control and self-awareness, rendering one unprepared when opportunity knocked. *Virtue*, however, became an empty word, a reassuring moral trope that people thought they understood, interpreting it according to their own tastes. Had the inspirational writers been specific about which virtues led to worldly success, they would have been ridiculed for being naive. Kind-

ness and generosity hardly led to wealth. "Virtue" served a psychological function, reassuring Americans that the new industrial society was
not as chaotic and arbitrary as it seemed, but it was not always realistic
career advice.

If Alger and others retained a Puritan residue in the success-story tradition, Andrew Carnegie purveyed a more tough-minded version that
emphasized work and hustle rather than other, softer virtues. Indeed,
with the appearance of social Darwinist ideas, the most ruthless compet-
itiveness could be seen as contributing to the greater good of society. Factory jobs depended on the creativity of individual industrialists, or so the
latter claimed. The benefactors in Alger novels were inevitably in "genteel" trade, while Carnegie (a poor Scotsman who came to the United
States in 1848 at age twelve) was in heavy industry. The "fortunes" of the
former were usually modest, in the tens of thousands of dollars, while
Carnegie's was as big as they came, in the hundreds of millions. In reality,
for middle-class clerks and salespeople, Alger's old-fangled virtues of
honesty, loyalty, dependability, and cleanliness were still business assets,
badges of respectability that customers and employers expected. But
their fantasies were about entrepreneurs who did not need to impress
superiors or anyone else, who instead needed to be ruthless in an era
of rapid industrial concentration. If Ben Franklin had been a model
of preindustrial success, Carnegie embodied industrial success. Both
shaped their own destinies through starting over, and both turned to public philanthropy only after they had attained considerable fortunes.

Carnegie's advice was closer than Alger's fantasies to a new genre
that emerged late in the century consisting of frank how-to guides to
success. The fortunes made in the decades following the Civil War differed from anything Americans had seen before, and they ignited the
popular imagination. There were a mere handful of millionaires at the
time of the war, but by the end of the century there were thousands,
whose exploits and lifestyles both fascinated and disgusted the public.
Success came to be defined more than ever in monetary terms. No wonder immigrants flooded into the country. Like Alger, most writers of
advice resisted the trend, praising the virtues of farm life and condemning the extravagances of city life, and recommending modest, steady
advancement rather than the dangers of sudden fortunes. Their urgent
need to write such cautions shows how little they were heeded. If nothing else, the rich embodied American fantasies of ultimate success.

Americans continued to believe they controlled their market fates,
even as the source of that control shifted from simple virtues to aggressive mind power. The industrialization and urbanization of the

nineteenth century left many Americans worried about their physical
health as well as their precarious economic destinies. Phineas Park-
hurst Quimby (1802–1866) developed a theory that disease was merely
a mental mistake, almost like an arithmetic error, and he attracted to
his Maine home a number of invalids who were "cured" through his
persuasion. The most famous, Mary Baker Eddy, founded a new religion, Christian Science, based on Quimby's principles. By her death in
1910, she had managed to attract one hundred thousand adherents to
her belief in the power of the human mind over the world around it, the
most successful of the many American religions and groups founded in
the last decades of the nineteenth century. Psychological power had replaced virtue, partly, but an individual's own choices were still thought
to determine his (and sometimes her) fate. A number of other groups
and individuals also saw intimate connections between individual will
and external, physical outcomes.

Economic success (of the material sort that had disturbed Quimby)
was soon included among the important outcomes of mind power. Frank
Channing Haddock wrote a series of self-help books beginning in 1907
with *Power of Will*, which sold nearly a million copies. Individuals, he
insisted, were masters of their fates:

He only is who wills to live
The best his nature prophesies:
Master of fate, executive
Of Self—a sovereign strong and wise.
Art thou a pigmy? Courage, soul!
For thee, as all, the Kingly goal.[4]

Haddock suggested specific exercises for training one's memory, attention, and other mental faculties. The most memorable advocate of such
exercises, perhaps because the simplest, was an immigrant, Emil Coué,
whose mantric refrain, "Day by day, in every way, I am getting better
and better," said often enough, was supposed to bring about just that result. Not all of these positive thinkers specified what "better" meant, but
this was not hard to figure out. Many were explicit. In *How to Win
Friends and Influence People* (1936), Dale Carnegie famously advised
readers on how to write business letters and make the right contacts,
following up on his earlier *Public Speaking and Influencing Men in Business*. Advertisements for his public talks candidly began, "Increase Your
Income." By the 1950s, positive thinkers had reinterpreted Christianity
in their own image. Dr. Norman Vincent Peale, whose radio and television shows, newspaper columns, magazines, tapes, and books reached

millions of Americans, taught a practical version of Christianity that could be applied to the modern world of business. Christian virtue could sell vacuum cleaners. Individual effort was still the centerpiece, however. God helped only if you called on him.

Psychotherapy, more popular in the United States than any other country, also grew out of the assumption that you could control yourself as well as the world around you, and that the world around you reflected how well you controlled yourself. Even Freud's concept of the unconscious, which Europeans found such a threat to social order with its sexuality and aggression, was just one more frontier for Americans to conquer in their quest for self-control, one more resource to use in self-improvement. Even a force that would seem to derail every promise of self-control could be transformed into a business asset, an advertising technique. One historian of psychotherapy compares European pessimism about the interior self with American optimism: "The European cure was to control through the practices of *self-domination;* the American cure, in contrast, was to control through expanding and revitalizing the self through the practices of *self-liberation.*"[5] Even the American unconscious was innocent and good.

Self-creation myths can be taken to extremes. Health and disease continue to be attributed to one's own actions, as reflected in the line of thought from Sylvester Graham (inventor of the famous cracker) through Mary Baker Eddy to popular spiritual healing and self-help techniques in today's United States. To take one recent case, therapists quote the adult son of a stroke victim as telling his father: "You look at television and you see people [without arms] who are painting oil paintings with the paintbrush held in their teeth. . . . I really think that if you wanted to, you could do a heck of a lot of things right now. I think it's a matter of saying, 'Damn it, I'm going to do this for myself because I want to do it.'"[6] Self-help books assure us that the right attitudes can defeat cancer and other illnesses. From EST to biofeedback, even our biology is, or should be, under our control.

Most of all, Americans continue to believe in economic mobility through individual effort. For those who don't win the lottery, there is always the slower route to wealth. In 1952, 88 percent of Americans believed that "there is plenty of opportunity, and anyone who works hard can go as far as he wants." In 1980, 70 percent still agreed with this. In a 1993 survey a whopping 94 percent agreed that hard work was crucial to success (followed by 53 percent who thought God's will was also crucial).[7] The poor are equally to blame for their plight. One study in the spring of 1969, at a time of relative liberalism in American political culture, found that individual reasons for poverty systematically out-ranked structural ones in American perceptions: the most-cited was lack of thrift (58 percent), followed in order by lack of effort, lack of ability, loose morals, sickness, and only then by low wages in some industries, lack of good schools, racial discrimination, the failure of private industry to provide enough jobs, exploitation by the rich, and plain bad luck (8 percent).[8] Interestingly, in contrast, serious studies of economic success and failure usually find that sheer luck explains more than anything else.

For an opposite view, reflecting both a different kind of economy as well as different cultural attitudes, we can turn to Russia. In a 1997 survey, Russians' favorite explanation of poverty was the economic system, although laziness and drinking were not far behind. Next came unequal opportunities and discrimination. Only then came a lack of effort and a lack of talents (fewer than half as many mentioned these as specified the economic system). Bad luck came last. Their favorite explanations for individual wealth were personal connections (cited by 88 percent), the economic system, dishonesty, and good opportunities, only then followed by talent, luck, and finally hard work (mentioned by only 39 percent). Russians reject individualist explanations that link success or failure either to virtues or to luck, focusing instead on aspects of the system such as inequality and discrimination.[9] Attitudes in most countries fall somewhere between Russian cynicism and American optimism.

One key belief has persisted across different images of American success: that individuals control their own destinies through maneuvering, movement, and starting over, again and again if necessary. All we need are equal opportunities. We see this optimism in the immigrants who uproot themselves and move thousands of miles, in the families and individuals who leave failing rural areas for the city, in the handful of boomtowners who strike gold, in the few who win the economic competition. The point of moving is to improve your chances in the great lottery.

Is our optimism justified? It may not matter. Americans would be just as stimulated by their dreams of economic success whether those dreams were mostly realistic or mostly illusionistic. The facts of mobility are simply not relevant to American expectations, for this is the land of the dream. Like those poor immigrants who insist they are doing well when they write home, most Americans need the reassurance that they could always start over if they had to. The worse they are doing, the more important this dream may be. If successful Americans like Houdini remain anxious about money, how deeply must unsuccessful ones feel the shame of being poor in the land of opportunity?

Overall, we are more optimistic than the facts warrant. Americans manage to move up the economic ladder, but only a few move very far or very fast. We have no more upward mobility than most other advanced industrial countries, despite our cherished image as the land of opportunity. Most of our immigrants do well, exploiting the cultural and financial capital they bring with them to advance beyond their artificially depressed starting jobs. As for our internal migrations, they lead to movement down as well as up, since people compete for a relatively fixed set of jobs. Despite our expectations, fresh starts don't always turn out to be better starts.

Throughout our history, most of those who dreamed of big success have been disappointed. As with all boomtowns, only a lucky few attain the success about which everyone dreams. The colonies, to start, simply did not offer many easy ways to accumulate wealth. One historian laments, "Very few people who migrated to English America during the seventeenth century ever acquired substantial wealth, and most of those did so in the West Indies. A far larger number of migrants were cruelly disappointed in their hopes, either dying early or never managing to get together the resources needed to make it out of servitude or dependency."[10] New England's settlers were more likely to arrive with families, and most managed to establish their children on small pieces of land—only to see those children push westward. In the southern colonies few lived long enough to do that. The lucky ones who managed to survive their bonded servitude found themselves free but impoverished in their late twenties or early thirties, after which they could expect to live only ten or fifteen years, in a society where women were still scarce. The lack of wives and regular family life further shortened men's life expectancies, giving them even less time to pursue their dreams.

Who managed to get rich? Mostly those who could find a way to create or exploit boomtown conditions—the Adolph Sutros of the world. For some, land speculation paid off, but most big fortunes had to await the era of industry, when market vicissitudes made and unmade people every day. Even then, it was those who owned railroads, developed the land along them, and otherwise helped to settle the continent who made the biggest fortunes. Many immigrants, less able to profit from the literal frontier, profited from the boomtown conditions created by later arrivals in the cities, selling them needed goods and services, just as Greek lunch counters catered to working-class immigrants. Most American fortunes were made by exploiting the restless dreams of others.

Many apparent exceptions are not so exceptional. Many southern planters, whose wealth would seem to depend on stable agriculture on the same land generation after generation (and the brutal exploitation of slaves), made a lot of money in other ways as well. In the colonial era many were given land grants on the frontier, which they rented, cleared, and sold at a profit to men like Bacon's followers. In many cases, the terms of the lease explicitly required that tenants improve the land in various ways, by not only clearing fields but planting orchards and erecting a certain number of buildings. The same planters often ran small stores for preying on those further down the economic ladder. They also thrived by offering credit, which they themselves were usually granted by English merchants. They dabbled in ironworks and other manufacturing. Other lucrative pursuits also depended on exploiting the young men flocking to boomtown conditions in the colonies. Many planters held government offices and practiced law, settling land disputes and the debt-collection lawsuits that naturally arose from so many loans.

Boomtowns offered diverse opportunities for wealth, but the best route was to combine a number of them. As an historian of Maryland and Virginia planters puts it, "In this milieu the lawyer had an enviable position," with a steady income ready to be put to opportunities as they arose, as well as "an intimate knowledge of the resources and dependability of the planters in the county. . . . Consequently he could take advantage of opportunities on the spot, whether they were bargains in land, sales of goods or produce, or tenants seeking leases." In other words he had sufficient liquidity to maneuver well in markets. "He could besides avoid the costs of litigation that inevitably arose as he involved himself in land speculation, lending, or merchandising, as many did."[11] In the North, too, merchants frequently benefited from speculating in land as well as supplying new arrivals, and there too lawyers did a thriving business settling the inevitable disputes of restless ambition. Boomtowns are litigious as well as violent.

We've seen that traditional constraints such as primogeniture, intended to keep a landed estate together despite the intentions of individual family members—a powerful constraint on restlessness—could not be transferred to the new colonies because younger generations could always find new lands. In direct contrast to the ruling families of Britain, success for the colonial elite often meant movement in search of new opportunities. "Since the land was quickly worn out," says Bernard Bailyn of colonial Virginia, "and since it was cheaper to acquire new land than to rejuvenate the worked soil by careful husbandry, geographical mobility, not stability, was the key to prosperity."[12] Because they had greater resources to help them profit from new boomtowns, elites often proved the most restless of all Americans. Whereas British merchants aspired to settle down on a landed estate and live like aristocrats, American landowners were ready to sell or mortgage their land in pursuit of new opportunities.

Even as the United States industrialized in the nineteenth century, almost all the bigger fortunes (and the associated companies) were generated by boomtown conditions, especially the railroads. Immigrants were usually quicker than others to see new opportunities. Immigrant John Jacob Astor's wealth was made from beaver pelts, although immigrant Stephen Girard amassed the early republic's other great fortune through banking and trade. The Du Pont family grew rich by manufacturing the black powder needed in mining and construction, especially of canals and then railroads. Carnegie made his first fortune in railroads, his second in the iron and steel needed for railroad bridges and rails. The railroads generated other fortunes as well: those of Forbes, Gould, Vanderbilt, Stanford, Huntington, and Morgan. The opening of the West to settlement stoked the dreams of millions of immigrants and native-born Americans, but in fact most of the land was given to railroads and thinly disguised (and wealthy) speculators. Of the twelve largest corporations in 1900—including American Steel, U.S. Leather, and U.S. Rubber—all but two involved raw-material extraction. Oil made John D. Rockefeller, of course. A generation later, automobiles would create more family fortunes and large corporations, not only making the cars but also the rubber tires. Real estate development continued to be a good path to wealth, only now in the cities filling with new immigrants rather than in the rich lands of the frontier. Through most of American history, reshaping the environment created new industries and fortunes.

However, *the surest road to wealth has always been inheritance.* Very few of the "robber barons" started off at the bottom of society; most merely invested and enhanced the wealth they inherited. For the most part only a few immigrants—Astor, Girard, Carnegie—worked their way from the bottom to the top.

Only in the fully industrialized economy since World War II has it been easier to make money by satisfying consumer tastes than by ransacking nature. (Today, only one of those twelve biggest companies from 1900 is still in existence.) The impact on nature is now frequently in the after-effects such as pollution rather than in the initial extraction of raw materials. With corporate consumerism, too, more wealth goes to bureaucrats than entrepreneurs. Those who climb the corporate ladder after Harvard Business School are the ones who land the jobs as CEOs making millions of dollars a year. One exception consists of those who can entertain us by making movies, playing sports, or attracting television viewers. But the most notable exception are the entrepreneurs of the computer industry, a sector filled with immigrants and the companies they have founded, from Intel's Andy Grove (a Hungarian) on down. Like the old West, Silicon Valley is filled with young men (nerds rather than cowboys) prospering from boomtown conditions.

Large fortunes, because they capture the American imagination, attract our attention even though only a tiny fraction of us ever attain them (mostly by starting with a lot of advantages). But what about more limited advances in income and status, the less dramatic forms of upward mobility that are open to more of us? Modest dreams are easier to attain. Even here, the picture is complex and less cheery than the optimistic dream would have us believe.

⌐⌐⌐⌐⌐⌐⌐⌐⌐⌐⌐⌐⌐⌐⌐⌐⌐⌐⌐⌐⌐⌐⌐⌐⌐⌐⌐⌐⌐⌐⌐⌐⌐⌐⌐⌐

If few Americans have won the lottery and gone from rags to riches, a large number have seen modest improvements in their situations, moving up the ladder by a rung or two. This is a common form of starting over. In the twentieth century, more men have moved up in occupations—relative to their fathers—than have moved down. One large study, which used five categories of occupational status (upper and lower white collar, upper and lower manual, and farm occupations, ranked in that order), found that 44 percent of men moved up in these categories, 20 percent moved down, and 36 percent remained in the same one.[13] Twice as many men moved up as down, but they were still a minority of all employed men. Women are even more likely to move up compared to their mothers, simply because they are more likely to have jobs than their mothers were (assuming that employment is a step up from homemaking). The upward movement of both sexes is almost entirely explained by shifting occupational structures, first away from farms, then away from manual work, and toward white-collar, service, and professional work. The changing economy has sucked everyone along with it. There is no evidence that the economy is sorting people according to their efforts and skills (if you start off in an upper middle class family, for example, you are two or three times as likely to end up there than if you begin in a blue-collar or farm family). If America is the land of opportunity, it is the land of modest opportunity.

Why are figures like these so at odds with American perceptions of great opportunity and mobility? Immigrant success, exaggerated though it is, has remained the core pillar of evidence supporting Americans' confidence that the dream works. Americans perceive more mobility than there is for other reasons as well. In addition to the movement into the United States, there is the geographic mobility within it, which allows occupational changes. Americans have always been quick to follow jobs that migrate, especially during the large but one-time movement off farms. Migration gives the illusion that things can get better—if only you move far enough west; if only you find out where the good jobs are. You *can* start over by moving. Unfortunately, that does not mean you won't make a mess of it again, but at least you have a chance. Or think you do. Starting over will not necessarily get you a better job, but it gives you another lottery drawing. It is easy to confuse geographic mobility with social mobility, and Americans assume that if people are moving around they must be moving up.

On top of this, there really is upward mobility, in that people tend to have nicer jobs and make more money than their ancestors. Thanks to immigrant ingenuity and to its vast natural wealth, the United States has become the world's wealthiest country. In addition, the job structure has constantly shifted upward, with better (in the sense of cleaner and less physically demanding) jobs constantly replacing worse ones. There is nothing particularly meritocratic about this, but we almost all benefit. It is not so different from what has happened throughout the world, but in the United States we interpret this improvement as a sign that virtue is rewarded, that opportunities are open.

More important than perceptions about the levels of mobility, which even experts have a hard time measuring clearly, is our culture's way of explaining who gets what, a view heavily affected by dreams, immigration, and internal movement. Not only do Americans overestimate how much mobility there is, they tend to see the patterns of mobility and immobility as fair. For much the same reason that we overestimate mobility, we attribute it to individual choice and effort, not to structural shifts. Most Americans tolerate inequality because they believe it comes from lotterylike market processes that offer everyone an equal opportunity.

We also confuse changes in the entire economic structure with changes of the positions of individuals within it. The biggest long-term structural trend through most of the last two hundred years has been the movement away from farming. We saw that this movement was even larger that the massive immigration into the United States. As agricultural jobs have almost entirely disappeared, as blue-collar manufacturing jobs have stagnated, and as white-collar jobs and the service sector have flourished, it looks as though people's occupations are improving—and they are—even though most individuals are staying in the same ranking relative to everyone else. This upgrading has occurred throughout the twentieth century. This is the famous expanding pie: you don't need to worry about distributional questions if everyone is continually making more and more money, getting better and better jobs. Everyone will be better off, even if none of their rewards are due to their own merits. In other words, enough absolute mobility for everyone can compensate for a lack of mobility relative to others.

Those who have won the lottery are especially pleased to interpret economic structure as individual merit, absolute mobility as relative mobility. In a nastier turn, even those who have done poorly tend to believe the system is fair, with the result that they harbor considerable self-blame and shame for having failed. For every structural impulse they have—blaming the Japanese, Mexicans, sometimes multinational corporations—they also think about what would have happened if they had stayed in school, not married young, not taken a dead-end job. Our culture bombards them with the message that individuals control their own destinies, facing the moral tests of drugs, alcohol, idleness, teenage sex, and pregnancy. Americans, characteristically blind to the structures affecting them, usually attribute their success or failure to their own efforts, not to demographic shifts or the economy's ever-changing occupational composition. Remarkably, many of those who feel they have failed are willing to blame themselves rather than look around for structural angles that would shift the responsibility.

Immigrants quickly embrace individual reasons for failure as well as success. Sarah Mahler's most surprising discovery about the poor Salvadorans on Long Island she studied was the degree to which they blamed themselves for not doing better in the United States. They identified their poor English, perhaps accurately, as a major reason for their lack of success. They rarely blamed discrimination, government policies, or even the state of the economy for their plight. The closest they came to a structural analysis was to blame the large flow of Latino immigrants like themselves for flooding the job market. Given the short time most had been in the United States and their isolation from American culture, it is farfetched that the Salvadorans had already picked up this self-blame from American culture. Yet it also seems unlikely they brought it with them. Something about the immigration experience seems to have created it. Mahler probed the reasons. Most immigrants pay high costs to come to America. Some are financial, some arise from psychic stress. Many feel strong obligations to send money home to their families or to pay off debts incurred in their migration. Psychologically, it would be nearly impossible for them to conclude it was all a big mistake, that America is not the land of opportunity they had believed. For one thing, no one would believe them when they returned. For another, they would have to borrow even more money to go home, where they would have even less chance to earn enough to pay it back. The result is that most are driven to work even harder, to prove to themselves as well as their families back home that they have not made a mistake. Others get desperate. As Mahler says, "When other strategies do not yield the desired results, immigrants often dream up get-rich-quick schemes, the most popular of which is the accident-related lawsuit. Almost everyone has heard a tale of an immigrant who won a large accident settlement and returned home to live like a king. Moreover, the Spanish-language media bombards its captive audience with advertisements from ambulance-chasing attorneys goading immigrants to sue for any wrong they may have suffered."[14] This is another source of distortion about the chances of getting rich in America, although one with a clear set of lawyers' interests behind it. But it is not just immigrants who dream of big lotteries when they realize that hard work is not paying off the way they had hoped.

No one would care about the American dream's exaggeration of mobility and merit, except that the perceived fairness is then thought to justify enormous inequalities. Americans allow the rich to keep a high proportion of their earnings, and we force the poor to lead lives, tortured in every way, that the rest of us would barely consider adequate to survival. Although older data are difficult to find or interpret, most scholars think that inequality increased during the industrialization of the late nineteenth century, which made vast fortunes possible. Since then it has probably been relatively constant, with minor ups and downs. Except for wars, which have a slight leveling effect, the only period in American history when inequality clearly declined was from World War II to the 1970s. In the last twenty years, there has been a pronounced increase again, which has wiped out most of the earlier postwar improvements.

American inequality has been well documented. Although there are different ways to measure it, the United States is *the most unequal country in the developed world.* A smaller proportion of our annual income goes to the bottom 10 or 20 percent of families and a higher portion to the top 1 percent, 5 percent, and 10 percent. The ratio of the income of the top fifth to that of the lowest fifth is around 9 to 1—comparable to the inequality found in poor nations like Zambia and Bolivia. Japan appears to be the most equal of the developed countries, with a ratio of just over 4, but diverse other industrial nations (Spain, Belgium, Sweden) have figures under 5. Among the industrial countries, only the United Kingdom and Switzerland are as unequal as the United States on this scale.[15] In certain states, and especially in cities, the ratio of the top to the bottom fifth reaches 20 (New York state) or 30 (Washington, D.C.).

Wealth is even less equally distributed than income. Today, the richest 10 percent of American families own about 70 percent of the country's total wealth. The top one-half of 1 percent—one family in two hundred—owns an astounding 30 percent. For certain assets, the inequality is even higher, with the top 10 percent of families owning 90 percent of stocks, bonds, and businesses. By most measures, the bottom half of American families have negative net worth: their debts are larger than their assets. For the families that do accumulate wealth, the process usually takes several generations, meaning it is rarely due to the actions of a single individual.

Under the umbrella of general inequality, the United States further specializes in the two extremes, with more super fortunes and more grinding poverty than other countries. Most striking at the top are the salaries of American corporate executives. The average pay for CEOs at the country's largest companies is more than $10 million a year—more than real lottery winners pocket in most states. (For comparison, the President of the United States makes $200,000 a year.) A standard statistic is the ratio of the average CEO's compensation to that of the average worker. In Japan the ratio is 16 to 1, in Germany 21 to 1, in the United Kingdom, 33 to 1. But in the United States it is a whopping 120 to 1 (and rising fast). Even within this select group of executives, the extremes are surprising. For instance, Walt Disney paid Michael Eisner $203 million in 1993 (a figure equal to 68 percent of Disney's profit that year!). Perhaps corporate executives do not seem overcompensated when we compare their earnings to the $550 million that bond trader Michael Milken made in 1987, a figure that came to light only because of Milken's subsequent criminal trial. Ironically, two of the biggest critics of Milken's salary were billionaires Donald Trump and David Rockefeller. Nor do Americans get upset by the golden parachutes given to executives for not working. Again Disney tops the charts, with the $90 million paid to Michael Ovitz when he left the company after working there only fourteen months. Our faith in markets is shaken only slightly by the compensation given executives who are clearly failing, such as CEO-celebrity William Agee, whose salary went from under $0.5 million to $2.4 million in the five years during which he nearly bankrupted Morrison Knudsen (apparently running the Idaho company from his mansion in Pebble Beach, California).

Even lavish spending can be justified, in many people's eyes, as the just desert of hard work. Not long ago a thirty-two-year-old banker was interviewed for the *New York Times*. He and his brother had just built a ten-million-dollar house in the Hamptons, complete with indoor and outdoor hot tubs, underwater sound system in the pool, and six suits of armor (the house was designed to mimic a medieval castle). He justified the expenditure as part of the American dream: "Especially considering that I'm the son of an immigrant who made $28.50 a week in his first job in this country." Although not all Americans would accept it, this man turned to the best argument for justifying such conspicuous consumption to Americans. He and his father had won the figurative lottery. (Less than a year later, the house was up for sale.)[16]

At the bottom of the ladder, the United States also has higher rates of poverty than other prosperous countries, even though it is the wealthiest of them (and hence has the means to do something if it wished). Depending on where the poverty line is drawn, between 10 and 20 percent of Americans fall below it. And none of the lines are very generous. Even full-time jobs are no guarantee of avoiding poverty. One in five Americans who work full time do not make enough money ($16,000) to keep a family of four above the poverty line. The difference between the United States and other advanced industrial countries is simple: *they have programs that compensate for market failures, and we do not*. In the absence of government programs, many other countries would have poverty rates like ours, but after government intervention none do. Other countries, less wealthy than the United States, simply try harder to keep their citizens out of poverty. It's a matter of will.

If the rich embody our dreams of winning the lottery, the poor represent our nightmares of failure. Well into the nineteenth century, Americans prided themselves on not having the kind of grinding poverty apparent in European cities. They conveniently overlooked black slaves, whom they apparently did not consider full Americans, as when William Penn praised America as "a good poor Man's country" or Jefferson spoke of its "lovely equality." When they developed their own large cities, with noticeable pockets of poverty, Americans had to explain what they considered an anomaly. Since then, in order to keep our dreams intact, we have castigated the poor, explaining their poverty as the result of vice and willful rejection of American opportunities. At the bottom, the lottery metaphor fails. Were we to think that "there but for the grace of God go I," we would have to admit that the system is not fair—and perhaps the winners would not deserve their winnings. We identify upward, but not downward. The rich are like us, but luckier. The poor are different, lacking ambition, unwilling to take advantage of the opportunities offered them. Invidious comparisons with successful immigrants, who did take advantage of the opportunities, allow us to condemn other poor Americans (including the immigrants who are still poor) even more strongly. Throughout American history, the poor have been condemned as lazy, addicted, bestial, and atheistic. In the eyes of most Americans, the only ingenuity the poor demonstrate is in cheating on welfare. The poor must get what they deserve, just as surely as the rich deserve what they get.

Such inequality has effects. Life expectancies differ enormously. In inner cities, in parts of the rural south, and on Indian reservations, poor men can expect to live to about sixty; elsewhere, they may live into their seventies. The author of the latest study said that the differences are comparable to those between wealthy Japan and impoverished Sierra Leone. Because the study used mortality rates by county, it could not link these differences directly to family incomes, but this clearly makes the difference.[17] Rich Americans get the world's best medical care; poor Americans do not.

Sadly, the greatest effect of inequality is on the opportunities available to the next generation, making the lottery extremely unfair. If you are born rich, it is hard for you to avoid wealth yourself. If you are born poor, you may be able to climb into respectability, but you are very unlikely to become rich. The greater the inequality in a society, the greater the differences in opportunities. One scholar even went back and examined data for the Jacksonian period, thought to be a time of social upheaval and mobility. His conclusion? "The pursuit of wealth in Jacksonian America was marked not by fluidity but by stability if not rigidity. Great fortunes earlier accumulated held their own through all manner of vicissitudes. The tax records indicate that the panic of 1837 appeared to have no effect on the minuscule rate by which the mighty fell or the puny rose during the years surrounding that economic convulsion."[18] Although Americans have moved up over time, they have moved up all together rather than as individuals or families.

In a lottery, you don't try to equalize the payoff among the contestants. You know the rules of the game in advance and accept them. Only a few win. Those who do not win can play again. Of course, life is not really a lottery, and few have the option of not "competing" in the economy. The losers face stiff penalties. American culture tolerates enormous rewards at the top and terrible suffering at the bottom. Americans recognize that not everyone is equally likely to win, but their biggest error lies in attributing people's chances to their own efforts. The reason? Our faith in markets.

Whether you think inequality is fair or unfair depends on your opinion of economic markets. Americans believe in the justice of market outcomes because they see markets as the simple aggregation of large numbers of individuals making informed, autonomous decisions, unconstrained by government policies or structural forces. As a result, they are responsible for what happens to them. Markets feel "natural" to Americans, since they were one of the first institutions we established. Many colonial Americans produced for markets who didn't belong to a church or have any contact with government. Markets are the social institution most compatible with restlessness, the one most opposed to place loyalty. Americans easily envision the whole world as one big market.

Colonial immigrants, we saw, established freer markets (especially but not only in land) than existed anywhere else on earth, and later immigrants have come here because of those freedoms. From the start, markets were well suited to people fleeing governments and societies they despised, who hoped to establish themselves here as individuals, and who had extensive natural resources with which to maneuver. It was hard to impose rules and traditions on people always ready to pick up and leave, heading for new land to the south or west. Government was poorly equipped to enforce contracts, which were treated as an act of individual will and choice earlier than in Britain. In the Old World, contracts were seen well into the eighteenth century as written expressions of traditional obligations and expectations. Although it would not triumph fully until the nineteenth century, the "modern" form of market contract developed in eighteenth-century America as an agreement between two individuals who were free to choose any arrangements they wished. Even military service was seen in the colonies as a form of contract, as British officers learned to their annoyance during the Seven Years' War of the 1750s, when colonial militia refused to obey orders they felt were not part of their agreements to serve.

The Revolution further encouraged markets, upending the personal, often paternalistic relationships which, although still individualistic, had moderated purely commercial motives in the colonial period. Although still largely rural, Americans entered into commercial contracts with even greater enthusiasm once royal patronage had been eliminated as an alternative source of wealth. Farm families eagerly produced goods for the market, often making more money that way than through agriculture. Said one visitor, "The American is always bargaining; he always has one bargain afoot, another just finished, and two or three he's thinking of. All that he has, all that he sees, is merchandise in his eyes."[19] As we have seen, Americans valued land, but were happy to mortgage or sell it if they saw greater opportunities in trade or industry. In America land and markets were fully compatible, whereas in Britain, and especially in the rest of Europe, land was still an aristocratic *alternative* to grubby market activity.

Even those Americans who desired to settle into self-sufficient family farming without additional market production were prevented from doing so. Large families constantly forced farmers to acquire new land on the open market. Eventually, this meant migration. Either their children migrated on their own, or the entire family moved to larger farms in the West. Most farmers were tempted by some crop—tobacco, later wheat—that could bring high prices on the market and by fancy, store-bought merchandise that required cash. Only the most isolated could avoid the market, and never for long.

If land was bought and sold on markets starting from the earliest colonies, so was labor. In the South a lively market soon developed for white bondservants, another for Africans. In New York, New Jersey, and Pennsylvania farmers took advantage of German and Irish labor in the eighteenth century. In Philadelphia, says one historian, "The ample supply of [immigrant] workers pushed down wage rates, thereby encouraging employers to replace bound men and women with free wage laborers."[20] Artisans could hire and fire these workers at will, something they could not have done (or not so easily) to family members. New Englanders came slightly later to markets in labor, preferring until after the Revolution to produce for the market with family labor. Cheap and plentiful immigrant labor was a constant threat to family cohesion.

The early nineteenth century saw the complete triumph of markets in America. The main function of government was to extend and preserve markets. At federal, state, and even local levels, as lawyers tightened their control over government, they initiated projects to move goods and help entrepreneurs. Corporations were chartered and protected; roads and canals were built; all impediments to free markets were attacked. Material progress, it was argued, benefited all Americans, and markets were the engines of that progress. Activist judges interpreted free markets to imply that they should remove protections for those who acted unwisely in markets, especially the poor, and federal courts overturned a number of state laws protecting bankrupt individuals. The restless were given free rein, and the reluctant were forced to follow along.

Only later in the century did modern economic theory develop as a way of legitimating and explaining these markets. Although primarily a British invention, modern economics fits well with American individualism because it portrays markets as large numbers of individuals haggling with each other over prices. The result of all these small deals is a common price for a commodity or service, as the pressure of Adam Smith's famous "invisible hand" brings everyone into line through competition. This hand works best when no players are large enough to affect prices; under perfect competition, everyone must accept the market's clearing price. If you try to charge more, no one will buy from you. If you charge less, you will go out of business or force other sellers to match your prices. Using the politically loaded term *free markets* for perfect competition, economists often overlook the effects of institutional players, notably state policies, on markets, or they criticize such intrusions as creating distortions and inefficiencies. In a country that idolizes freedom, "free" markets must be good—and economists and Americans define free markets as lacking government intervention.

Rewards, in this system, go to those who can command them. Those who have invented a new product or technology "reap" the profits (a wholesome agricultural metaphor), at least until competitors catch up. They are filling a genuine social need. If they were not, no one would buy what they had to sell. Beyond that, people make money by selling their skills for the going price, and by working as many hours as they want. The system is ruthlessly fair, rewarding those (and only those) who have something that others want to buy, whether land, skill, or ingenuity. The market, supposedly, does not care about race, gender, or family background. It is as blind as a lottery.

This simplified market vision is close to Americans' utopian view of what society should be like: no constraints imposed by government, no markets dominated by large corporations, no professional groups inflating their members' salaries. Immigration to the United States, like migration within it, has been motivated by efforts to flee just these kinds of institutional constraints, and the apparent ease of movement seems to suggest that structures are not so important. From the immigrant responding to an advertisement placed by a large American company to his descendant cruising down the interstate highway, we are good at ignoring the very structures that aid our movement.

Perfectly competitive free markets have never existed, nor could they. Currencies depend on governments, as do roads and trains, enforcement of contracts, stock markets. Almost all economic behavior is shaped by laws and other regulations. The colonists created governments for themselves precisely to protect markets from taxes and other intrusions of the British crown, and Americans have used their government ever since to manipulate markets—partly, and ironically, to maintain an illusion of free markets.

The main distortions in American markets, however, come from corporations rather than government. Since the late nineteenth century a large number of basic industries have been dominated by one, two, or a handful of enormous companies, large bureaucracies that shape markets as much as they react to them, that influence government policies toward their own industries and create consumer needs as much as responding to them. An appropriate level of suspicion of these behemoths has surfaced from time to time in our history, notably in populism and progressivism at the turn of the century. Yet we tend to misread these organizations, insisting despite all evidence that they are the work of creative individuals. From Andrew Carnegie and Henry Ford to Lee Iacocca and Michael Eisner, we see individuals at the top, running the largest corporation the way Mom and Pop run their corner grocery store. There is no solid evidence that CEOs matter to the profitability of their companies, but we insist on seeing the largest companies as the personal projects of their leaders. We have a cult of "leadership," through which we credit all sorts of charisma to powerful CEOs, sure that this filters down to the shop floor. Why else would Americans stand for annual compensation of two hundred million dollars for the CEO of a "publicly" owned corporation?

Individualism and markets are connected. In the market vision, it is easy to lose sight of the connections between people, the emotional loyalties, but also the deployment of power, and the political and economic structures that shape our lives. In preindustrial societies, these ties, this place in the social structure, define one's identity. With the emphasis on money that accompanies markets, this is no longer the case. Increasingly, people define themselves in terms of how much money they make and how much they spend. Both production and consumption get reduced to money values. This obviously involves a great deal of freedom, more choice about how to live one's life, more options, more mobility. But it also brings with it a kind of impoverishment of the activities that make up one's life. The activities have less value in and of themselves;

they are valuable only for the amount of money they involve.

Money is easy to take with you when you move. The more we focus on money, and define ourselves in terms of it, the less attention we give to our political, social, and personal connections with other people. Critics of American culture have argued that these nonmonetary, interpersonal connections have atrophied, that money erodes all other bonds, destroys them, leaving us with only the "cash nexus" as a way of relating to each other. Restlessness does often sever these connections, but for the most part, the ties of families, friendships, and other social networks are still there. Americans, men especially, just don't recognize their importance: consider Fred Douglass's wife, who financed his escape, Jim's constant support for Huck, or the keys Houdini's wife slipped him. Restless men do not like to admit any dependence on others. Picturing society as composed of disconnected individuals makes it easier to judge the value of people, of activities, and of themselves in terms of money. They always know how they are doing, even if they are never doing well enough.

The American vision of the market, with individuals making choices and controlling their own fates, lends itself to something psychologists have called the "just world hypothesis": the basic assumption that individuals get what they deserve. It is an appealing view, for it suggests that you have control over what happens to you, rather than being buffeted by chance and accident. Fatalism was appropriate for peasants, perhaps, or fishermen and others who derive their livelihoods from nature; storms and mudslides, for example, are beyond our control. But in industrial societies, where we have a choice of jobs and careers, we need to feel that our choices matter. Many people in industrial societies believe in a just world, but nowhere as strongly as in the United States.

Even among Americans, however, not everyone is equally likely to believe that the world is just. Those most likely to believe in a just world include those who have orthodox Christian views, in which God actively intervenes in human life; those who are politically conservative, especially if they believe the poor deserve their fate; and those who have attained some upward mobility or who believe that they will. Just-worlders are also more likely to favor capital punishment (perhaps the ultimate in getting one's desert, at least in this world), to believe that social inequalities are small, and to see those which do exist as fair or inevitable. Although it is hard to say which of these beliefs cause the others, they form a familiar cluster, a typically American cluster.

Members of groups who have faced active discrimination, such as women or racial minorities, are less likely to believe that the world is just, understandably enough, since they have seen injustice firsthand.

They are more likely to see structural forces invisible to other Americans. Not everyone has the same beliefs, but almost all Americans (especially men) share some of this market vision.

━━

The confidence man is an interesting image in American culture, one of the few criminals we typically like, at least in the movies. We admire him (and less frequently her) for his individual initiative in getting ahead. Like the private eye, the con man is often portrayed as working against the kind of sinister powers that we especially fear and dislike (when we believe in them, as we must in the paranoid world of novels and movies). Many, like the amiable con artists in the movie *The Sting*, take money from more hardened—and violent—criminals. Others prove to have a kind heart, as in *Traveller* or *Paper Moon*. But mostly they are models of personal initiative, like O. Henry's character Jeff Peters, who took a dollar in another man's pocket as a personal offense. Con men know how to take care of themselves and sometimes even the women and children around them. Even some forms of criminal behavior are vaguely acceptable in the pursuit of worldly success.

The outward trappings of material success are especially important in a culture on the move, where we encounter strangers and look for quick signs of what kind of people they are. If we stayed longer and knew them better we might judge them by their moral habits or special skills. But we do not stay put long enough for that. Sociologist Michèle Lamont, who has extensively compared French and American culture, found Americans to care much more about material success, which she related to their geographic mobility: "Income is more likely to act as a central determinant of status in mobile and anonymous societies because consumption of durable consumer goods permits immediate signaling of one's status."[21] In some versions Americans are worth what they make; in others they are worth what they spend. Either way, the metric is money. (Although Americans' obsession with personal appearance may also reflect the need to impress strangers quickly.)

Not stopping to rest is the literal meaning of "restless." Because they care so much about material success, Americans work more hours per year than the citizens of any other advanced industrial country, with relatively few choosing part-time work. Their productivity per *worker* is higher than that of any other country, but not per *hour:* Americans are more productive in part because they work more. The United States is one of the few countries without any national legislation providing vacations to its citizens. (Throughout most of Europe, in contrast, na-

tional legislation guarantees at least a month of paid vacation to everyone, and union contracts often add a week or two more—in several
countries two months off is now standard). Most European governments restrict the hours and days that shops can be open, a limit on aggressive work that could hardly be imagined in America (in France you
can be fined for working more than 39 hours in a week). Long hours of
hard work characterize boomtowns, where money must be made fast.
Immigrants bring this hardworking drive with them to the United
States, and they force other Americans to adopt it if they are to keep up.
Especially in manual jobs, it only takes a few rate-busters to change the
standards for everyone. Americans' anxiety over how well they are doing, since they believe their success reflects their inner worth, is a further prod. In their fight to get ahead, they may simply not have the time
to build ties with other people. This is especially true for men, who are
still often expected to be the primary breadwinners and still define
themselves through their work more than women do.

It is hard not to admire the economy Americans have created. Even
Henry David Thoreau, who had little use for its products, prized its creativity and energy. For most of our history, our wealth came from the
enthusiastic exploitation of our natural wealth. In the twentieth century, it came more from ingenuity in recognizing needs and in developing and marketing new products. In both phases, the enthusiastic
energy and flexibility of immigrants contributed enormously. Their
vision of their surroundings as an opportunity for enrichment was
self-fulfilling. They valued material success and worked hard to attain
it—and in the process set up competitive structures that forced most
everyone else to work hard too or suffer enormously. Markets were as
much a stick as a carrot.

But how do Americans explain their powerful economy? The same
dynamic we saw in popular images of immigrants' success is replicated
in how we understand society as a whole. A whole series of structural
factors, from government subsidies to an expanding economy, fade
from sight, leaving us with individual actions and their consequences.
We believe in the justice of markets because we think markets result
from individual choices, not from power. For most Americans, moving
around and starting over encourage us to believe in better starts. Becoming rich is the ultimate dream, but doing better will at least do. Our
economic restlessness leads us to tolerate actions we would normally be
repulsed by, from con games to executive overcompensation. Houdini
could be a hero to millions, despite his unpleasant personality, because
he was successful and (pretty much the same thing) rich.

The Spanish-born Harvard philosopher George Santayana once said that the American is an "idealist working on matter," someone for whom moral goodness and material wealth were connected. To Americans who believe in a just world, wealth is still a sign of moral virtue. If you are rich, you (or at least your ancestors) must have done something important and good for society. Like the immigrants who cannot admit that the United States is not the land of gold they had expected, we cannot recognize unexpected barriers to advancement. Instead, we blame ourselves and congratulate the rich. Because we only see individuals, and thus misread the nature of social mobility, we see merit everywhere. Those who succeed apparently have it; those who stagnate (a form of failure in American eyes) must not. Life is a lottery that only the virtuous can play.

Even as boomtowns faded in importance in American history, market values remained strong, and they still shape the way most Americans view the world. There have always been some dissenters, to be sure, from those who have looked nostalgically backwards to Southern plantations to those who have looked forward to socialist utopias. Those Americans who were ambivalent about markets are the subject of my sequel, and all I'll say now is that their voices have had little effect.

Markets are a natural part of Americans' image of the world, since our institutions and culture were worked out during the same period that markets were being established in Europe and the regions it controlled. Markets were created in the United States before government was, and they took deeper root. Our Revolution was a rejection of governmental intrusion, at a time when government consisted of an offensive royal family thousands of miles away. Central government, we'll see in the next chapter, has struck us as alien ever since. The flip side of seeing life as a market or lottery composed of individuals is that we fail to see the structural forces that establish that lottery. Just as governments set up and regulate lotteries today, they are responsible for much of the economic life of markets. But when you ask Americans to see the world as consisting of something in addition to individuals, we are blind. We see a number of institutional and structural entities—government, demography, community, tradition—only as bad, if we recognize their existence at all. They can only constrain our movement, not aid it. The biggest casualty of restlessness is our sense of moral and political obligation to a community, any community, and to the formal institutions that could represent it. If markets are our utopia, government is our dystopia.

Many nineteenth-century landscapes show enthusiasm for the clearing of the wilderness and the trains that were connecting the United States. The lithograph by Currier and Ives (top), based on a painting by Frances Flora Palmer, *Across the Continent: "Westward the Course of Empire Takes Its Way,"* shows no qualms. And in *The Lackawanna Valley*, George Inness had good reason to make the locomotive and its roundhouse such gorgeous objects of contemplation for the reclining figure in the foreground: the painting had been commissioned by the Delaware, Lackawanna, and Western Railroad. Like other Americans, artists traveled thousands of miles to paint the new land, led by immigrants John James Audubon and Thomas Cole. *Across the Continent* reproduced by permission of the Gilcrease Museum, Tulsa, Oklahoma; *The Lackawanna Valley* reproduced by permission of the National Gallery of Art, Washington, D.C. © Board of Trustees, National Gallery of Art.

Frances Gumm on the Yellow Brick Road. Courtesy of the Museum of Modern Art, New York.

Marion Michael Morrison and Claire Wemlinger in *Stagecoach*. Courtesy of the Museum of Modern Art, New York.

David Daniel Kaminsky. Courtesy of AP/Wide World Photos.

Detroit Red. Courtesy of
AP/Wide World Photos.

Robert Allen Zimmerman.
Courtesy of AP/Wide World
Photos.

America is a nation of name changing, perhaps the easiest way to craft a new identity. Immigrants and entertainers are most likely to seek new names, but many other Americans have done the same. If you wish to become a new person, it is good to have a new label. It worked well for Judy Garland, John "Duke" Wayne, Claire Trevor, Danny Kaye, Malcolm X, and Bob Dylan.

Not all Americans start over as individuals. Sometimes entire utopian groups move to new places to transform themselves together, often with strict discipline and surveillance. Utopian communities were one of the easiest places for women to start over, which may be the reason that the Oneida women look happier than the men or children in this photo (at least it was not one of the celibate communities). Of the tens of thousands of such efforts, not many lasted more than a few years. The same centrifugal forces that led people to leave their routines to start over together led them out of the group to start over again as individuals and families. Reproduced by permission of the Oneida Community Mansion House.

Sam Clemens never tired of new identities. In this 1894 photo, taken when he was 59, he has raised his chin in a dignified fashion to match the persona "S. L. Clemens," the form of his name he often used in later years. Fascinated by photography, Clemens carefully staged each image of himself for the public. One would never know from this photo that he was in the midst of bankruptcy proceedings. Despite occasional setbacks, he had come a long way from W. Epaminondas Adrastus Blab, one of his earliest pseudonyms. Reproduced by permission of the Mark Twain House, Hartford, Connecticut.

On the right is Erich Weiss, better known as Harry Houdini but here described as one of the "Rahners" (his wife Bess's maiden name), in 1894. Perhaps the first publicity photo of the pair, it was also one of the last in which Bess had equal billing with Harry. She gradually faded in prominence in stories and publicity about him, even though she remained his partner and was a crucial part of his act, especially if (as many suspect) she slipped him keys during difficult escapes. Although Houdini already seems to show self-confidence, if not arrogance, the "comedy act" description shows that he had not yet settled on his escape routines; they were still following the normal route of entertainers of the time, mixing acting, acrobatics, comedy, and anything else that would pay.

As part of their fascination with markets and success, Americans love the initiative of con artists, who inevitably have hearts of gold and prey on violent, hardened criminals (such as the character played by Robert Shaw, hovering over Paul Newman and Robert Redford in this scene from *The Sting*). They are capable, too, of taking care of those they love. Here we see Ryan and Tatum O'Neal in *Paper Moon*. Although she claims to have his jaw, he never admits to being her father. But he takes her with him, in part because she is much better at con games than he is. She rejects settled life with an aunt just as Huck Finn fled Aunt Polly. Photos courtesy of the Museum of Modern Art, New York.

The citizens of Hadleyville in *High Noon* represent organized social life as portrayed in Westerns: moralistic, weak, corrupt. They are too cowardly to help Will Kane (Gary Cooper) in his showdown with the villain Frank Miller (a convicted murderer whom corrupt "politicians" from "up north" have pardoned). Even though his new (Quaker) bride (Grace Kelly) is opposed to violence, she comes around in time to help him kill Miller and his gang. At the end, the hero and his love must leave the town and live by themselves ("all alone on the prairie") to maintain their purity. This heroine is lucky: the typical gunslinger sets off with only his horse. Photos courtesy of the Museum of Modern Art, New York.

THE "BRAINS"

The most famous American political cartoonist of all time was probably Thomas Nast, born in the German Palatinate in 1840. He published more than three thousand drawings, most of them appearing in *Harper's Weekly*, as this one did, between 1862 and 1885. Although his anti-Catholic images are now thankfully forgotten, his Republican elephant, Democratic donkey, and rotund, bearded Santa still flourish. As Reconstruction floundered, Nast's early immigrant optimism gave way to cynicism about government. In this simple 1871 drawing of boss Tweed, head of the Tammany machine, the politician is an arrogant fatcat, portrayed in the style others would use to describe capitalists. Big government was as scary and corrupt to him as big business. Courtesy of the Mariners' Museum, Newport News, Virginia.

Early in American history, these young men would have gone to the frontier and knifed each other in fights. After the 1960s, they turned their aggression toward African Americans, gays, and feminists, and voted for antigovernment candidates like George Wallace and Ronald Reagan. Courtesy of Corbis/Owen Franken.

Critics of the American dream have usually attacked materialism and greed on the grounds of an even deeper individualism, a line that stretches from Ralph Waldo Emerson to the hard-boiled detective. In the latter, Emerson's optimism has given way to cynicism, for private eyes have seen too much "civilization." Philip Marlowe is Huck Finn with a hard shell. In this still for *The Maltese Falcon*, Sam Spade (Humphrey Bogart) eyes the bird that everyone has been killing for. All too often, "the stuff that dreams are made of" turns out to be lead, not gold. Courtesy of the Museum of Modern Art, New York.

Like the Emersonian tradition in the arts, American religion has frequently criticized materialism while fostering other forms of restlessness. Early in the nineteenth century, circuit riders (like this fictitious one from the cover of *Harper's Weekly*) covered tens of thousands of miles each year to convert frontier souls. Carrying little more than a Bible and a bottle of rum, and certainly not a change of clothes or soap, no wonder they looked wild. Manners and education would have alienated them from their audiences; they were more credible when a bit rough. These preachers, mostly Methodists and Baptists but only loosely affiliated with church hierarchies, set the United States on the road to becoming the most Christian of modern nations. Courtesy of the Mariners' Museum, Newport News, Virginia.

THE CIRCUIT PREACHER.—DRAWN BY A. R. WAUD.—[SEE NEXT PAGE.]

6 An Alien Power

> So far as a man has the power to think or not to think, to move or
> not to move, according to the preference or direction of his own
> mind, so far is a man free.
> —*John Locke*

> Nothing is more striking to an European traveller in the United
> States than the absence of what we term Government, or the Ad-
> ministration.
> —*Alexis de Toqueville*

Around the corner from my New York apartment is a Dominican who
rolls cigars by hand. I like to watch him work with his enormous, soft
leaves of tobacco, and he makes pretty good cigars. There are only a
handful of shops like this left in the city. At one time, in the late nineteenth century, New York boasted tens of thousands of cigarmakers,
almost all of them immigrants. Until 1868 they were highly skilled
craftsmen, but in that year the invention of the cigar mold made it possible for just about anyone to make cigars. The new products were not
as good, but they were cheaper. Entire families, especially from Bohemia,
began making cigars in their tenement apartments. In a small replica-
tion of American economic history, new immigrants were willing to
work for less money than established immigrants or the native-born,
and their competition drove down everyone's wages. Many immigrants
were sympathetic to unions but simultaneously undercut them by tol-
erating poor conditions, long hours, and low pay.

One of the old-style cigarmakers, Samuel Gompers, was born in the
Spitalfields neighborhood of London's East End in 1850, the son of
Dutch-Jewish immigrants. Although he left school at age ten to help his
father make cigars, he continued to hear lectures, attend night school,
and pursue every means he could find for self-improvement. Driven by

poverty, Gompers's parents brought him and his four brothers to New York in 1863. The English cigarmakers' union paid part of their passage, realizing that emigration was good for those who stayed behind as well as those who left. The voyage took seven weeks, not much better than two hundred years earlier. The family had to cook their own food, which consisted mostly of salt beef, dried vegetables, and pickled red cabbage. They were mid-ocean on July fourth, but all assembled on deck for a celebration, at the end of which "all saluted the Stars and Stripes—the beautiful emblem of America that was then in a mighty contest for human freedom."[1] Rather than condemning the United States for having allowed slavery to persist for so long, this immigrant saw the Civil War as a triumph for freedom. The family settled on Houston Street in New York's Lower East Side, with the stench of a slaughterhouse across the street and that of a brewery out back.

In New York Gompers kept helping his father at his trade in their tiny apartment. He also continued to educate himself through an odd assortment of lectures, classes, debating clubs, and union meetings. He was married before he turned seventeen and lived briefly in Hackensack, then Lambertsville, New Jersey. By his early twenties he had joined or founded a dizzying array of clubs, including the Odd Fellows and the Ancient Order of Foresters. From 1873 to 1878 he worked at the city's only union cigar shop, owned by a German immigrant sympathetic to socialism.

In good American style Gompers wrote an autobiography near the end of his life, where he described the dreams he formed in childhood. Some he attributed to his grandfather. Gompers recounted that his grandfather traveled frequently, often for months at a time, and that he had left his trade, calico printing, to become an antique dealer because he could not stand to "work for a boss." Gompers himself reported that "my nature has been in conflict with the restriction of sects, against conformity to ritual or the idea of authority vested in superiors."[2] Gompers's autobiography was also in the tradition of exaggerating early hardships, as he doubled the length of his late-night walks from the Battery up to East Houston Street into five-mile excursions. Writing when he was the patriarch of the American Federation of Labor, he expressed modest goals he thought were due all working men: "All my life I had wanted a home surrounded by grass and trees, where I could hear the birds night and morning."[3] Gompers had come to the right country, even though by American standards his dreams were modest.

Gompers did not expect much help from the city, state, or federal government in his struggle for labor. He saw this government in action in 1874, when New York police attacked a peaceful demonstration of the unemployed in Tompkins Square. The largest working-class gathering in the city to that time, the crowd expected to hear a speech by the mayor, who not only changed his mind at the last minute but decided to prohibit the meeting altogether. The police viciously descended on the crowd, injuring hundreds of men, women, and children with their billy clubs. For hours they chased down and beat small groups on the Lower East Side. Gompers, who barely escaped harm by hiding in a cellar, decided that radicalism was too dangerous for the embryonic labor movement. For months afterward, the police assiduously broke up even private meetings of workers.

With the cigar mold, production shifted rapidly from centralized shops to families working out of their tenements, who were making half of all cigars by 1875. Relatively unskilled children could now contribute to their production. The cigarmakers' union fell from 1,700 members in 1873 to a mere handful in 1875, split among German, Bohemian, and English-speaking sections. Along with another immigrant, Hungarian Adolph Strasser, Gompers set about trying to reorganize and strengthen the union, beginning with their own local 144, organized in 1875. They soon had a test, a strike in 1877 inspired by a railroad strike that crippled the country's rail system, which Gompers referred to as "a declaration of protest in the name of American manhood against conditions that nullified the rights of American citizens . . . the tocsin that sounded a ringing message of hope to us all."[4] The cigarworkers' strike lasted 107 days, and did little for their manhood. They lost badly, gaining no concessions. But Gompers insisted that the solidarity and sense of power forged in that strike were crucial to building the union.

In 1879 Gompers, Strasser, and others reorganized the union along "business principles," emphasizing health and death benefits, high dues to build up a reserve fund, central control of assets, and the equalization of finances across locals. They also established a fund to help journeymen travel in search of work. The union abandoned secret handshakes and rituals, but also the socialist goal of self-employment in cooperatives. They wanted to focus on "practical methods" and "immediate demands." Many of the new ideas were Gompers's interpretation of English union practices. Even more, these two immigrants were proposing labor practices appropriate to American culture.

Unions would operate on principles that would allow them to maneuver as though they were businesses in markets, giving up hope of an ultimate escape from markets. By organizing skilled workers only, unions could take advantage of whatever market power those workers had, regardless of the effect on the broader solidarity of labor. The focus on immediate gains had characterized mainstream American labor for decades, despite frequent efforts to build more communally minded unions. Immigrants did not want or expect to remain in the working class, and so were most concerned with getting the wages that would help them move up and out. Moreover, with so much geographic mobility and so many new immigrant arrivals, it was hard to build the emotional loyalties that labor solidarity required. Like everyone else, American workers believed in markets.

The unions soon gave up not only radicalism but, most fatefully, any efforts to use the political system to attain their goals. The cigarmakers had tried working through governmental channels. Although federal protective legislation failed, the New York State legislature passed restrictions on tenement manufacturing in 1873, just as Gompers was becoming seriously involved in union activism. But the regulations were almost immediately overturned by the federal courts. A more tightly worded act the following year met the same fate. Across the country, conservative courts struck down pro-labor legislation on the grounds that it interfered with markets. If government was not going to help organized labor, unions might as well battle employers directly rather than working through the political system. The United States was to be the *only industrial country without a progressive political party* devoted to the poor and working classes.

The new model of "business unionism" caught on. The cigarmakers, well represented at a national meeting of trade unionists in 1881, persuaded the group to adopt the spirit of their principles: attention to immediate bread-and-butter issues of "less hours and better pay." As Strasser put it, "The working class pays attention to those things which may be achieved immediately: provision of jobs, high wages, short working-time, support in case of unemployment and illness."[5] These were also things that helped individual workers, not the working class as a whole in its legal or political status. The convention rejected proposals from the Knights of Labor for government ownership of transportation and communication systems. In 1886, the group changed its name to the American Federation of Labor (AFL), becoming the organization that would most influence the tactics and demands of the American working class.

If Gompers was wary of communal group solidarity, the press was much more so. There was already considerable red-baiting in the newspapers, with most efforts at unionization being dismissed as communistic and un-American. Even the nasty depression of the mid-1870s was not seen as the result of structural forces outside of workers' control but attributed to individual vice. In the eyes of most Americans, the unemployed needed moral guidance, not handouts. In several decades of struggle, organized segments of the working class came more and more to accept this individualistic interpretation of the market. They decided to concentrate on increasing their gains within the system. Unlike its European counterpart, the American working class did not develop a sweeping program to use government to constrain or restructure markets, or to own and operate enterprises itself. Led by restless immigrants, the bottom of American society as well as the top has accepted the market vision as well as its obverse, a deep fear of government.

Two big, complementary ideas emerged during the Renaissance that helped define the modern world: the individual and the state. The *autonomous individual*, free to act and make choices, unconstrained by tradition or inherited status, struck the imagination of those who had previously lacked such freedom. People were no longer so thoroughly defined by their membership in a corporate body, such as a guild, or by feudal obligations to their lord. Many escaped from the countryside to towns and cities, where new personal freedoms were being invented. The modern individual was increasingly free to define himself (and later herself). Many kinds of individuals would proliferate in the centuries to follow, including the world explorer, the market competitor, the truth-seeking scientist, and the passionate Romantic artist, but all would be driven by a remarkable faith in the spirit of the individual. This striking individualism had roots in Christianity, especially as reinterpreted during the Reformation. It was also intimately involved in the rise of modern science, based on new philosophies that saw the individual as the starting point for knowledge as well as politics. (John Locke, an influential example, believed that true knowledge came from individuals' direct sensory contact with the world around them, unmediated by authorities or institutions.) Intellectuals were increasingly expected to question authority, thinking for themselves. Most of all, perhaps, individuals were expected to pursue their own interests through economic markets.

At the same time there appeared the image and reality of the sovereign *nation-state*, along with its prince, able to make choices and maneuver among other such states. Nations were no longer defined as part of the Holy Roman Empire or subordinated in any way to religious leaders. Parallel to its external autonomy, the national state increased its control over and penetration of its own territory. Police were eventually deployed to make the countryside safer, for instance, suppressing banditry, family vendettas, and marauding knights. The modern individual and the modern state were well suited to each other, as the citizen's loyalties were now directly to the nation rather than to a hierarchy of intermediaries. Likewise the state, as it became more centralized and bureaucratic, began to count individuals and mobilize them for various purposes, especially warfare. Eventually the state would assume considerable responsibility for the health, education, and welfare of those who inhabited its territory. Increasingly the sovereign's legitimacy would come, not from his relationship to God, but from his relationship to his subjects. Metaphorically, too, the sovereign had the same autonomy in relation to other sovereigns that the new individual had in relation to other individuals.

Individuals and governments had of course existed before the Renaissance, but around the sixteenth century they were transformed into something like the images we have of them today. Each gained new powers and status, a new sense of agency. Although we perceive an inherent tension between the rights of the individual and the power of the state, they developed together and required each other to be fully defined. Individual rights are granted and protected by the state; at the same time they are primarily rights *to be free from* state interference and oppression. The more self-interested the state, the more individual freedoms suffer. But in the absence of the modern state, individuals suffered other depredations. As the state's powers for surveillance and control increased, so—at least in the West—did citizens' legal (although not always enforced) rights.

The American colonies were settled as these new concepts of the individual and the state were being worked out in Europe, but when they were transported to the new world, *one gained a positive and the other a negative symbolic charge.* As we have seen, individual freedoms and the economic markets necessary for their full extension were eventually written into laws and cultivated as new traditions. Although these freedoms took (slightly) varied forms, they are what immigrants have always sought in coming to America: the freedom to move, to start again, to abandon the constraints of one's past.

The strong unitary state, on the other hand, was what most immigrants were fleeing, whether it represented religious conformity, economic constraints, or a corrupt, ensconced elite. To the extent that the image of a powerful modern state became part of American culture, it was as a negative referent, a kind of demon to be castigated in political arguments. Government and corruption became almost synonymous for the colonists. While the British debated the divine right of kings versus the popular sovereignty of a commonwealth, the colonists sided with the latter; authors such as Locke who upheld the popular origins of government were extremely influential in the colonies. They "emphasized the dangers to the sovereignty of the people from ambitious executives: the people must be ever watchful against abuses of power but especially of executive power. Colonial assemblies were therefore suspicious to the point of paranoia of every move a governor made, and their suspicions were heightened by the fact that royal commissions and instructions seemed to convey to governors more authority than any governor was able in practice to exercise."[6] Personified by royal governors, whose official power grew steadily after Berkeley's bumpy days in early Virginia, government was an alien force to early Americans, who recognized the legitimacy of only the most locally elected representatives. Their own colonial assemblies were seen as a force for opposing government, established as a counterweight to royal power rather than as part of it. Royal government could never seem an organic part of American society.

In Europe, the ruling lineages predated not only markets but societies and territories, all of which dukes and princes had to fight to consolidate; they created the nations they would then rule. To make

John Locke (1632–1704) was the philosopher whose ideas had the greatest influence in the creation of American political institutions. He held several government posts dealing with colonial affairs and wrote a constitution for the Carolina colony (although, like most utopian plans, it was never adopted). He never visited America, but he knew what it was to move. To avoid political repression, he spent four years in France and five in Holland, returning from the latter in 1689 after the Glorious Revolution that he helped to justify in his famous *Second Treatise of Government*. We examined his justification for private property in chapter 4, but his rationale for government was equally influential. In the *Second Treatise* this hinged on "tacit consent," the idea that a people could implicitly consent to their government even in the absence of an explicit vote. Just as citizens had certain rights to overthrow an unjust government, so they accepted a just one in part simply by living in its territory. Why? Because a citizen "is at liberty to go and incorporate himself into any other commonwealth, or to agree with others to begin a new one *in vacuis locis,* in any part of the world they can find free and unpossessed." As long as he refrains from migration, he accepts his government. Locke's influential theory of legitimate government rests on the possibility for dissenters to start over in America and places like it.

modern Spain, for instance, the kingdom of León had to be absorbed by Castile, and Valencia by Aragon; Castile and Aragon had to be joined through marriage in 1479; the southern kingdoms had to be seized from the Moors; Navarre was annexed from France. Catalonia and the Basque region have never been thoroughly digested. The other large European countries arose from similar series of uneasy and often violent consolidations. No one could doubt the central role of the sovereign in creating the nation; it was hard to think that government came "from the people." (The tough men who managed to vanquish their competitors and create these nations, while ruthless, tended to be more competent than their descendants would ever be.) Such conquest and consolidation persisted through most of North America's colonial period, driving many of the defeated to emigrate here.

Even though European rulers established American colonies as part of their newfound power, they remained an alien, external spur (and later hindrance) rather than an integral, even defining, component of the new societies. Their rule was easily seen as artificial and false, imposed from the outside rather than grown from within. Rather than parading in carriages through the streets, the rulers lived in palaces three thousand miles away and never visited their colonies. More important were the expectations of colonists, who hoped to avoid strong governments. Even today other countries refer to their government as the *state*, a word that implies a coherence and purpose, but Americans prefer the word *government*, a more amorphous image.

Spanish and English monarchs took a special interest in their American colonies. In the early years they financed exploration and piracy. Later they often circumvented other branches of their own governments in dealing with the colonies. In the English colonies this special relationship took unusual twists in the seventeenth century. In the early part of the century, the Crown was willing to grant private charters for colonies and to concede considerable freedoms in order to entice settlement. During the interregnum from 1649 to 1660, little attention was paid to Virginia, Maryland, and New England, where colonists grew even more accustomed to managing their own affairs. Granted unusual liberties from the start, the colonists grabbed even more because of the availability of land and the scant oversight possible in such a sparsely settled area. As late as 1681, William Penn was awarded enormous discretion to establish a colonial government that fit his Quaker sensibilities, and he allowed the assembled representatives to write their own constitution and grant themselves unprecedented powers. Charles II was generous in giving such latitude to his favorites.

North American colonists faced the most advanced state in the world, the British Crown, which came to represent every manner of evil to many of them—especially taxes, which from Bacon onward represented unwarranted governmental intrusion. As one of Berkeley's successors commented, colonial legislators shared "a received opinion among them, that he is the best Patriot that most violently opposes all Overtures for raising money."[7] The *Declaration of Independence* reads like a screed against essential strands of modern government, such as standing armies, increased taxes, and administrative bureaucracies. Colonists saw these as dangerous burdens.

Part of American hatred of British regimes came from deep allegiance to Britain's liberal *ideals*, which allowed the reality to be judged harshly. Extremely modern in its bureaucracy, military, and legal system, the British state was almost unique in not moving toward an absolute monarchy in the seventeenth and eighteenth centuries. Its citizens were proud of their English liberties, in contrast to the oppressive regimes on the continent. This was an ideal imported early to America, becoming part of the utopian expectations of all immigrants. But conceptions of freedom tend to expand, and colonists soon turned those ideals against the British government, especially its colonial administration. They took the abstract ideal seriously. In asking why so little legitimacy was granted to politics in the colonies, Kenneth Lockridge finds that the colonists, especially New Englanders, brought old English traditions of localism with them: "It was an English tradition of local resistance to the emerging national state. It was the congregationalism which was the religious expression of that tradition."[8] From the earliest colonies, political authority was centrifugal, pulled apart by restless, idealist Americans.

Unstable from the start, colonists' relationship with the Crown deteriorated inexorably. At the same time that Charles II was rewarding his favorites, the more bureaucratic segment of the British state, recognizing the growing economic possibilities of the colonies, tried to tighten its grip. The Navigation Acts of 1660 and 1663 defined the colonies as a source of raw materials, a market for British manufactured goods, and little else. Existing charters began to be revoked, and royal governors were sent to manage the colonies with vast formal powers—often without any official provision for local representation. To make matters worse, governors received many explicit instructions from London bureaucrats ignorant of local conditions, often precluding local negotiation and compromise. Such intervention was clumsy and rigid, hampered by slow communications across the Atlantic (it took four to six months for a boat to go to England and return with a response). Royal governors had little patronage to distribute to win local favor, and at any rate their average appointment only lasted five years. James II's overthrow in 1688 did not remove the impulse for greater control, only its most insensitive implementation. Most royal governors were smart enough to work out informal ways of living with colonial assemblies, but heavy-handed interventions from Britain remained frequent enough to remind colonists that they were governed by an alien power. A pragmatic modus vivendi lasted until Britain tried again to increase the benefits it was deriving from the colonies by imposing the Sugar Act of 1764 and the Stamp Act of 1765, resistance to which had its familiar result in the 1770s.

Colonists had a rich tradition of antigovernment rhetoric with which to craft their own images of British misrule. Priding themselves on being English, the colonists were quick to perceive threats to their freedoms. They found one in the idea of conspiracy, elaborated by opposition politicians in Britain, who portrayed the King as surrounded by ministers constantly betraying his will with corrupt and sinister "designs" on government. Colonists who had faith in the individual when it came to markets and religion thought that, once placed in positions of governmental power, the same individual would inevitably abuse that power in pursuit of his own personal ends (which he was expected and encouraged to pursue in markets). Whereas coffeehouse radicals in London were saying *this* government (specifically Robert Walpole's, from 1721 to 1742) was corrupt, American colonists concluded that *all* government was corrupt. Given that many governors accepted their posts in the colonies with the ambition (like everyone else) of enriching themselves, this was a reasonable conclusion.

The American Revolution occurred after years of accelerating immigration. By 1776 the colonies were flooded with young men who had just rejected Britain in favor of new prospects in North America and did not appreciate the King's long reach. As always, they did not take kindly to authority. Part of the problem, Bernard Bailyn argues, was that colonial governments had to play a greater role in citizens' lives than the home government did in those of British citizens. Economic, political, and social institutions were being created from scratch every day in the colonies, whereas the main function of the British government in the relative stability of the eighteenth century was primarily to administer existing laws and institutions. In the colonies, government had to play a role in dividing up the largesse that immigrants were arriving to pursue, from land to trading and slaving privileges. What were typically private matters in Britain were public in the colonies, where legislatures had "the power of controlling the initial distribution of the primary resource of the society: land. . . . Much of colonial politics was concerned with the efforts of individuals and groups to gain the benefits of these bestowals."[9] In a society devoted to economic gain, government was unavoidably drawn into the game—a game that was inevitably corrupting. Even so, colonists clearly distinguished locally elected assemblies from the representatives of (often arbitrary, always distant) royal power. The colonists were pleased to throw off that part of the government which they felt in every way to be artificial.

But what could they replace it with? Unlike most countries, the United States had no ancient traditions or imagined blood lines that could command authority for their new government. If the colonists had any indigenous political tradition at all, it was one of opposition to government. American dislike of political authority was obvious from the first debates over the new Constitution, as the newly freed colonies tried to establish some sort of common system of government. What they managed to create was stronger than most Americans wanted, but far weaker than any European government. Each colony, wary of federal interference, had to be appeased. To ensure that the new government continued to reflect the "will of the people," the Constitution's framers made sure that no single branch could grow inordinately. Thus the most anti-institutional sentiments of the age were incorporated in a document that would itself take on a sacred aura; Americans have more respect for a piece of paper than for the apparatus it created. If all else failed, the governments of the colonies-turned-states (the very term Europeans would use to designate their newly powerful governments) could always reassert themselves. At the same time that absolute monarchs in much of Europe were streamlining their governments in order to exert greater control, Americans established what John Quincy Adams would call "the most complicated government on the face of the globe." Observing European, especially British, movement toward centralization, Americans laid down some formidable obstacles to the same process here.

The founding documents explicitly limited the power of government, especially Congress. The first ten amendments, ratified collectively as the Bill of Rights in 1791, are all framed negatively. From free speech to bearing arms to the powers of juries, they arose out of fears of what government, especially central government, might do. The first sets the tone: "Congress shall make no law respecting an establishment of religion, or prohibiting the free exercise thereof; or abridging the freedom of speech, or of the press, or the right of the people peaceably to assemble, and to petition the government for a redress of grievances." The rest follow with additional prohibitions on federal action, culminating in the tenth: "The powers not delegated to the United States by the Constitution, nor prohibited by it to the States, are reserved to the States respectively, or to the people." Although open to continual reinterpretation, the amendments clearly view federal government as an extraneous, potentially abusive intrusion. They differ strikingly from the Declaration of the Rights of Man and the Citizen passed two years earlier by the Constituent Assembly in the French Revolution. The French document leaves open considerable action by the state, and it recognizes collective interests as well as purely individual ones (it sees the two as complementary). It frequently turns to the state to limit what the state can do, a preposterous idea to Americans.

Despite occasional efforts to strengthen it, in most arenas the new American government remained almost as weak as intended through most of the nineteenth century. (The Civil War was a notable exception, but the state apparatus built to win the war, including national military conscription, a national income tax, monetary controls, and a kind of welfare bureau for former slaves, was at first resisted by Supreme Court Head Justice Roger Taney and then largely dismantled in the 1870s.) The power vacuum of the nineteenth century was filled by two institutions. Political parties linked local, state, and federal levels of government and, beginning in the 1830s, brought some measure of stability to national politics. These parties were good at mobilizing voters with torchlit parades, rallies, and long speeches, but they had costs. As Stephen Skowronek has pointed out, their need to mobilize diverse segments of voters, especially cutting across the nasty North-South divide, meant that "the organized forces of democracy in America came to represent only the most general policy preferences."[10] Blunt as a form of ideological expression, parties were, at the local level, corrupt sources of jobs and other economic benefits. For a nation obsessed with economic advancement, parties were one more path for individuals who wished to enrich themselves. This did little to foster respect for governmental authority.

Power also accumulated in the courts. Just as colonists had used the courts to pursue land claims, debt collection, and other economic disputes, their descendants continued to see them as a means for economic redress. Like government itself, lawyers were despised yet utilized frequently in trying to get ahead. Courts supposedly develop no substantive policies of their own, but only respond to issues brought before them. In this way they were just what Americans wanted from their government at all its levels. Government was there to police the competition of markets when it got out of hand. Courts were especially good at declaring winners and losers, and distributing rewards among them. Lawyers, who dominated the United States government from the beginning, proved especially loyal to markets and their dynamics, to the extent that they have been called the "shock troops" of capitalism. The free, unfettered individual assumed by contract law is the model of the restless American.

The nineteenth-century federal government, although limited compared to its European counterparts, was never as weak as Americans thought. It negotiated treaties, bought new territories, conducted wars, encouraged the development of rail and telegraph systems, and grabbed land from Mexicans and Indians. It operated an efficient postal system that helped to open up the continent, and it imposed a thorough system of tariffs on foreign trade. Most of all, perhaps, the federal government opened up vast new lands to settlers, operated land offices, and enforced titles. It accommodated both individual settlers and the new rail systems. The federal government's important interventions in markets during the first decades of the century were made by Republicans such as Jefferson, Madison, and Monroe, who were committed, at least in theory, to an ideology of limited government.

State and local governments did far more, especially in the realm of promoting immigration and economic development. State-level officials and legislators avidly granted special charters, monopolies, tax exemptions, and loans to private corporations, supposedly in the public interest as a means for economic development, but also as a way to enrich themselves and their cronies. Legislatures even authorized lotteries to benefit private endeavors. Canals and railroads were built by the companies that benefited from all these interventions. Courts were the means by which the companies' behavior was regulated, to the extent that it was regulated at all; usually, the courts were used to extend the rights of business. Government was there as an adjunct to, if not an engine for, business boosterism, protecting capital investments and moderating—minimally—the competition. What Americans thought they saw, however, were the "natural" forces of markets at work.

The federal government grew steadily during the twentieth century to meet the demands of modern complexity, but it has never fully established its legitimacy for most Americans. No politician has ever won national office on a platform of expanding government, not even Franklin Roosevelt (even though he later did just that). But many have run

Ronald Reagan perfected antigovernment rhetoric even as he vastly increased military spending and the size of the federal deficit. He talked about states' rights while using federal power to bully state legislatures that disagreed with his agenda. Most of all, Reagan continued a rhetoric perfected by Phyllis Schlafly and George Wallace, associating government spending with aid to the poor. Wallace and Reagan managed to link two of the things that Americans fear and despise the most. Americans want to punish the poor, not help them; the only government programs they want for poor people are prisons. Politicians themselves are even described as the only ones who benefit from government spending, so that Schlafly could ask in 1998, after pointing out that federal spending (other than defense) was 17 percent of the gross domestic product (which is very low by international standards), "Why are we continuing to support the Washington politicians in the rich style to which they've become accustomed?" Politicians regularly manipulate to their own advantage American suspicions of politicians.

successful campaigns on the idea of reducing it, and a large number have positioned themselves as "outsiders" ready to "clean up" Washington. Third-party challenges have appeared regularly as the ultimate form of "outsiderness." Even an oddball like Ross Perot can attract millions of votes. The politicians most opposed to government often have strong restless credentials. Many, like Ronald Reagan, are divorced men who run on platforms that feature family values. Others, like Newt Gingrich and Bob Barr, are not only divorced but have moved from one region of the country to try their hand at politics in another.

Only twice in American history has there been political support for intentionally expanding the federal government during peacetime. In the 1930s a charismatic president, even though he had campaigned on a balanced-budget platform in 1932, established the basic framework of social protections, centered around Social Security, that we enjoy today, and which not even Reagan questioned. The Depression provided a clear sense of crisis and urgency, and Roosevelt could turn to a Congress dominated not only by Democrats (unusual enough), but by Democrats from the more urban, industrialized parts of the country. Even the New Deal retained considerable respect for markets. For instance, in the National Labor Relations Act, the government only mediates the market conflict between business and labor, especially keeping union elections fair, rather than intervening in the contract itself. In the 1960s, racial tensions fostered another impression of crisis, which allowed Lyndon Johnson to strong-arm Congress into passing additional "Great Society" measures.

Both rounds of federal expansion required an unusual combination of crisis, electoral alignments, and a clever political strategist in the White House. In other periods when Democrats have dominated Congress, the Southern wing of the party has voted with the most conservative Republicans against any federal expansion. In most of American history, the norm has been suspicion and restraint of government, although it tends to grow even in the face of rhetoric and policies to the contrary.

Times of war seem to be the exception, when citizens have rallied around their government as it mobilized to fight external villains. And wars have been the biggest source of (unplanned, unintended) federal expansion. But every serious war this country has fought has been unpopular, at least initially, with large numbers of Americans. In some cases the reason has been sympathy for the opponent, as in the War of 1812 and World War I. In others, it was isolationism or simple lack of interest in the cause. Despite Hitler's aggression, Roosevelt could persuade Americans to enter what would become the most popular war in our history only after the embarrassment of Pearl Harbor. In many cases, immigrants and Protestant fundamentalists have been the backbone of antiwar sentiment; Irish and German immigrants filled the ranks of the Copperheads, northern Democrats opposed to the Civil War, along with a few rural, evangelical counties. In almost all cases there has been a sense that the federal government was embarking on a *venture of its own* rather than fully representing the will of the people. Only since World War II has the isolationist feeling that we should avoid foreign entanglements as corrupting given way to the idea that we owe it to the world to bring our special gifts to other countries. In all these cases, many Americans feel, evildoers abroad draw virtuous Americans into their corrupt conflicts.

American foreign policy has often been guided by a familiar boomtown machismo. Americans have little tolerance for subtle negotiations. They prefer firepower, deployed with enough force to win quickly against any opponent. We dislike long entanglements or holding operations. Fascination with the most advanced technology—the equivalent of being the fastest draw in the West—is balanced by admiration for individual war heroes, especially commanding generals, many of whom we have elected president. We don't like to become embroiled with foreign allies, especially European nations seen as corrupt or international governing bodies seen as overly powerful. We fight on the basis of principles, and hope to remain morally pure. Foreign wars are about fighting, not government.

The quieter, nurturing work of foreign aid interests most Americans even less. We give away a lower proportion of our national income than any other advanced industrial country, a mere one-tenth of 1 percent of gross domestic product. This is half what the next stingiest country (Italy) contributes, and one-tenth what generous Denmark does. We feel toward the foreign poor as unfavorably as we do toward our own. To many Americans, international aid only means another government bureaucracy.

Because deep in their culture there is no clear place for government, Americans have been shocked to discover its role in their lives. Political scientists and pop analysts of recent decades have written with dismay about the bureaucratic state, the therapeutic state, the capitalist state, the corporate state, the welfare state, and so on ad nauseam. Even though their government is generally less intrusive than most, Americans are surprised to find themselves with a government that makes any demands of them at all. Even today right-wing crusades question the legality of the income tax or the jurisdiction of federal courts. What H. G. Wells said in 1906, that "the typical American has no 'sense of the state,'" remains true, unless that sense turns the state into a demon. We find it easier to picture our government as a meddlesome bureaucracy than a provider of roads, schools, and Social Security.

Politicians themselves do not seem to have much respect for government. Many appear to be driven by personal rewards, either monetary payoffs or the pleasures of fame and power. When these are not the draw, politicians seem to yearn for the private life. Thomas Jefferson insisted that all he really wished was to be a farmer. He wrote in 1795, "It is now more than a year that I have withdrawn myself from public affairs, which I never liked in my life, but was drawn into by emergencies which threatened our country with slavery, but ended in establishing it free. I have returned, with infinite appetite, to the enjoyment of my farm, my family and my books, and . . . determined to meddle in nothing beyond their limits." Ironies, if not self-deception, abound, from his application of the term *slavery* to white Americans but not black to the fact that only five years later he would be elected president. His point was that farming is natural to Americans, politics is not. He only entered politics because his rural way of life was threatened. As Leo Marx puts it, "Seen from this vantage the forces which make politics necessary are not truly American; they always originate somewhere else." Government and politics are a form of corruption, which cannot arise among innocent Americans. They are an alien imposition.[11]

Governments are organized by fixed territories and boundaries, which can only constrain movement. Migration, conversely, can only undermine political loyalties. Governments are not for the restless.

The result of all this mistrust is that government plays less of a role in the lives of American citizens, especially economically, than in the lives of citizens of other industrial countries. Government's reach has increased steadily throughout the industrialized world, and at almost every point the United States has lagged behind. In 1870, government spending in the United States represented less than 4 percent of the gross domestic product (GDP), while the average throughout the industrial world was already over 8 percent. By 1920 American government spending had grown to 7 percent of the GDP, compared to over 15 percent on average. By 1937 the Great Depression had raised our figure to 9 percent and the average to 18 percent. In 1960 our spending (27 percent) was close to the rest of the industrial world's, but ours has barely risen since then, while the average has continued upward. Today, the figures are 33 and 46 percent. No fully industrialized nation has a lower figure than the United States.

Most of this growth in government, here as elsewhere, is due to transfer payments: support for the disabled, the elderly, the sick, the unemployed, and the poor. Except for Social Security, this is where the American government is cheapest, compared to other countries, because most American voters do not demand or even tolerate generous transfer payments. Because we believe in markets, we expect them to take care of us. Those who fare poorly in markets, we feel, probably don't deserve help anyway. They must learn to adjust to market demands as the rest of us have. The result is the greatest inequality in the industrial world. Other nations have less inequality because they use their governments to adjust and equalize market outcomes. Our reverence for markets and suspicion of government prevent us from doing the same, despite our greater wealth per capita.

American expectations that government's role is primarily to regulate the natural economic competition of markets is reflected in the relatively low voter turnout rates that have persisted throughout much of the nation's history, despite an inclusive franchise. By the end of the colonial period more than half of all white men were eligible to vote, in part because so many owned property. But few exercised this right. Voting usually took place in the county seat, a great distance over bad roads for most voters, and contests usually pitted one wealthy family against another without any issues to divide them. One study of Rhode Island in the 1760s found turnout rates almost identical to today's, ranging from 38 to 52 percent of eligible voters.[12] Turnout improved in the party systems of the nineteenth century, especially under the influence of big-city political machines. Florid rhetoric, torchlit parades, marching bands, and other spectacles increased participation at the local level even in the absence of much interest in national policy.

This voting regime was dismantled in the early twentieth century. Republicans, dominating state legislatures in most of the North, and Democrats, hegemonic throughout the South, gradually tightened registration requirements in the states they respectively controlled. The elites who ran each party had little desire for interference from below. Voters now had to register longer in advance, so that lively campaigns could no longer inspire last-minute registration. In many states voters had to reregister annually, and to do so, they often had to travel to distant centralized offices. At the extreme, registration might require a reading test, an interpretation of the Constitution, or payment of a poll tax. In many states even today, a convicted felon forfeits the right to vote, not just while in prison, but for the rest of his or her life (we are the only country in the world with such a restriction). Under this assault, voter turnout dropped dramatically, from 79 percent in the hotly contested election of 1896 to 49 percent in 1920 and 1924. The main targets of these attacks were urban immigrants and southern blacks, but also the poor more generally—in other words those most likely to see electoral politics as a means of restraining markets in the pursuit of social justice. For most other Americans, federal government remained irrelevant or potentially dangerous.

Turnout for national elections in the United States has remained low ever since, and today it is the lowest of any industrial nation (except Switzerland, where national elections are relatively unimportant). Most European countries have rates above 80 percent, while Americans consider it a good showing if half the potential voters participate in a presidential election (one-third in off-year Congressional elections). But the rate of voting among registered voters, as opposed to eligible ones, is above 80 percent in the United States, the only country with elaborate registration requirements. Only 60 percent of those Americans eligible to vote are actually registered.

American movement is a key underlying cause of low registration, and hence voting, rates. In the colonies, relatively few of those who voted in one election were around to vote in the next. Large numbers had moved on to other colonies or jurisdictions, where they might or might not be eligible to vote. The eligibility restrictions that appeared in the early twentieth century were especially hard on those who moved. They had to register in their new towns or neighborhoods, often two months before the election. Continual reregistration is still required today. It is cumbersome to reregister in each new district or even, in some states, for each new change of address. Recent legislation, recognizing what really matters to Americans, allows them to register when they renew their automobile driver's licenses—ironically pegging registration on the same centrifugal force that helps Americans move so often in the first place. (It has improved registration rates some, but getting a new driver's license isn't always that easy either.)

Cynicism about government is another reason many Americans don't vote. We expect politicians to be crooks, which means that on one level they all seem alike, ready to pursue their own interests rather than ours. We are not surprised by Nixon's dishonesty or Clinton's sleaze. In the broader landscape of self-interest, Republicans and Democrats do not seem to offer a real choice. A 1994 Harris Poll found that 82 percent of Americans did not think their government represented their interests; instead they overwhelmingly believed that it represented particular "special interests." In another recent survey, Americans were asked whether United States senators—in some ways the most dignified of national politicians—had "very high ethical standards." Only 2 percent thought so.

American trust in markets and suspicion of government help explain why the working class has had so little sustained influence on our national politics, the kind of influence that might have moderated our inequality. No political party has lasted long in the United States with social justice or benefits for labor as its primary target, in sharp contrast to the ongoing labor, social-democratic, and socialist parties of Europe. This lack of a powerful socialist effort was the puzzle that originally spurred discussions of "American exceptionalism" early in the twentieth century. It is less of an issue now that European socialist parties have begun to look like the American Democrats: a loose grab-bag of interests designed to appeal to the broadest possible coalition in order to win general elections. But our unique lack of a left-leaning party throughout the twentieth century helps explain why we have so little state intervention in the American economy, for even as the socialist parties of Europe become less socialist, they leave behind an abiding legacy of government programs to compensate for the inequalities of markets.

American parties have never been representatives of distinct class interests. Because of our geographic diversity, they have been more apt to represent regional interests, with the Democrats (until recently) dominating the South and industrial cities, and the Republicans the rest. The urban working class, which supported the Democrats from the 1930s to the 1960s, had to deal with a monolithic block of conservatives—within their own party—who hated federal government. Yet government is the only conceivable counterweight to continually growing corporate power and market inequality. Without its intervention, little can be done to alleviate the inequalities of markets.

Immigration has also helped prevent the formation of a leftist political party. Although some immigrants around the turn of this century brought with them socialist ideas and union sympathies, they had trouble persuading many of their fellow workers (even their fellow immigrants) to join them in organizing. Instead, immigration contributed to the fragmentation of the working class. If a working-class or socialist party was ever going to form, it would have been in the big industrial cities in the decades around 1900. This is when and where the leftist parties of Europe developed. There, workers acquired intense solidarities with their emerging class, through a strong culture that developed in their neighborhoods and reinforced the bonds of the workplace. But in the United States, the same workers who were massed by the thousand in factories during the day went home at night to ethnic neighborhoods, read newspapers in their native languages, and attended churches of their national origin. Economically the working class was united; culturally it was divided.

At the same time, the political machines that dominated industrial cities organized people at the level of blocks and wards, not workplaces. As a result, says one student of the phenomenon, "The machine at the mass level defined the realities of politics as being about ethnicity and territoriality rather than about capital and class, and it reproduced and reinforced the segmented-ward principle of political organization."[13] Not coincidentally, these machines had their heyday from 1880 to 1920, exactly at the peak of European immigration and exactly when efforts arose to form a working-class political party. The diverse nationalities of immigrants reinforced a political system that privileged neighborhood over class. Despite considerable radicalism and some powerful efforts to found socialist or populist parties, no party was able to emerge that would speak for the entire American working class.

Certain immigrant groups retained special traditions that reinforced this cultural and political fragmentation. The Irish brought traditions of loyalty to the parish and its priest, as well as a separate system of Catholic schools, which other Catholic immigrants often adopted. They developed special access to urban police forces and political machines that split their interests from those of other groups. Jewish immigrants from eastern Europe, especially Poland and Russia, were accustomed to living in fairly autonomous communities, with their own schools, political leadership, and other traditions, and easily adapted to American cities. The larger the numbers of any arriving group, the easier it was for them to establish their own insular community. For a brief, key period, ironically, immigrants were not individualistic enough.

Some of the fragmentation due to immigration operated in the workplace, too, purposely encouraged by factory owners who feared a united workforce. Factory owners and their hired Pinkertons (the company was founded by Allan Pinkerton, himself a Scottish immigrant) could exacerbate the fragmentation by stoking the suspicions of one group against another, or by feeding conflicting information to various foreign-language newspapers. Rumors of strike-breaking by another group were always a winner. If these tricks failed, employers could always play their best trump: bringing secret boxcars of African Americans from the South to help break strikes.

Unions themselves made matters worse. Many excluded immigrants, who in response sometimes created their own competing organizations. Terence Powderly, leader of the Knights of Labor, was the son of an Irish immigrant who nonetheless detested more recent arrivals, whom he denounced in 1890: "The class of immigrants that come now are not as good as those of twenty years ago."[14] Existing unions refused to organize them, effectively undermining their own otherwise heroic efforts. Sometimes the lines of prejudice seem to have been quite arbitrary. When eight hundred Japanese and four hundred Mexican farm workers went out on strike in 1903, a local AFL organizer petitioned his organization to grant them a charter. The letter he received in response was willing to charter the smaller group of Mexicans, but "with the express understanding that under no circumstances shall you take into your union any Chinese or Japanese." The letter was from Samuel Gompers.[15]

As we saw, trade unions were not very successful when they did engage in party politics, in part because of the dominant role the courts had assumed in an otherwise weak political system. The courts remained the strongest institutional defender of the market vision—along with the rights of employers, the sanctity of contracts, and the fundamental importance of economic development—well into the twentieth century. Many of organized labor's legislative triumphs—like the cigar-makers' New York regulations—were undone by judges. During most of the nineteenth century, the courts banned unions as criminal conspiracies, and in the 1890s they began issuing injunctions against strikes and boycotts as restrictions of free trade. The structure of the American state thus confirmed unionists' gut suspicions about politics, reinforcing labor's predilection to battle with employers on the terrain of market power through strikes and boycotts. With the state as the only possible counterweight to corporations, the unions' refusal or inability to use that power condemned them to relative impotence.

Gompers was not alone in seeing labor organizing as an issue of American "manhood," a vague concept which to him combined market success, the ability to support a family, and freedom to move around. The Miners' National Progressive Union, an AFL affiliate, also saw market strength as manly, and reliance on government intervention as unmanly: "Upon matters of wages and obnoxious rules that oppress and rob us, we should not look to legislative bodies for protection. It would be unmanly for us as miners to ask either national or state legislators to exercise a paternal surveillance over us and the difficulties which we ourselves can supervise and control."[16] If markets are a fair and manly competition, real men must apparently take their lumps when they lose.

In addition to their political effects, immigrants have reduced the market power of organized labor by supplying American companies with an almost infinite flow of cheap labor, undercutting union efforts to place demands on employers. Even in the colonial period, a steady flow of Irish and Germans helped Philadelphia manufacturers remain profitable, allowing them to respond to market fluctuations. The United States industrialized so rapidly in the late nineteenth century because tens of millions of immigrants made up the labor gap that rural migrants could not fill, with each new wave willing to work for lower wages than the last. For every German cigarmaker, there was a large Bohemian family willing to work more cheaply in their tenement apartment. Gompers and the AFL knew what they were doing when they pushed for restrictions on immigration in 1918, even though Gompers and AFL Secretary Frank Morrison, both of whom testified before Congress, were immigrants themselves.

Although ideological debates swirl around the economic effects of immigration, a fairly clear image emerges from research, which (like most good social science) confirms common sense. Immigrants have positive effects on the overall American economy, boosting growth and flexibility, bringing new skills and creativity, and keeping the population younger. But at the bottom of the job hierarchy, they keep wages low. They work harder and longer for less money, they are less likely to be unionized or to complain, and as a result they frequently take jobs from the native-born. When low-paid workers must compete with each other for jobs, this guarantees they will remain low-paid. During most of American history the supply of people at the bottom has been endless because of immigration. The wages of labor have been suppressed.

The effect of immigration on black Americans, who have faced extreme racism as well as wage competition, has been especially severe. Frederick Douglass described how, even in the 1830s, white immigrant workers beat up and chased away black competitors for shipyard jobs; the Draft Riots of 1863 (in full swing the month Gompers arrived in the United States) saw Irish immigrants kill more than one hundred black New Yorkers in a frenzy related to job competition. After Emancipation such brutality only increased. Concludes one student of immigration, "In a cold, economic sense, the steady flow of foreign workers had left the United States—other than southern plantation owners—with little need of the labor of its black citizens."[17]

On the lower rungs of the economic ladder the same dynamic continues today. In some cities the flow of immigrants has forced many native-born Americans to move elsewhere for a fresh start; one study found that "the effect of immigrant arrivals on native workers was so large that the natives' migratory responses more than totally offset any arrival of immigrants. . . . This is a startling finding."[18] According to a 1996 United Nations study, one-third of the recent decline in the wages of Americans without a high-school education is due to competition from low-skilled immigrants. In some industries, especially agriculture, the effect is even greater. A number of trade unions, especially in construction, continue to favor immigrants over African Americans, as do many employers (those who own capital benefit the most from immigration, a number of studies have found). Many immigrants qualify for affirmative action, taking spots that would otherwise go to native-born blacks. Most Americans benefit from immigration, but a significant number at the bottom suffer.

As usual, political decisions often influence the dynamics of the labor market. Since the 1970s many city governments have replaced unionized workers (often disproportionately African American) with small, contracted companies frequently employing immigrants. A few workers and companies willing to do more for less quickly force everyone to do the same—or be pushed out of the market. Throughout American history, our flow of immigration has meant more workers scrambling for jobs at the bottom of the heap; without it, employers in many periods would have been forced to raise wages to attract sufficient numbers of employees to those jobs, and government might have been pressured to do more for those at the bottom. (This effect would have been worse except that so many immigrants come with skills they eventually can put to work; they compete with the bottom tier of American workers for only a short time.)

The weak bargaining power of so many American workers has constantly undermined trade unions, which reached the pinnacle of their power in the 1950s after three decades of curtailed immigration. Even in 1955, when one-third of Americans belonged to unions, that figure was lower than the comparable rates in other industrial countries. Today only 14 percent of employed Americans belong, compared to around 40 percent in western Europe (where almost twice that many are covered by collective bargaining agreements, even if they do not belong to unions). To some extent, American workers apply to their own unions the cynicism they have for all bureaucracies. In addition, government policies have rarely encouraged unionization, and they have frequently allowed companies to practice dirty tricks against unions. *Unions are for those who stay put,* slowly climbing job ladders and taking advantage of the benefits of seniority; their rules hurt those who move from job to job and place to place. (Economists have shown that older workers, who are less mobile, are more active in union affairs.) Immigration and internal migration are not the whole reason for weak American unions, but they are part of the story. We should not be surprised that organized labor has traditionally opposed immigration while big business has favored it.

The fragmentation of labor brought on by immigration and migration along with labor's reluctance to use political mechanisms helps explain America's conservative politics. But other factors are involved too. Vast numbers of workers, both immigrants and native-born, believe in the cluster of values I have dubbed restlessness. They move in pursuit of a better job but still blame their own poor choices or lack of skills when they do not find the job they want. They see their environment as a set of resources to exploit and do not want interference in that exploitation. They trust markets and mistrust government intervention. Yes, as leftists point out, capitalists manipulate union elections; yes, monied lobbyists affect legislation in Washington. But the individualism of American character still explains a large part of our conservative politics. Usually, Americans get the kind of policies most of them want.

Government intervention is the only way to help those who have been hurt by market dynamics. In some European countries, Tory parties, linked to aristocratic feelings of noblesse oblige, are willing to intervene to help those at the bottom, but the United States has never had this kind of conservative party. Instead, we have had a Republican party tied to big business, with an interest in preserving pure market outcomes. Without a strong leftist party as balance, there have been few challenges to inequality, few serious efforts to help those at the bottom.

American mistrust of government is part of a broader suspicion of authority that goes along with a headstrong restlessness. When that suspicion is directed at elites instead of government, it has often pushed in a less conservative direction. Doctors, lawyers, ministers, professors, and experts of every sort have been regular demons in American history, for they set themselves up as authorities with the right to tell other Americans what to believe and how to behave. More than anything else, restless people fear dependency, since that entails obligations and needs that might tie them down. In the 1830s, 1890s, and 1930s, populist suspicion of elites had egalitarian intentions, aimed at bringing the mighty into line. In periods like these, the wealthy have been seen as obstacles to upward mobility instead of embodiments of the American dream. We have always been individualists, but individualism is not always conservative.

Almost every recurrent trend in American history has undermined respect for authority, especially but not only for government. Immigrants have come here to escape legal, cultural, religious, and economic authorities who constrained them. Refuge from the same kinds of authorities has motivated Americans to migrate in the hope of starting over. In boomtowns young men take the law into their own hands not only to protect their earnings but to enforce their ideas of honor. They hate governments which, concerned with stability, sometimes try to protect the environment, if only to stretch out its exploitation. And governments, at least viewed in the abstract, sometimes interfere with other ways of making money, the ultimate American obsession (although more often government is used as a means to that very end). There is little to commend the idea of government to Americans, although considerably more to recommend the actual practice.

The essence of individualism is that we do not like to be told what to do, even by our own government—or what to believe. Americans take some pride in believing outlandish claims precisely because the authorities tell us not to. Even morality has no higher (human) authority; it is ours to work out for ourselves. If we don't like what our minister tells us, we find another; if we cannot find a suitable replacement, we found our own church. We pay little attention to pointy-headed intellectuals who tell us that UFOs do not exist, that Satanists do not abuse our children, or that Vietnam is not holding hundreds of MIAs. We do not believe what authorities tell us simply because they have impressive institutional affiliations. In fact those affiliations often undermine their credibility.

Americans sometimes follow demagogues precisely because they stand outside of institutional constraints. We trust them as individuals, even when a Jim Jones leads us into the jungles of Guyana. We don't trust them—in fact we mistrust them—in their role as representatives of institutions. Those bureaucratic assemblages that might discipline and control their representatives (a church hierarchy, say) are precisely what we so often reject, and thus we leave ourselves vulnerable to charismatic individuals operating outside them.

What do we lose in ignoring, despising, or fleeing authority? One student of the matter insists, "Our rejection is not connected to our seeing a better image of authority in the mind's eye. And our need for authority as such remains. Desires for guidance, security, and stability do not disappear when they are unsatisfied."[19] He sees an authority as someone who disciplines us, leads us to improve ourselves by reference to some higher standard. In addition to the negative constraint that Americans perceive in authority, there is a positive—and possibly necessary—dimension of encouragement. Authorities force us to be better selves. When we restlessly escape or reject them, we are free to remain kids. No one can force maturity on us.

Americans tend to trust markets but question government and authorities because they think through individuals. They understand a lot that happens in the world in terms of the actions and choices of individuals. Our restless market vision helps us view the whole world through the lens of individuals, not corporations, or technologies, or government incentives. We even view government as a collection of self-interested individuals, looking for opportunities as they would in a market. In many cultures, the state is a symbol of the community. Hegel argued that it was the only institution that could rise above special interests and represent the needs of the entire nation. Americans take the opposite view, that government is a bunch of scoundrels who pursue their own interests and those of their pals just as enthusiastically as other Americans pursue their own interests in markets.

_____

An American economist named Albert Hirschman (a German immigrant) once argued that people can respond to things they do not like in three different ways, which he dubbed exit, voice, and loyalty. They can switch to a new product, get a new job, move to a new town or country. Or they can stay and complain in the hopes that what they dislike will be changed. Or, finally, they can swallow their discontent and accept the changes they dislike, allowing loyalty to alleviate their discontent. Exit behavior is inspired by markets: when you don't like one brand of raisin bran, you switch to another. Voice is more political, since it requires an articulation of your values and an argument capable of persuading others to change the way they do things. Loyalty relies on feelings of emotional and moral obligation and solidarity. Hirschman thought there were trade-offs between the approaches, especially between exit and voice: people who were prevented from exiting would be more likely to use voice to express their complaints; people without ready mechanisms for voicing discontent would be forced to exit. In fact, loyalty to a company, a group, or a country makes voice more likely, for your commitment makes you want to improve the entity to which you are loyal. You do not like to see it deteriorate.

The relevance of Hirschman's model is obvious: *Americans are quick to exit.* Their market vision consists of mobile individuals, not groups organized for collective protest or formal organizations which set the terms of the debate. They are always ready to move on. They are slow to feel or appreciate obligations toward one another or toward organizations. This also means they are uncomfortable using politics as a means of getting what they want. They are more loyal to an ideal image of America than to its concrete embodiments in actual American institutions, especially government. American politics is not about voice, expressing moral views; or about loyalty, the recognition of abiding bonds with others; but about grabbing what you can for yourself. This is a vicious circle: Americans are cynical about government, so when they are appointed or elected to office, they frequently use their offices in cynical ways. This behavior, when revealed, nurtures further cynicism.

Economic activity somehow seems natural, primordial to Americans, and governmental action seems artificial. For Europeans, however, the state is a natural, even the preeminent, economic player. In the United States we are repulsed by the idea of government interference in "natural" markets, although we also watch for opportunities to turn that interference to our own advantage. We are not going to let ideology get in the way of economic advantage. So, despite their assumptions and ideologies, Americans happily use government when they can for their own purposes. Although political scientists refer to the American federal government as a "weak state," it is anything but weak in select arenas. Making war is one, so long as Americans are convinced the war is a moral crusade against an evil villain. Interfering in the personal lives of citizens—especially poor citizens—with moral prohibitions and pronouncements is another. For the most part, though, we don't like to admit these strong uses of government. Ever since Nathaniel Bacon, Americans have resisted taxes because they have disliked government. Not only do governments represent all sorts of constraints that people came to the United States to escape, but they also represent interferences in markets that, in American eyes, are doing well.

When they look around them, most Americans see a society of unconnected individuals, not a community of people who feel some obligation to one another. When Americans help someone else, they want to do it from a sense of altruism that makes them feel good, not from a sense of responsibility that shames them into it. Millions of Americans volunteer in soup kitchens, or Amnesty International, or neighborhood associations, activities which they insist are not political—politics for them being the use of partisan elections and offices to advance one's own interests. They volunteer as individuals, refusing to see their work as related to a broader culture or society. We do good because it feels good—and only as long as it does not tie us down. In the words of one scholar of American volunteerism, "Compassion is possible in an individualistic society like ours because we limit it to what we can handle and still maintain our own individual needs and life-styles."[20] An imagined community is the biggest victim of restlessness.

There are exceptions to American individualism. Women, we shall see later, are more likely than men to appreciate the bonds that unite people and obligate them to one another. Immigrants are not all alike, and for every super-individualist like philosopher Ayn Rand there is a collectively oriented Joel Hägglund, better known to Americans as Joe Hill. Other exceptions include the utopian communities that Americans have established, the fraternal brotherhoods of the nineteenth century in which men swore secret oaths of mutual loyalty, the thick communal ties of African Americans, the protest groups through which other Americans have resisted many dominant cultural images. Their very belief in starting over has led numerous Americans to try to lead lives that take community seriously. Even so, restlessness always threatens these efforts, always draws some individuals out of the community, and eventually destroys the community itself. Few American communes have lasted more than a few years. Even many fraternal societies were aimed mostly at social advancement for their members. Community is not impossible, but it is always fragile—and usually temporary.

Place is important primarily because it supports a sense of community. We feel more connected to our families because we have shared homes with them, sat around tables with them, gone on walks in the countryside with them. We consider people our neighbors because we have lived next to them, watched their children and ours play together in the park, served on the PTA together, attended rallies to save the local playground. We do things with other people, and the places where we do them help remind us of the activities. Places carry our memories. When those memories are good ones, places offer a sense of security and belonging. They remind us of our attachment to others. But Americans rarely stay in one place long enough to collect those associations, so we may not feel those bonds as strongly.

In American imagery, markets and governments (exit and voice) are seen as opposed, with more of one leading to less of the other. These intuitions have changed little over time, even though in the twentieth century more and more Americans concluded that government interference in markets had desirable benefits (even though the two are more closely intertwined than ever). Faith in markets and suspicion of government are central aspects of restlessness that have faded only slightly in recent decades. In fact the 1970s and 1980s saw their resurgence under the careful manipulation of the religious right, the Republican party, and Ronald Reagan.

So far we have examined a number of factors that have fragmented American society, especially economically and politically: the dream of self-advancement, the flow of immigrants well positioned to pursue their dreams, the belief in remaking oneself, a vision of the environment as a set of resources to exploit, faith in the justice of markets, and apprehensions about government and authority. There has been a failure of imagination when it comes to seeing community rather than individuals. It is now time to look for alternatives, symbols and sentiments that might temper our restlessness, link us together with others in some kind of community. One logical place to look for such an antidote is our culture, especially art and religion. But we shall see that they also encourage Americans to start over.

The Culture of Flight

No less than Tom Paine or Thomas Jefferson, populist Christians
of the early Republic sought to start the world over again.
—*Nathan Hatch*

Allons! we must not stop here,
However sweet these laid-up stores, however convenient this
    dwelling we cannot remain here,
However shelter'd this port and however calm these waters we
    must not anchor here,
However welcome the hospitality that surrounds us we are
    permitted to receive it but a little while.
—*Walt Whitman*

A moral dilemma dogged Huck on his southbound raft. Jim was a fugitive slave, and every lesson that Huck had been given, in church, school, and home, said to turn in escaped slaves. Huck wrestled with this issue, sincerely expecting to rot in Hell for eternity if he continued to aid Jim's flight. In the end he listened to a voice deep inside him, a fragile impulse that amounted to little more than the fact that he liked Jim and did not trust "sivilization." He turned to no external authority in wrestling with his decision; he found no body of rules, or adult role models, or even literary heroes to reinforce his intuition. His choice, to the contrary, flew in the face of every authority he knew. But as an American, he weighed his own conscience, confused and unprincipled though it was, more heavily than all the world's institutional authorities.

We began this book with three Americans in flight: Huck, Jim, and Fred Douglass. Of the three, only Huck endured a deep interior struggle. Jim and Fred both knew what they were doing and why—although they struggled enough in arriving at their decision to flee. Huckleberry Finn's dilemma, and especially his resolution of it, are a fine expression of the romantic tradition that has dominated American art and culture. It concentrates on the individual and his (rarely her) conscience and choices and boils morality down to individual impulses. The way to deal with repulsive situations is not to fight but to flee. Just as Huck and Jim skip out of St. Petersberg, Huck will later escape to the territories. Since it does not fit this model of the unencumbered individual, we hear little of Jim's reason for flight, which was to rejoin his wife. This escapist vision is often critical of core American traditions, especially the concern with material success, but it offers no practical alternatives. The individual is always better than institutions. As Walt Whitman put it, "What have I to do with institutions?"

The solitary individual is at the center of American high art. Much is missing from Huck's dilemma and from the novel named after him. We find little sense of slavery as a social and political system, little description of Jim as a human being, with a wife he loves so much he risks death to be with her. The broader implications of Huck's decision disappear, and it boils down to his own feelings, his own impulses and intuitions. He frees Jim because he feels like it. Just as there is no broader context, there is little sense of broader responsibilities or reverberations. Huck must decide what *he* will do about Jim. Jim has little choice in the matter, as is clear at the end when Huck and Tom Sawyer keep Jim locked in a horrible cell even after he is a free man.

Huck's and Jim's innocence is a central theme of the novel. Huck seems to be a natural human, good precisely *because* he is unaffected by society, which can't possibly have anything admirable or permanent to offer him. Organized society only claims to be civilized, whereas the raft actually is. Because Huck and Jim are better than the society around them, we are not bothered by their lawlessness, the way in which they live off the land by taking a chicken here or a watermelon there (although they do not own these things by *either* of Locke's definitions of property). Just as Huck lives outside the law, he is unconcerned with changing society's institutions. They are irrelevant to him, so irrelevant that he cannot even bother to develop a critique of them. He does not link his own dilemma with other people's challenges. He does not see any connection between his own private troubles and the public issues of the day.

From Huck's point of view, slavery is his own private burden. This self-centered view is that of a child not fully aware of or attached to the broader social world. Huck remains a child throughout the novel. Despite all his *movement,* at the end there has been little sense of *passage* for him, little change or development. How could there be, since Huck already had more goodness than any of the adults around him (except for Jim, even more primitive than Huck in Clemens's view of the world). What could they teach him? They could only corrupt him. If Huck ended up on another raft with another runaway slave, he'd possibly go through the same agony. If he didn't know the slave well, he might even turn him in. At the end of the novel, Huck is still a boy, still immature. His experience has not transformed him in any way. He is about to light out for the territory, where he can continue to avoid civilizing influences in the boomtowns of the frontier. He is unready to accept any responsible role in society. The only thing he has learned from his adventure is that society is corrupt, a lesson that only confirms his individualism. In the American artistic tradition, one's deep interior self is not subject to evolution or rationalization, processes that would merely pollute one's natural intuitions. Efforts to impose even the rules of reason are suspect, for they would interfere with the purity of feelings.

Surprisingly, Frederick Douglass is not changed much by his escape either. He knew the truth about slavery all along, so his story could only be one of eventual triumph over it. His inner self could not be changed, although it might be allowed to flourish. More generally, the American story of success and self-making rarely involves much transformation. The inner self remains intact, and the story concerns triumphs over barriers to fulfillment that the external world throws in one's path. From the start the hero knows who he is and what he wants. As always, the individual is prior to society and not much shaped by it.

The idea of escape is hardly unique to *Huckleberry Finn,* or to boys. Nor is it confined to the nineteenth century. When, in John Updike's *Rabbit at Rest,* the women in Rabbit's life pressure him to face up to his social and familial responsibilities, he responds like any idealization of an American man: he gets in his car and heads for I-95. Updike has portrayed him in a self-conscious parallel with Huck, leaving behind any kind of adult responsibility, with the broad highway replacing the Mississippi. Any number of fictional characters have acted the same way: Natty Bumppo slips back into the woods; Ishmael ships out with Ahab; Christopher Newman sails for Europe; Holden Caulfield drops out; Sal Paradise and Dean Moriarty take to the road. Such characters, like most of their authors, believe in starting over somewhere else.

Because it features only individuals, American culture provides few ways of thinking about our private troubles that would link them to broader public issues. When we have moral passages, if we can even call them that, they leave us in more or less the same place—even when they take place on the road. We don't have cultural images that would help us identify with other people in similar circumstances. We don't have much language for talking about social structures that affect large numbers of people in the same way, or about the intimate relationships between people.

A central part of our American (male) self-understanding is that we're innocent, which means we do not have complex relationships with other people, we do not have political entanglements, we do not face unresolvable tragic choices between competing demands. Instead we have our inner self, each of us, in a kind of presocial form, existing before there are rules and attachments to others. We believe in America's freshness, a persistent belief that we are different from the corrupt, encrusted Old World—and not just America as a whole, but each of us as an individual. There is something inside each American, a soul if you want to call it that, which is pure and presocial. All social connections— political connections, family ties, love and friendships—are ultimately irrelevant to this inner self. This is the essence of individualism.

Our innocence is that of children, who are thought to inhabit a world of fantasy and fiction. The setting of *Huckleberry Finn* is in some ways as familiar to us as our own childhoods. This is the fantasy world we grew up with, a simple, personalized world of picket fences and imaginative adventures. It's a fairly clear world, which exists precisely because of novels like this one, which have created this world alongside real life. It is the safe but adventuresome world of Nancy Drew and the Hardy boys, or the suburban sidewalks of Charlie Brown and Calvin and Hobbes. As fine a novel as it is, *Huckleberry Finn* is still a boy's book, with all the illusions of boys' adventures. Throughout the book Clemens parodies the romantic boy's adventure novel, which Tom Sawyer is always trying to live out. But Clemens seems to accept the main illusion of this tradition, that humans (or at least children) are unencumbered by social expectations, customs, manners. They are even outside the law. It is fantasy for boys more than for girls, for whites more than blacks, but it has been with us for two hundred years.

Of all the places we might look in American history for an alternative to rampant individualism, suspicion of authority, and boomtown restlessness, two logical candidates are religion and the arts. Culture, after all, should bind us together as a community or a people, remind us of our shared traditions and meanings. And religion might seem as though it were about the obligations of one member of the community to the rest, about submission to legitimate authority. Surely here we might find a counterweight to all the seeking and striving we have seen so far, discover some sense of connectedness to people and place.

American religious and artistic traditions have indeed been critical of the world they saw around them. The jeremiad has always been a popular form of sermon, denouncing the sins and corruptions of materialism, the lawless violence of boomtowns, the flight from family responsibilities. Camp meetings and revivals have long tried to save sinners. There can be no salvation without sin, in fact, and the deeper the sin, the more glorious Christ's saving power. Artists, too, have railed against the shallowness of their fellow Americans, against the commercialism that distracts us from more elevated concerns. But in both cases the attacks were on our materialism, not our individualism. Rejecting the dominant American concern with money has not been easy, to give generations of efforts their due. But the way that artistic and religious leaders have criticized this, when they *have* criticized it, has been by appealing to an even deeper individualism. American religion and art have both been grounded in the individual soul, which, freed from context and history, had to be pure and good. Rather than providing a balm for our restlessness, religion and art have reinforced it.

Since its first great flowering in the 1840s and 1850s, American "high" art has been characterized by a deeply romantic sensibility that pits the good individual and the natural world (both inner nature and outer nature) against the corrupt society (which is counter to nature). Americans already had seen government as an alien force, but in this new vision social life itself, with its bonds and obligations, was also external and threatening to the lone individual. On the side of the intrusive state would be lumped family, tradition, organized religion, even business. This romantic vision can be suspicious of boomtown materialism, which threatens to destroy the integrity of the individual and the healing powers of nature. But, driven by an even deeper individualism, romanticism has difficulty sustaining a critique of that materialism. Its preferred response is flight. It is one more form of starting over.

As Ralph Waldo Emerson and others first articulated this sensibility, one must listen to one's own inner voice in order to see the world freshly, untainted by the corroding layers of traditions and institutions. Here was a vision through which American painters and writers could distinguish their art from European traditions in a positive manner: they celebrated nature, innocence, and the sublime grandeur of the wilderness in contrast to the courts, traditions, and civilization of the Old World. For a new country seeking an artistic identity that would compare favorably with Europe's (Americans already had a political identity), the romantic glorification of natural beauty provided a perfect set of images and arguments, and American artists created a tradition celebrating the American land as an expression of the American soul. Nature could be allied with the self-images of Americans as new, young, and virtuous.

Although John Locke and other English philosophers had developed a benevolent view of human nature by rejecting Christian original-sin theologies, it was a francophone Swiss, Jean Jacques Rousseau, who, in the decades preceding the American Revolution, presented the West with the definitive image of the noble savage, alone gathering his food, satisfied and free. Rousseau, himself a retiring man more comfortable walking through the countryside than negotiating social settings, saw nothing peculiar about linking freedom with solitude. He almost certainly had America in mind. It was Europe's idealized America, populated by noble savages and settlers who lived almost like them on the frontier. But this was also one of America's self-images, used to attack European corruption and defend American virtue. In the nineteenth century it could also be used by Emerson and others to attack the new world of "commerce."

Romanticism first developed in Europe as a complex reaction to the Enlightenment's enthusiasm for scientific observation and measurement, to the unsettling horrors of the industrial revolution, and to the initial excitement but ultimate disappointment of the French Revolution. If the Enlightenment had looked to nature as a source of scientific understanding and instrumental control (even for politics and morality), the romantics hoped to save nature as a source of spiritual inspiration. After the collapse of the French Revolution, hope for revolutionary change took an inward turn: rather than sudden political change, poets and artists began to look for individual, spiritual change. But not an explicitly religious change: they replaced traditional religion with art, which for them was the new home of the soul, the new articulation of hopes and feelings. Indeed, a new emphasis on the importance of art in human life was a key trait of the romantics in both Europe and America. If philosophers and scientists (the line between them was not so clear then) had articulated the Enlightenment view that the frontiers of darkness were gradually being pushed back, it was the artist who embodied the romantic hope for a revolution of the imagination. The artist was of a specific kind: struggling, soul-searching, anguished, but a kind of isolated genius, often misunderstood by the rest of society—someone trying to express his or her innermost feelings. Ever since then, modern societies have granted enormous respect to people who spend their lives working out problems of sensibility, of inner feelings, and who try to impose artistic form on these feelings. In all of human history the status of the artist has never been so high.

In the United States the romantic mood arrived late, but it was still a response to a series of related changes that took place during the nineteenth century. This momentous "great transformation" included the accelerated growth of cities, the expansion of national markets, technological improvements (especially in transportation), continued immigration and population growth, and the emergence of large factories and corporations. These changes were well underway in the Northeast by the 1830s. A society of small producers faded as the economic reality, even as it embedded itself more deeply in myth. As we saw in chapter 5, Americans desperately wanted to believe that virtue led to success. But the autonomy, freedom, and integrity of these artisans was already becoming a nostalgic image from the past when Longfellow wrote "The Village Blacksmith" in 1839:

His brow is wet with honest sweat,
He earns whate'er he can,
And looks the whole world in the face,
For he owes not any man.

Even as they scrambled to take advantage of it, Americans frequently bemoaned the new economic order. The large, anonymous cities seemed sure to undermine America's imagined virtues. If your customers no longer knew you personally, then it mattered little whether you maintained a Franklinesque personal reputation for all the right Protestant habits. You now sold to customers rather than to friends and neighbors, and all you wanted was to make money off them. This critique, which had more than a little truth to it, saw Protestant virtues like trust, honesty, and diligent hard work becoming less important in daily life. Hard work was now good only if you needed it to make money; if you could find other ways to get rich, so much the better. And there were more and more of these other ways.

Disturbing social divisions also increased. The home and the workplace were now in different places, and a clearer division of labor between men and women emerged. At least among the middle class, who worked hard to impose their ideal on the rest of society, men went off to work someplace else, a factory or store in a different part of town, while women stayed home to raise children. Even more alarming to those who believed in opportunity for all (all men), there was an increasing division of labor within the workplace, in the new factories. In contrast to the older artisanal system of small-scale production, the new factories and corporations had a clear distinction between owners and workers, with little opportunity to move from one to the other. Apprentices' dreams of being their own masters became more and more an illusion. Anxieties over declining mobility, we saw, led to an even greater allegiance to the *ideal* of the self-made man.

Many Americans began to rethink their attitudes toward nature, which some now saw as benevolent if not sacred. This was a view available to those who lived in the relatively tame East, for whom nature had been effectively neutralized, rather than to those on the frontier, who still battled it daily. The middle class no longer grew crops or raised animals. Their livelihoods no longer depended on nature and could no longer be ruined by it. They were freed to see its beauty, and eventually most came to see it as good, as a source of spiritual healing, even as pleasant and safe. Native Indians, no longer a threat to most Americans, could similarly be transformed into the noble savage, a figurative transformation for which James Fenimore Cooper was largely responsible. Once nature was no longer an active threat in people's lives, they began to remind themselves of nature's spiritual and aesthetic beauty by keeping small emblems of it, such as pets, landscape paintings, and the suburban yard with its patch of grass and garden.

The revaluation applied to inner as well as outer nature. The romantics adopted the Puritan emphasis on the integrity of the individual soul, but they thought that untutored instincts were likely to be good rather than reflections of original sin that had to be disciplined. While most nineteenth-century Americans still saw (inner and outer) nature as something to be conquered, a growing minority saw it as a source of the divine. In the established Protestant denominations this vision gradually overturned Calvinist ideas of a stern God, predestination, and original sin in favor of a kinder God out to reward believers for their own acts of kindness toward others. Everyone contained a spark of the divine that only had to be encouraged.

New ideas about human nature entailed a rethinking of manhood and womanhood. Both ideals flourished in natural opposition to one another. As women's role came to be seen as emotional sensitivity and the moral training of the next generation, restricted to the domestic sphere, men's contrasting role was to go out and compete in the growing marketplace. (American men had always done this, but without claiming it as their exclusive prerogative.) The romantics rejected part of this dominant conception, insisting instead that the true, self-reliant individual—a real man—had more important things to do with his time than work in the dull bureaucracies then taking over production. This was an acute issue for "serious" writers in the nineteenth century, most of whom were dismal financial failures. No wonder they soured on the commercial system in which they fared so poorly. Even worse for their self-images, the most popular writers of the time, and most of the readers, were women, so that male writers had to defend their cross-gendered activity.

The romantics began to question the commercialism that treated the new cities as though they were, like boomtowns, merely a means for getting rich. Many artists, ministers, and philosophers were horrified by the new bourgeois society, the market-oriented system of commercial competition. They quickly came to recognize and condemn the new way of life for being crass and materialist, for encouraging people to care only about themselves and not others, and for ignoring the "higher" things in life. The result of this new point of view was the first flowering of the arts in America, especially in painting and literature, which gave rise not only to Cooper, Emerson, and Thoreau, but to Hawthorne, Melville, and Whitman, to name the most famous writers.

Almost all these writers shared several characteristics. They rejected the dominant commercial culture, in which manliness and self-worth were defined by how much money a man made. But they retained an extreme individualism, believing that men (and they meant men) could remake themselves in whatever style they wanted. Their critique of commercialism was largely that it discouraged this remaking, this taking control of one's own life. From Emerson on, there would be a sneaking suspicion that making money was a form of overconformity, threatening the American individualism of real men. Yet these men remained concerned with proving their masculinity. Rather than challenging the idea that men and women were so different, they tried to redefine what it was to be manly, to prove that they were men even though they were writing poetry rather than making money. For them manliness was a combination of remaking themselves—recall that each of these writers changed his name (and thus his identity) in some small way—with a lack of concern for others. You make it on your own, by consulting your own conscience, and you do not have to worry about others. American artists are restless deep in their souls.

The inner voyage matters to them more than any outward success. Melville said it was better to fail by being too original than to succeed by imitating others. This is a romantic sentiment, in which popular success is a sign that one's genius is not original enough. This was a convenient stance for writers like Melville, Thoreau, and Whitman, who had little popular success during their own lives. Yet they traveled far, both inside themselves and on the high seas.

Ralph Waldo Emerson (1803–1882) was the original of this tradition. Disliking his first name, he had people call him Waldo. Even the lax doctrines of Unitarianism were too orthodox for him, and he resigned his ministry over doubts about holy communion. In 1835, Emerson retreated to Concord, Massachusetts, to work out his own intuitions about religion, nature, and human society. It was twenty miles, three hours by stagecoach, from Boston (where he had grown up): far enough to feel as if he were in a different world. His move allowed him a new start of a strange kind, a position from which he could criticize fresh starts. Concord was his ancestral home, where his grandfather had built the Old Manse on the Concord River. Despite the deep roots on his father's side, however, Emerson had been raised by his immigrant mother, since his father had died when he was only eight. Perhaps for that reason he showed little loyalty to Concord as a place, dismissively writing to Carlyle that "utterance is place enough."[1]

As industry came to Massachusetts in the 1830s, Emerson and a loose group of his acquaintances began to coalesce into what would be known as Transcendentalism. Most were refugees from the Unitarianism that dominated Boston. If there was an idea that united them, it was that nature, including human nature, could be interpreted in such a way as to yield truth. This intuition resolved theological debates over what kind of truth the Christian Bible held, and how it could still be true even though it had been written for an ancient, not a modern, society. Nature could now parallel the Bible as a moral authority. (The risk, of course, was that it could replace the Bible, leading many out of Christianity altogether.) Like many in this movement, Emerson came from a family of ministers (five generations in all), and so reacted to the new commercialism he saw around him with concern for the soul of modern humans, his own foremost. The death of his father left the family financially strapped, a situation that could not have helped Emerson's opinion of market societies. His optimism was moral, not material, centering on the idea that salvation was possible if one paid attention to nurturing the soul.

The other transcendentalists were more literally restless than Emerson. Orestes Brownson changed denominations almost as fast as he changed towns, moving throughout New England and New York in the 1820s and 30s, clinging at each stage to a deep optimism about human nature—but not much else. Bronson Alcott (born Amos B. Alcox) had also lived in a number of cities, working as a teacher, before he landed in Concord, transforming his school and his family into a commune. Elizabeth Peabody and Margaret Fuller, who moved less often, were attracted by the seeming egalitarianism of the new sentiments, and transcendentalist conversations usually included them and other women. Transcendentalism emerged from a self-conscious effort, a kind of club that began meeting in 1836, partly driven by Emerson's feeling that, "Twas pity that in this Titanic continent where nature is so grand, Genius should be so tame."[2] Americans needed to cultivate their inner nature to match the grandeur of external nature.

Emerson's essay "Self-Reliance" was one of the most famous statements of the new romanticism. "To believe your own thought, to believe that what is true for you in your private heart is true for all men—that is genius. Speak your latent conviction, and it shall be the universal sense; for the inmost in due time becomes the outmost, and our first thought is rendered back to us by the trumpets of the Last Judgment." Then, "Trust thyself: every heart vibrates to that iron string." And later: "No law can be sacred to me but that of my nature." Inner human nature, lodged in the individual, has even displaced religion. The first romantic trait we notice, in addition to Emerson's concern with genius, is his turning inward to see what's inside him, with complete confidence that what he finds there will be good.[3]

Individuals and their souls are good, while society is bad, Emerson tells us, and he equates society with commercial society: "The [inner] voices which we hear in solitude . . . grow faint and inaudible as we enter into the world. Society everywhere is in conspiracy against the manhood of every one of its members. Society is a joint-stock company, in which the members agree, for the better securing of his bread to each shareholder, to surrender the liberty and culture of the eater. The virtue in most request is conformity. Self-reliance is its aversion. It loves not realities and creators, but names and customs." Here is the familiar artistic rebellion against commercialism. But instead of calling for communalism or political resistance, Emerson attacks commercialism in the name of an even greater liberty and a more profound individualism. He calls for rejection and escape. Emerson equates self-reliant individualism with manliness: "Whoso would be a man must be a nonconformist."[4] There is more to life than making money.

Emerson has astounding faith in the individual's abilities, especially his own, commenting in his voluminous journal (basically an extended autobiography) in 1839, "The new individual must work out the whole problem of science, letters and theology for himself; can owe his fathers nothing. There is no history, only biography."[5] Start over from scratch, free yourself from all of society and history. Create yourself. Despite his claim to originality, Emerson stands in a straight line stretching from Franklin to Houdini.

Emerson's confidence in the inherent goodness of the individual suggests that you stand up to society's institutions, to secular authorities, if you disagree with them strongly. His protégé Henry David Thoreau took this idea to heart and refused to pay taxes to fuel the war with Mexico. He was briefly jailed for this. Emerson was shocked, but Thoreau's action was true to their shared philosophy. If you believe you have moral truth deep inside you, no external authority can persuade you otherwise. This tradition of "civil disobedience" has a long Protestant lineage in people like Anne Hutchinson, who trusted their own hearts rather than their preachers, as well as a legacy in the nonviolent protest of recent decades. When Emerson visited Thoreau and asked him why he was in jail, Thoreau asked why Emerson was not in jail, implying that moral obligation was binding on others. But Emerson was the deeper individualist, and Thoreau's arguments did not persuade him.

In the romantic view, emotion and intuition are often more accurate, because more honest, than logical thought, which so often represses or rechannels feelings. Everyone has important talents and capacities that must be nurtured. If we listen to our own hearts, we can be confident in our judgments. In some ways romantic individualism fits well with other kinds of individualism—for example, in lacking clear ties to others. But it contradicts other American trends, especially the urge to work hard. It is hard to express yourself, after all, when you are repressing everything in order to be productive. These contradictions would explode most fully in the counterculture of the 1960s.

As we look more closely, Emerson's criticism of the prevalent restlessness is not all it seems. "Traveling is a fool's paradise," he says. "But the rage of traveling is a symptom of a deeper unsoundness affecting the whole intellectual action. The intellect is vagabond, and our system of education fosters restlessness. Our minds travel when our bodies are forced to stay at home. We imitate; and what is our imitation but the traveling of the mind? Our houses are built with foreign taste; our shelves are garnished with foreign ornaments; our opinions, our tastes, our faculties, lean, and follow the Past and the Distant. . . . Insist on yourself; never imitate."[6] Characteristically, Emerson is criticizing a superficial restlessness in favor of a deeper kind. The wrong kind of quest—for money, possessions, and status—is an endless distraction that will always prevent us from knowing ourselves. We are distracted by fashion, losing track of our own tastes. Again, true individualist striving cannot be bothered with what others do and think. If we search deep within ourselves we will find a better anchor to keep us steady against the winds of fashion.

But Emerson's inner quest could involve considerable physical travel. He spent years on the lyceum lecture circuit. In 1867, the year he turned sixty-four, he gave eighty lectures in fourteen states, as far west as Minnesota and Missouri. Four years later, almost as soon as the transcontinental railroad was completed, he went to California, stopping to meet Brigham Young along the way. He was impressed by the redwoods and the spirit of California, from which he thought no young man would ever voluntarily return. America, he said, was a country of young men. Emerson exulted in "railroad iron" as "a magician's rod" with the "power to evoke the sleeping energies of land and water," appropriate for a "country of beginnings, of projects, of vast designs and expectations." After all, he recognized, "Trade planted America."[7] Place and movement apparently were more to him than simply utterances.

The spiritual dimension of nature stands starkly opposed to its exploitation in boomtowns; Emerson hoped "to account for nature by other principles than those of carpentry and chemistry."[8] Thoreau would echo this sentiment loudly in his famous statement, "In Wildness is the preservation of the world." He wandered the woods and fields of Concord, measured the depths of Walden Pond, and did all he could to dig into the mud of his hometown. While Emerson wrote about an abstraction called "nature," Thoreau wrote about Walden, the Maine woods, the Concord and Merrimack rivers. He was searching, every bit as thoroughly, if not as anxiously, as most. When he recrafted his name by switching the order of his first and middle names, his Concord neighbors teased Thoreau for not letting them call him David, as they had all his life. God knows what they thought when he retreated to the woods. He was searching for Heaven, only he thought it "is under our feet as well as over our heads," so he looked for it in the deep waters of Walden Pond, in the melting ice and snow, in ants, and loons, and old birches. He thought he found it when a sparrow alighted on his shoulder or when he abstained from tea or animal flesh. And human institutions, especially government, were about as useful to him as to a young boomtowner: "Wherever a man goes, men will pursue and paw him with their dirty institutions, and, if they can, constrain him to belong to their desperate odd-fellow society. . . . I was never molested by any person but those who represented the state." He too rejected all social institutions as irrelevant to his real self.[9]

Romantic inner quests rarely attract the poor, for whom material success remains more urgent. For those born to genteel comfort, even when (or perhaps especially when) that comfort seems threatened, explorations of the mind or the soul satisfy restlessness better than westward migration and boomtown competition. Emerson was born and raised at a relative low point for American immigration, but he wrote when immigration was picking up rapidly, part of the whirl of crass materialism he (sometimes) disliked. The best solution was an inner voyage where immigrants and businessmen could not follow, or did not care to. Romanticism is not legally restricted to the affluent, however, and an occasional oddball like Walt Whitman appears with his own reasons for rebellion.

Walter Whitman Junior (1819–1892), who shortened his name when his first book of poems was published, found the peripatetic life more pleasing than Emerson claimed to. He loved ferries, roads, and bridges, not for how he could profit from his movement but for the connections he could make through it, to places as well as people. More than Emerson, Whitman showed the romantic's delight in the variety and plenitude of the world around him, the opposite of the boomtown's pragmatism but just as enthusiastic. This joy in hearing, smelling, and seeing America meant that Whitman would never stop moving, never settle down. Movement itself is the key to Whitman's self-expression, infinitely more important than what he might find upon arrival. Whitman sought contact, but the most fleeting contact was enough to touch his soul. He opens "Song of the Open Road" as follows:

> Afoot and light-hearted I take to the open road,
> Healthy, free, the world before me
> The long brown path before me leading wherever I choose.[10]

What is important is certainly not the destination, or even (in a way) the road, but the choice. The open road provides for choice. It is a state of being, not a process of becoming. Whitman is healthy and free because of that road.

Remarkably, Whitman's journeys are not about change or growth; he is already fine as he is. He has little to discover in himself; he only needs to express or fulfil his inner self by connecting with the world around him. His enthusiasm is so great that he cannot even bother to criticize the vapid commercialism that exercised Emerson; it is beside the point and beneath Whitman's lofty vision. As are all formal institutions, all politics:

> I hear it was charged against me that I sought to destroy
>   institutions,
> But really I am neither for nor against institutions,
> (What indeed have I in common with them? or what with the
>   destruction of them?)

Huckleberry Finn was at least bothered enough by organized social life to flee it; Whitman finds it so alien that he cannot even see its horrors (although he flees it nonetheless). What he hopes to establish instead, he says, is

> Without edifices or rules or trustees or any argument,
> The institution of the dear love of comrades.[11]

With edifices (and other forms of place) go rules and constraints that might interfere with freely given love and movement. In "Facing West from California's Shores," Whitman recognizes American restlessness as he (or Adam) stands at its western limits:

> Facing west from California's shores,
> Inquiring, tireless, seeking what is yet unfound,
> I, a child, very old, over waves, towards the house of maternity, the
>   land of migrations, look afar, . . .
> Long having wander'd since, round the earth having wander'd,
> Now I face home again, very pleas'd and joyous,
> (But where is what I started for so long ago?
> And why is it yet unfound?)[12]

The newest American is like the oldest man, pure and natural, full of promise and at the same time the fulfillment of that promise. An entire human history of wandering has reached its end in America. Happy though he is to be home, he also recognizes that his restless journeys have not attained what he had sought. The poem recognizes material progress and the exploration of the globe, but still feels a spiritual lack. The journey itself is close to the point. But the real point of restlessness is that *it can never be satisfied*. Just as materialists can never be rich enough, romantics can never be pure enough.

The connections Whitman sought with others were his own form of American idealism. They were his personal dream of American fulfillment, to which he clung dearly. They were deep friendships, not long ones. And they were deep because he imagined them as deep. They involved no lasting obligations, only poetic fancy. They existed foremost in Whitman's own imagination. But in the romantic tradition, this inner self is the only thing that matters.

The romantic culture of movement and escape is especially apparent in the most homegrown American arts. In literature, we see it in the Western and the detective novel. In music, it is obvious in jazz and the blues, rock 'n' roll, and country and western. And of course we find it in film, the most popular American product in the world. Let's examine a few of these restless genres.

The lone heroes of most American Western novels and especially movies have personified themes of unattached restlessness. The have-gun-will-travel rider who saves the day is associated with wilderness, not domesticity; he knows the ways of animals and Indians. Whether a "leatherstocking" like Daniel Boone or Natty Bumppo or a later gunslinger on horseback, he stands outside normal civilization. As a solitary individual, he is superior to organized social life. Characters in Westerns are on the move. James Fenimore Cooper started the genre, says one commentator, when he "placed his characters in motion across the wilderness, involving them in what became the Western's characteristic rhythm of chase and pursuit."[13] These men never talk much, as conversation is a form of attachment.

The Western hero typically arrives just in time to save a town from a group of powerful villains, often cattle ranchers who want to ride their herds over the lands of honest farmers. In some cases the townspeople themselves are too venal or weak to support the gunfighter in his climactic battle; at the end of *High Noon* Gary Cooper throws his sheriff's badge in the dust, disgusted with the cowardly townsfolk for whom he and Grace Kelly have just slain four bad guys. Worst of all, often, are Easterners—usually arrogant but cowardly. In its Old World artifice, corruption, and weakness, the East stands to the West as Europe to America. For some writers, the settlement of the frontier appears in a positive light, while for more romantic (and usually more sophisticated) writers, it also represents the loss of important values. Fenimore Cooper himself shifted from one stance to the other as his Leatherstocking novels appeared—and as he became disillusioned with western annexations and boomtowns. Whichever inflection one gave them, the great open spaces of the west had a mythic quality: "Into that space went wandering a road, over a hill and down out of sight," wrote Owen

The man responsible for making the Western into a serious movie genre in the 1920s and 1930s was Sean Aloysius Feeney, son of immigrants from Galway, who changed his name to Jack Ford and then to John Ford. This was the surname chosen by his older brother, apparently a customary substitute for Feeney. Ford, who went to Hollywood at age eighteen to make money, was notoriously driven and hard on his actors. He remade the Western by centering it on movement, not only motion on the screen but movement across a landscape. Films like *Stagecoach* (1939), *The Searchers* (1956), and *The Man Who Shot Liberty Valance* (1962), as well as some non-Westerns like *The Grapes of Wrath* (1940), were about journeys and arrivals. His films were also about the tension between the individual and the community. The latter is more pure when it consists of travelers thrown together temporarily, like the passengers on the *Stagecoach*, than when represented by settled towns like Lordsburg, the stagecoach's destination. Ford's two themes come together in his frequent movies of capture and escape, tapping anxieties over male freedom much as Houdini did. Ford loved America, and he loved to show the flag, literally and figuratively, in his movies. He also worked and reworked a favorite American story line until it was even more American. The main thing missing, from his life and his work, was a stable relationship between a mature man and woman.

Wister in *The Virginian*, "a land without end, a space across which Noah and Adam might have come straight from Genesis." In these settings even the flora—tumbleweeds—are on the move.

Westerns are stories for boys and men, celebrating the restless abandonment—but also the protection—of women and civilization. Historian Henry Nash Smith condemned them: "Devoid alike of ethical and social meaning, the Western story could develop in no direction save that of a straining and exaggeration of its formulas. It abandoned all effort to be serious, and by 1889 . . . it had sunk to the near-juvenile level it was to occupy with virtually no change down to our present day."[14] The majority were simplistic adolescent escapism.

More complex Western movies have emerged since the 1950s, sometimes featuring a group of buddies rather than a lone rider as heroes. Driven partly by the need for more complex plots and partly by the greater cynicism of audiences, these bands are more cynical about the social groups they protect and save, less driven by a concern for truth and justice. Some, like Butch Cassidy's Hole-in-the-Wall Gang, are even on the "wrong" side of the law, and others are rather reluctant protectors. Yet certain features remain the same: organized social life is seen as uninteresting compared to life with the boys; individual gang members still have special talents that set them apart (although sometimes now these talents are leadership and humor rather than deadly accuracy with a gun; Sundance even kids Butch about being a good talker). If earlier Westerns dealt with the simple setting of farmers and Indian wars, the newer ones discovered the titillating potential of boomtowns. In some, such as *McCabe and Mrs. Miller,* corporations—railroads, mining companies—are the villains, ruthlessly imposing "civilization" on simple young men of the Huck Finn variety. Violence, of which the cowboy hero is the master, is an expression of his superior individual moral judgment—when he uses it. By the time we get to Sergio Leone and Clint Eastwood, the towns are so corrupt that we wish for their destruction, not their saving. The only hope lies in a powerful, good leader, who can establish his own justice outside the official "law" (just like Godfather Corleone in a parallel genre!). Despite all these variations, the scariest thing in a Western remains settled, rooted town life.

Most detective stories have a hero just as alienated from social life as the gunslinger. In the standard detective novel, a private eye wanders around, constantly on the move, noticing things and talking to a variety of people. American Edgar Allan Poe helped create the genre in the 1840s, but it took on an especially American style only with the emergence of the "hard-boiled" detective story in the 1920s. One of the most famous writers in this genre was Raymond Chandler, born in Chicago but raised in Ireland, who invented the character of Philip Marlowe. Like most hard-boiled heroes, Marlowe is suspicious of the world, especially of local authorities, who are inevitably brutal and corrupt. In fact, it usually transpires that the hard-boiled detective was once a cop himself, a good cop forced off the force for refusing a bribe. He has been reborn as a private eye. Hotel lobbies and bars are a favorite setting, full of strangers, transience, and movement. And misinformation: the hero's environment is treacherous, with people lying to him, waiting to slip him a Mickey Finn. Most clues turn out to be misleading. Often the evil conspiracy reaches to the wealthiest strata and the top politicians. As a result the detective repeatedly has to mete out justice himself, killing the bad guys like a Western gunslinger. He can't even trust anyone else to narrate his story, so that many of these novels are in the first person (with voice-overs in the movies), in the individualist tradition of Emerson and Whitman.

The hard-boiled hero is a restless rebel against society and its materialism. Says Marlowe,

> The other part of me wanted to get out and stay out, but this was the part I never listened to. Because if I ever had I would have

stayed in the [unnamed] town where I was born and worked in the hardware store and married the boss's daughter and had five kids and read them the funny paper on Sunday morning and smacked their heads when they got out of line and squabbled with the wife and how much money they were to get and what programs they could have on the radio and TV set. I might even have got rich— small town rich, an eight-room house, two cars in the garage, chicken every Sunday and the *Reader's Digest* on the living room table, the wife with a cast-iron permanent and me with a brain like a sack of Portland cement. You take it, friend.[15]

Real wealth, lottery-winning wealth, might tempt him, but small-town wealth isn't worth the price of corruption that goes with settled social life.

These guys, usually too old to believe much in their own dreams any more, are threatened especially by women. Usually it is a beautiful and aggressive blonde, who comes to the detective for help but turns out to be part of the evil plotting. Huck Finn the boy-child would see through her immediately, but it takes longer for a fully grown man with the usual desires. As ever, attachments to women are dangerous, in this case possibly fatal. No one can be trusted. Not only lovers, but even friends may betray him.

Inhabiting the city rather than the prairie, the private eye replaces the gunfighter as the solitary individual who can set things right, a moral man in the middle of society's immorality. But in American mythology cities can never be made entirely right, so the hard-boiled detective must often satisfy himself with merely knowing the truth rather than setting things right. As in immigrant Roman Polanski's *Chinatown*, the truth can sometimes appall even someone who has seen it all. Because the private eye is associated with the city, he can never be entirely pure. He must be cynical—especially about the American dream. In *The Maltese Falcon*, Sam Spade refers to the eponymous statue as "the stuff that dreams are made of." Everyone believes it is made of gold and jewels, but this embodiment of the American dream turns out to be made of lead. Living in Los Angeles, a city in constant motion yet the place where the dream of moving west comes to a stop, Spade and his brethren have seen enough to develop a veneer of tough cynicism, as necessary as a handgun for a romantic to survive in the corrupt world of organized society. Huck Finn with a hard shell.

Movies are notorious for twisting the tone and plots of novels in systematic ways, simplifying their moral quandaries, focusing on individuals, adding happy endings. John Ford's version of *The Grapes of Wrath* ends on a much more hopeful note than Steinbeck's grim story, to take just one example. Hollywood "Americanizes" stories, but its movies are one of this country's most successful exports. And no wonder: the American movie industry and Hollywood itself were created almost entirely by immigrants, who knew how to package this country and its myths for export. Some of the most famous stars and directors have been immigrants. Even more, the big studio producers were, to an astounding degree, Eastern European Jews: Carl Laemmle, founder of Universal Pictures; Louis B. Mayer, head of Metro-Goldwyn-Mayer; Adolph Zukor of Paramount; Lewis Selznick. Others, like William Fox, Harry Cohn, and the four Warner Brothers, were the sons of Jewish immigrants. (Budd Schulberg, son of Paramount's production head, drew a crude portrait of their ruthless ambition in the person of Sammy Glick in *What Makes Sammy Run?* He makes it clear that Sammy was running from his past.) Most thoroughly hid their pasts, including often their families, in order to become the most pure Americans. They were free to create a new industry from scratch, on the far fringe of the American West, an industry that was all about starting over and happy endings. (Even the theaters themselves, early in the century, were palaces of dream and escape.) Hollywood escapism continues to appeal to Americans, who today go to the movies more than twice as often as Europeans.

The most indigenous American music, jazz, was born in movement, as a number of New Orleans musicians moved north and west in 1917, a migration forced on them when the U.S. Navy shut down the red-light district of Storyville. Many went straight north to Chicago, others to Kansas City, Los Angeles, New York. None other than Louis Armstrong insisted that migration was the soul of jazz. He likened himself to Huck Finn, as he and many others played on Mississippi riverboats. One historian of jazz comments, "Travel is frequently a way of life for most musicians [especially American musicians], but what made turn-of-the-century black musicians and their music special, was that the music captured and carried the experiences of migrating black audiences, and eventually, the shifting fortunes of the nation at large."[16] What makes jazz (and blues) different is the sense of the place left behind, an image of home and community. Black Americans moved north in the twentieth century, but they retained a sense of their southern roots. Most American arts do not look back.

Jazz was not the only American music to be associated with nonconformity, social protest, and perpetual youth: all of them have been, most notably rock 'n' roll, which panicked adults from the very start by its association with restless youth. Yet other adults remain lifelong fans. The British rock critic Simon Frith once wrote that in the United States youth is a state of mind, not a demographic category. In Britain only young people buy rock music, which has been an integral part of generations of British youth cultures.[17] In the United States rock is played everywhere, including at sports events. Rock 'n' roll, in contrast to pop music, is the artistic expression of rebellious youth, connoting authenticity and a rejection of commercialism. It is no accident that there have been frequent moral panics over rock, for its intent is to attack the way things are. It is also no surprise that its roots are American.

Bruce Springsteen, for one, continues the classic traditions of American rock. His music is about cars, and dreams, and movement, even though he attacks the dream of mobility through his portraits of losers who keep dreaming and hoping—and losing. Their very rebelliousness almost guarantees they will lose. In his most famous song, "Born to Run," he sings of "The highways jammed with broken heroes / On a last chance power drive." Their tragic heroism comes from their lonely desperation. Springsteen celebrates the poetry of their lives: "In the day we sweat it out in the streets of a runaway American dream / At night we ride through mansions of glory in suicide machines." Even those who can pierce the myth of success still rebel through a restless, desperate drive (literally) for glory and freedom. In standard romantic fashion, his heroes "bust out of class" and learn more from three-minute songs than from school. Emerson would (perhaps) approve.

But rock isn't for everyone who is young at heart. It appeals especially to the male heart. It is an entire genre of art that captures Huck Finn's fear of institutionalized social life. It also adopts the seamier side of boomtowns: the fascination with violence, the image of women as sexual trophies to be abandoned when inconvenient, the horror of settled family life.

Country music and western music, often combined into one marketing category, have a number of characteristic American themes. Country was established as a commercial genre in the 1920s on the basis of the perceived "authenticity" of rural folk like hillbillies and cowboys. Like Huckleberry, they were unsullied by civilization. Most country songs are about love, but not of a stable, reassuring sort. They are about men who cheat, men who leave, men who hurt (and a large number of women who do the same). The connections between people are real but fragile—real enough to hurt badly when they are severed. A large number feature women as dangerous, as a "Devil Woman," to use the title of a popular 1962 song: women who can tempt a man away from domestic stability. When they aren't breaking hearts, the characters in these songs are trying to make it big, American-style, like Glen Campbell's "Rhinestone Cowboy," who comes to New York to sing. Some try to make it through illegal means and must pay the price, like the condemned prisoner who can at least boast, "I Never Picked Cotton." Besides singing, there seem to be only two occupations portrayed in these songs: rodeo cowboy and long-haul truck driver. Being constantly on the move, as both are, provides opportunity for cheating, heartbreak, and loneliness. Even the narrator of Merle Haggard's "Workin' Man Blues," who toils at a dead-end job to support his wife and nine children, sings, "Sometimes I think about leaving, do a little bumming around / I want to throw my bills out the window, catch a train to another town." These characters dream of, and sometimes set out for, Alaska or Mexico. They have "Ramblin' Fever," title of another Haggard song. "It's good times here," sang Jimmie Rodgers, "but it's better down the road." Highways, backroads, winding roads, dirt roads have all been subject and setting for country music. The musicians say they are "on the road" when they are performing, and often refer to the employees who tour with them as their family. A "country girl" who is "restless"— in a song by that name—goes to a Greyhound counter and asks for a ticket to anyplace because she's "gotta get out of town." Those who have lost out in American markets continue to hope their next lottery ticket will pay off.

It usually takes two or three generations to move from the material striving of the immigrant to the romantic self-expression of his grandchildren. Henry James's grandfather arrived in the United States in 1789, settling first in New York, then in Albany, where he made considerable money at a series of occupations, including saltmaking, banking, and of course land speculation. When he died in 1832, he instructed the trustees of his estate to "discourage prodigality and vice and furnish an incentive to economy and usefulness" among his heirs, who (being full-blooded Americans) went to court and had the will broken.[18] Their grandfather's wealth enabled Henry's generation to abandon material striving for the exploration of inner experience, which Henry pursued through novels and his brother William through psychology and philosophy. Even for them, however, inner exploration meant travel.

Henry James meditated on American character in his novels, especially *The American,* whose hero is the aptly named Christopher (as in Columbus, get it?) Newman (too obvious to miss). He is introduced, a handsome naïf in the Louvre, as filling out "the national mold" with an "almost ideal completeness." Newman admits to being a good worker but a poor loafer, yet he has every confidence that he can learn to loaf (perhaps not as well as Walt Whitman, but well for an American businessman). It turns out he is wrong, as he remains too restless for true aristocratic loafing. He is intelligent, virtuous, and assured—and completely ignorant of culture. He has come to Paris to see and do "all the great things." Material strivers rarely turn into romantic expressionists, but Newman has undergone this conversion in a carriage on his way to do a deal on Wall Street. "At all events I woke up suddenly, from a sleep or from a kind of a reverie, with the most extraordinary feeling in the world—a mortal disgust for the thing I was going to do." He has the driver take him to Long Island, where (prefiguring Gatsby) he spends the morning "looking at the first green leaves." He decides to transform himself, and immediately sails for Europe.

Henry James is often seen as a novelist of manners in the tradition of Jane Austen, and he is a shrewd observer of social life. But unlike Austen, for whom people exist only in their social roles and settings, James pits the individual *against* society, innocence against corruption. James is on the same side of the Atlantic as Emerson and Whitman when it comes to picturing the unencumbered individual as the ideal, but his years of exile in Europe have left him pessimistic about its attainment.

Americans' restlessness can take them away, just as it brought so many here. Some leave to make money, others to keep what they make. More Americans leave in order to discover or express their inner selves, and corrupt old Europe is the favorite destination. James wrote *The American* in 1876, the first year of his own long sojourn abroad. He was part of a flood of American travelers, to whom Europe connoted not just traditional images of corruption or decadence, but also elegance, glamour, and polish; art and culture; and finally personal fulfillment, often erotic fulfillment. American writers and nonwriters churned out travel books and magazine articles at an increasing pace during the nineteenth century, leading one of them to comment in 1865, "The American is a migratory animal. He walks the streets of London, Paris, St. Petersburg, Berlin, Vienna, Naples, Rome, Constantinople, Canton, and even the causeways of Japan, with as confident a step as he treads the pavements of Broadway."[19] Of the century's major writers, only Whitman, Thoreau, and Dickinson seem to have avoided European travel. For some Americans, the trip was part of their mobility into the middle class; for others, a way to develop and demonstrate "sensitivity." For those of a romantic cast of mind, it was a "flight from various distasteful aspects of life at home."[20] Traveling and writing about it were a means to explore the world and the self.

By the twentieth century—perhaps because more Americans had wealthy grandfathers—the expatriate artist would be almost a cliché. Isadora Duncan believed she was taking the virtues of America, and California especially, to the rest of the world. Josephine Baker, Richard Wright, and other African Americans hoped to escape the bounds of American racism. Gertrude Stein, Ernest Hemingway, Ford Madox Ford, F. Scott Fitzgerald (who once wrote, "Americans have no repose"), Ezra Pound, and many more were looking for freedom and inspiration. Some, like T. S. Eliot, never returned. This migration went in the opposite of the traditional direction, and many eventually returned, but these Americans still thought they should move if they wanted to recreate themselves.

Sometimes the wandering helped them create better art. William Faulkner, whom we associate more closely with a single place (in his case Mississippi) than any other writer, not only traveled Europe but lived for periods in that non-place, Hollywood. In the words of one commentator, "The wandering is of the life and the career and not of the work: the work is much steadier in development and pursued in a far more consistent manner."[21] Faulkner's migrations gave him the perspective he needed to write so perceptively about Yoknapatawpha County. But the restlessness in Faulkner's novels is all the more striking because of its contrast with the settled place where it occurs: he wrote about people moving to, from, or through that place: Thomas Sutpen arriving with his wagonful of slaves in *Absalom! Absalom!;* the epic journey and sufferings of the Bundrens in *As I Lay Dying;* Joe Christmas and Lena, two orphans who separately wander into Jefferson in *Light in August.* These are characters on the move, usually starting over. Then there is the parody of a voyage: Benjy, in the wagon at the end of *The Sound and the Fury,* whose mental handicap makes him—perhaps alone among American literary characters—incapable of leaving home or starting over.

Shorter trips are also possible, including the meandering of backpacking youth. The impulse behind this form of travel is still Emersonian: to learn, develop, find out things about one's inner self. It involves self-improvement of a nonmaterial sort. This style of listening to the inner self has migrated downward in the class structure. Tourism, which to Henry James still had the traditional European flavor of a leisurely grand tour, a liberal education that might last a year or two, became among less affluent but equally restless Americans a one-great-European capital-per-day bus blitz. It was Americans' love of the automobile and its cousin the bus that transformed travel from a form of education into a means of frenzied exhaustion.

Today, most American tourists are not young people trying to learn something about their inner selves, but older people afraid they have missed something important. They have had their careers, and no longer fret over their relative economic success. They have started over when they retired at age sixty-five, and they are unlikely to do it again (at least not in this world), but travel satisfies some bit of their residual restlessness. It is never too late for self-improvement, a modest form of starting over.

⸗⸗⸗⸗⸗⸗⸗⸗⸗⸗⸗⸗⸗⸗⸗⸗⸗⸗⸗⸗⸗⸗⸗⸗⸗⸗⸗⸗⸗

If Walt Whitman's poems often feel as though they were hurriedly jotted down directly from life, Jack Kerouac's novels more or less were. Kerouac believed in "spontaneous prose," in which he only needed to record the life he and his friends were living in the 1950s, changing the names slightly. He saw spontaneous prose as a technique parallel to improvisation in jazz, a way of letting artistic truth emerge untrammeled by formal constraints. ("Action painters" like Jackson Pollock, in this era of triumph for the romantic vision, also saw themselves as letting the unconscious self shine through.) He claimed to have written *The Subterraneans* in three nights, *On the Road* in three weeks. Benzedrine seems to have helped him do it. No wonder he managed to write eighteen books before he died in 1969, at age forty-seven, taking time out from writing only to live the life he wanted to write about. In fine romantic tradition, the real work of art was the life itself. The books that emanated were merely the record for posterity (as well as Kerouac's effort at prosperity).

What kind of life was it? Restless, to be sure. Kerouac lasted a few semesters at Columbia before shipping out in 1942 with the Merchant Marine and then the U.S. Navy. He returned to New York two years later and fell in with the writers who would help define the "beat generation," including William Burroughs and Allen Ginsberg. He also met a charismatic young drifter named Neal Cassady, who introduced him to the "purity of the road" and the joys of cross-country road trips, and who became Dean Moriarty in *On the Road*. Kerouac's letters were filled with youthful idealism and plans for the future. In one he wrote, "My subject as a writer is of course America, and simply, I must know everything about it."[22] Many were simply childish. Adolescent grandiosity and self-absorption permeated his novels as well, leading *Time* magazine to accuse *On the Road* of creating "a rationale for the fevered young."

"The road" was more a character than a setting for Kerouac's novels, and much of his work dealt with this peculiar suspended place where the point was adventure. *On the Road* opens with a description of Dean Moriarty, "the perfect guy for the road because he actually was born on the road, when his parents were passing through Salt Lake City in 1926, in a jalopy, on their way to Los Angeles." There was "talk" that he had "just married a girl called Marylou." That he was a criminal made him all the more exciting: "He was simply a youth tremendously excited with life, and though he was a con-man, he was only conning because he wanted so much to live and to get involved with people who would otherwise pay no attention to him." The real-life Cassady became a hero to the middle-class beats, a symbol of the freedoms of the low life. His "intelligence was every bit as formal and shining and complete, without the tedious intellectualness. And his 'criminality' was not something that sulked and sneered; it was a wild yea-saying overburst of American joy; it was Western, the west wind, an ode from the Plains, something new, long-prophesied, long a-coming (he only stole cars for joy rides)." Nothing so sinister as stealing cars for profit. This is the lawlessness of Huck and Jim, who take only what they need, no more: a raft here, a chicken there. The American admiration for con men as entrepreneurs bubbles up: "I suddenly began to realize that everybody in America is a natural-born thief. I was getting the bug myself." In fact, Cassady seems to have been interested mostly in getting laid. But he embodies the road. Writes Kerouac, "I was a young writer and I wanted to take off. Somewhere along the line I knew there'd be girls, visions, everything; somewhere along the line the pearl would be handed to me." He was leaving the "east of my youth" for the "West of my future." The two encounter girls and many other characters on their trip, most of whom they sneak out on early in the morning: "I realized I would never see any of them again, but that's the way it was." More sophomoric than profound.[23]

Religion was not incompatible with the beats' aggressive self-indulgence. Several were especially interested in Buddhism, which Kerouac summed up in bizarre American fashion as "Your own private mind is greater than all." Even the most nihilistic of the world's religions can be translated by romantics into a celebration of the individual.

In a brilliant pairing apparently arranged by Grove Press, Jack Kerouac drove the Swiss-born photographer Robert Frank from New York to Florida. Frank was taking snapshots for his book *The Americans,* published in 1960. Kerouac admired Frank's eye for details, especially with cars and roads, as well as Frank's frequent snapping of photos from their own moving car. Kerouac describes a shot Frank took from inside a Delaware diner: "From the counter where we sat, he had turned and taken a picture of a big car-trailer piled with cars, two tiers, pulling in the gravel driveyard, but through the window and right over a scene of leftovers and dishes where a family had just vacated a booth and got in their car and driven off, and the waitress not had time yet to clear the dishes. The combination of that, plus the movement outside, and further parked cars, and reflections everywhere in chrome, glass and steel of cars, cars, road, road, I suddenly realized I was taking a trip with a genuine artist and that he was expressing himself in an art-form that was not unlike my own." Kerouac asked Frank why he took so many pictures of cars: "He answers, shrugging, 'It's all I see everywhere . . . look for yourself.'" And Kerouac did: "Sunday, the road to Daytona Beach, the fraternity boys in the Ford with bare feet up on the dashboard, they love that car so much they even lie on top of it at the beach. Americans, you can't separate them from their cars even at the most beautiful natural beach in the world, there they are taking lovely sunbaths practically under the oil pans of their perpetually new cars."

Quotations from *The Portable Jack Kerouac,* 501, 505.

These men who were trying to craft identities for themselves through travel adventures were not, whatever their mental age, adolescents. By the time he wrote his most famous novel, Kerouac was already on his second wife, who had their daughter the following year. Cassady too had a daughter, whom he visited periodically but had no means of supporting. Most of the women who show up in Kerouac's novels are casual flings on the road, reflecting his attitude, "I know cunt is all, I live cunt and always will and always have."[24] Married men, on the road, trying to pick up girls. In *On the Road,* Cassady, Kerouac, and Cassady's wife (whom the two have picked up along the way) arrive in San Francisco and have just unloaded the car (onto the sidewalk!) when, "Suddenly Dean [Cassady] was saying good-by. He was bursting to see Camille and find out what had happened. Marylou and I stood dumbly in the street and watched him drive away. 'You see what a bastard he is?' said Marylou. 'Dean will leave you out in the cold any time it's in his interest.'"[25] Attitudes toward women may have actually deteriorated since Huck Finn.

Kerouac's spirit is alive and well. Sometimes it seems as though most American novels are about boys or men in boats or cars, traveling around and having adventures, learning little or nothing along the way. A recent contribution to the genre, Frederick Barthelme's *Painted Desert*, innovates in having a girlfriend along, who brings a tiny television and access to the latest information from the Internet. The two of them romp through the great Southwest in an enormous Lincoln Town Car, seeing broad chunks of American pop culture such as the O. J. trial and Roswell, New Mexico (what they see in person and on television are not distinguished). At the end of the novel it is deep night. "I was out of the car too, standing in the road. There was nobody as far as the eye could see in front of us or behind us on the highway, no lights, nothing but a few insistent stars and the craggy silhouettes of dark desert rock against a still-sleepy sky. I couldn't see anything anywhere. Jen was walking around kicking up dust on the shoulder of the road. The dirt-covered Lincoln was idling there." They decide to drive off the road and straight into the desert. They are as restless at the end of a novel's worth of adventures as they were at the beginning. "I kept hitting the button, but I couldn't find anything that made sense to listen to, so I left it on Autoseek— ten seconds of every station. For a minute all I could think of was what we must look like from the sky, the black Lincoln, the two splintered headlights shooting out into nothing, the two taillights glowing red tracers behind us, the big flat space everywhere and all this dust swelling around us like a land-speed-record attempt. We rocketed across that desert sand."

For those who dream of it, artistic self-expression is as urgent as making money is for other Americans. It seems distant from the material concerns of most immigrants, but it leads just as surely to starting over.

Religion has been no better than the arts at calming the inner restlessness of American men. It too has criticized materialism, also in the name of a deeper individualism. Pilgrims and Puritans came to New England to start over, free from the institutional corruptions they saw in the Church of England. Initially their journeys were collective, but as new lands opened up for later generations, farms were farther and farther from towns and churches. Plentiful land encouraged boomtown aggression, not piety. And the kind of religious faith brought to America, with its radical questioning of authority, had its own centrifugal force. Dissenters like Roger Williams and Anne Hutchinson were a problem from the start. At first they could be banished or sent back to

England—demonstrating a continued faith in the value of starting over in a new place. But Americans quickly learned to start their own colonies, denominations, and entirely new religions. The very strength of their faith made religious Americans willing to leave and start over as both individuals and sects, confident of forging a better relationship with God.

As the early Puritans faded from memory, none of the colonies proved especially religious. Settlers were too busy establishing themselves on farms, speculating in land, producing for and trading on the gradually spreading markets. Overall, no more than one in five colonists were full members of a church. The colonies were a frontier, full of the carousing young men we saw in chapter 4. Commenting on similarly low church attendance in the colonies and the later "Wild West," two scholars ask, "Why should it have been any different when the frontier boom towns were New York or Charleston? It wasn't. On any given Sunday morning there were at least as many people recovering from late Saturday nights in the taverns of these seaport towns as were in church."[26] Young single men are not big churchgoers—unless they launch their own sects.

Joseph Smith was only fourteen (according to his own later autobiography) when he first heard God's voice, and only twenty-four when he founded what would become America's most successful indigenous religion, the Church of Jesus Christ of Latter-day Saints. Rejecting all existing versions of Christianity, he downplayed original sin and played up the kind of earthy pleasures a young boomtown man might relish, to the extent of making polygamy a matter of doctrine. Like his contemporary, Waldo Emerson, Smith thought that every man contained a spark of the divine. Making money was a sign of God's blessing, although Smith would have done better at this had he not listened to God's advice so often. He led his growing flock on a long westward search for land and freedom, crossing paths with the young Sam Clemens in Missouri. When Smith was murdered in Illinois in 1844, one-third of his followers were restless immigrants, happy to follow Brigham Young even farther west to Utah (although other factions did not).

Like many other American cults—thousands have been founded here—the Mormons tended to see themselves as the only pure church and also as the only true Americans. Even the federal government was not truly American, but a fallen and corrupt institution. America was an ideal that no reality could match. Any man who felt an inner calling could declare himself the true prophet and try to attract converts. The less educated he was, the more successful he was likely to be. The further from civilized ways, the more natural the man and the more pure his soul.

Religion became a marketplace in the early decades of the Republic, with hundreds of denominations and thousands of preachers competing for souls, and every one ready to start a new sect if no existing one suited. In the greatest period of Christianization any modern country has seen, circuit riders traveled thousands of miles a year to make converts in the American backwoods at the beginning of the nineteenth century. They took little with them except a Bible and a bottle of rum—certainly not soap or a change of clothes. Like other forms of restless culture, there was great emphasis on youth, free speech, and the individual conscience, and not much on the niceties of civilization. Cutting religion loose from state support after the Revolution only made it more popular, as preachers competed for followers by specializing according to style and doctrine. There was a sect for every taste.

Protestantism has been the main choice of most Americans, appropriately for its emphasis on trusting one's own reading of the Bible more than that of official churches and ministers. When Joseph Smith sought the truth, he went off and read the Bible, concluding that every man (not woman) should be his own minister. There are no rules to govern whose interpretation of the Bible is the right one, to sort better from worse opinions. Everyone's version is equally good, and everyone can believe what he wishes. Many observers have noted the affinities between Protestantism and markets, in that individuals and their choices are central to both. Christianity more generally has been the faith of people on the move, upwardly mobile, not of peasants tied to the soil. It entails faith in sudden transformation (when Christ returns), and in flight and movement, as in the book of Exodus. In the concept of being "born again," it is *the* faith for starting over. Movement will set us free.

American-style Protestantism and democracy went hand in hand. The seeds were there before the Revolution, but the fervor that Christianized Americans was spurred by the Revolution. The impulse behind both was to trust one's own heart and to suspect anyone who tried to tell you what to believe. Although many enthusiasts saw Christianity as a great force unifying the new country, there was little unity in this version of it. Rather, as the historian Gordon Wood concludes, "The outpouring of religious feeling in the early decades of the nineteenth century—called the Second Great Awakening—actually did not bring people together as much as it helped to legitimate their separation and make morally possible their new participation in an impersonal marketplace."

As Americans made their own choices, religion no longer helped pull towns together socially but rather helped divide them. It was a purely personal choice. Interestingly, Wood links this to a detached sense of place: "The church became for many little more than the building in which religious services were conducted, and church membership was based less on people's position in the social hierarchy and more on their evangelical fellowship."[27] For revival meetings held in fields, even the building could be dispensed with. The physical place for meetings was an empty shell, with no organic connection to spiritual or social life. If church buildings could be deprived of spiritual meaning, any place could.

Sects proliferate because Americans switch happily from one to another, seeking a spiritual fresh start. Switching varies across denominations, with only one in five Catholics switching to another faith but nearly half of those in the mainline Protestant denominations switching in or out. People often switch when they marry someone from another denomination, but large numbers convert on their own, in the classic Protestant "born-again" pattern of deciding one's faith as an adult. In some cases, adopting a new denomination is part of upward mobility. Denomination switchers tend to be more religious, not less, than those who stay put. Because Americans care about their religion, they make it a matter of individual choice, not inherited social custom.

Other patterns established in the early nineteenth century continue today. "Respectable" denominations like the Lutherans or Episcopalians decline in numbers, while smaller, more fervent denominations proliferate. By a conservative estimate, no fewer than sixteen hundred different religions and denominations exist in the United States today, most of them founded here. The pace of foundings has not slowed, either: half of these were started after 1965.

Of all the advanced industrial countries, the United States is the only one to have grown more religious over the last two hundred years rather than less. While at least half of Americans attend regular services, the comparable figures for equally industrialized countries range from 25 percent in Canada and Australia (frontier territories like ours) to 10 percent in England and down to 5 percent in Scandinavia. Among young people, 41 percent of Americans said in a recent poll that religion should be "very important" in life, compared to less than 10 percent in France, Germany, and Britain.[28] In all of Europe, only Ireland has comparable levels of religious belief. (The only chink in American religion has emerged since the 1960s, as increasing numbers of educated Americans have abandoned religious beliefs and practices; until then, college-educated Americans had similar rates of belief as others.) What is more,

63 percent believe that religion can solve the vast majority of the country's social problems, a figure which has remained stable in recent decades. Who needs government?

There are even contemporary equivalents of the old circuit riders. In the great open spaces of the West, churches are widely spaced, and because of rural depopulation, congregations are small. One preacher may tend six or eight flocks, putting ten or twenty thousand miles a year on his sport utility vehicle as he moves between them. At least one preacher has a chapel inside an eighteen-wheel truck, which he drives from truck stop to truck stop, ministering to the most mobile of all Americans. Other clergy follow Americans to the beach, hold services in flea markets, and proselytize at horse shows. Southern Baptists in particular have retained their skill at following Americans as they move about.

Place remains irrelevant to our spiritual life. Few religious sites in the United States have the aura of a healing shrine to a saint, or the palpable sanctity of a gothic cathedral. Our sacred places, if we have them, are more likely to be natural parks, not churches. We attend religious services in hideous hangarlike buildings because the buildings do not matter. Some Americans even attend services in their cars, perhaps as close as we get to a sacred place—and in good individualist fashion, it is a place they can take home with them after the service.

Romantics and most of today's Christians share a faith in the inner self as good, pure, and at its best when uncontaminated by institutions and civilization. Because it is divine, it needs room for fulfillment, not development or change. This faith can sometimes be critical of boomtown materialism, but more often its own urgent restlessness allows little time for criticism. If nothing else, belief in an afterlife is the ultimate form of American optimism (especially since 94 percent of Americans think they are going to heaven, not hell). It is the most important fresh start of all.

Carl Sandburg wrote, "America has many businessmen but no poets. The reason for this is that we are a nation of hustlers and no poet can really be a hustler." He was being coy, for he himself was quite a hustler, reading poems on the Ed Sullivan Show and writing them for Gene Kelly dances. American poets are not businessmen, but they are restless seekers nonetheless. The vision of a tiny minority in the nineteenth century, the romantic view has grown steadily stronger ever since, with a big boost in the affluent 1950s and 60s. More young people than ever before dream of being musicians, painters, or filmmakers, and many go to

New York, or Los Angeles, or elsewhere to pursue those dreams. The flow is not as large as that of immigrants to the United States or of farmers coming to the cities, but large numbers of people have dreams that involve movement for self-expression rather than wealth (although if they are successful, wealth follows). Never before in history have so many believed their deepest destiny to be individual self-exploration. Romanticism's sensitivity to inner needs also received a big boost with the development in the twentieth century of therapeutic language dedicated to precisely that end. Today, more Americans work in the arts than in boomtowns.

Boomtowners and romantics share more than just hustle. They are equally suspicious of cities and civilization, where women seem to dominate. Huck Finn is a romantic hero who will end up in a boomtown. Good American heroes continue to live in the woods, on the vast sea, or on rafts (or, today, in vans). When American novelists write about cities, it is most likely to damn their central characters as lost souls. Cities are now the place for worldly success, which in the romantic view exacts its price. One major tradition in American novels portrays a hero whose rise, like that of the paradigmatic Faust, is based on the collapse of his moral center. Sometimes his flaw is professional hubris, like the doctor in Hawthorne's story "The Birthmark," who insists on removing the one "flaw" in his wife's beauty—and in doing so kills her. At other times it is political ambition, a theme that dovetails neatly with American suspicion of all politicians. The usual image of corrupt success, however, is the man of wealth, and in this critique the romantic parts company with the boomtowner.

The romantic cult of the artist's inner self, if pushed to its extreme, implies that the artist is more important than his art, or that his life is his most important product. In Europe there was a cult of artists who died young, even in their teen years, before they could produce any serious work at all; they were pure sensibility and expressive impulse. They never had to submit themselves to the alien discipline of artistic forms. This vision fell in naturally with American idealism: if this was the perfect, pure, natural environment, Americans must themselves be its perfect products. They are themselves works of art. Thus our greatest works of art have frequently been accounts of American lives: Crèvecoeur's letters, Franklin's autobiography, Thoreau's *Walden*. The purity of American life needs no artificial artistic embellishments. Kerouac's barely fictionalized accounts of his life follow in this line. Young people are the most pure, the least affected by society's corruption, from Joseph Smith to Huck Finn to Neal Cassady.

The writers of the American Renaissance in the 1850s grafted onto American culture an attack on some mainstream bourgeois values. Their rejection of commercialism and materialism, their celebration of poetry and laziness, went hand in hand with more formal, "modernist" assaults on the expectations of their readers (who responded predictably by ignoring the new books). The writers began to mix genres, abandoned morally inspirational tales, eventually broke down consistent characters and even normal rules of time and place. By William Faulkner's time, multiple narrators would be telling stories from different points of view.

In the end, romanticism is a significant departure from the macho violence of boomtowns and the widespread enthusiasm for material gain. Many of the men in this tradition worried deeply about their manliness as a result. Of those who did *not*, a few were gay, like Whitman or Ginsberg. A few were celibate, like Thoreau. Some were both, as Henry James probably was. It is possible that a different orientation toward sexual relations, different patterns of desire and connection, could have helped more artists break free—partly—from the spell of restless masculinity that has long dominated American culture.

Religion and romanticism contain a sentiment that, if nourished, promises to undo those traditions' individualism. It requires a rare maturing of Huck's impulses. Whitman pushed individualism far enough that he was no longer anxious about the opinions of others, as Emerson still so patently was. Emerson was concerned to prove his individualism through the greatness of his soul, but when Whitman looked inside himself, he was content with whatever he found there. He even wrote,

I loafe and invite my soul,

I lean and loafe at my ease observing a spear of summer grass.[29]

The true inner soul needs no improvement; once you have found it you need not work to change it in any way. Just sit back and enjoy. This idea harks back to Anne Hutchinson, who thought that those with true inner faith need not do anything to demonstrate it to others. But Whitman found something else inside him when he probed his inner self: a desire for companionship, which he wanted "to plant thick as trees along all the rivers of America." Pushing American individualism to its antinomian extreme, Whitman came up with glimmers of something else, of a world in which people deeply needed one another, in which the solitary individual was not a happy individual. He pointed toward a truth that most American women had known all along: restless individualism overlooked something important in human nature. Connection with others may be one of our deepest (if suppressed) impulses.

8 Fleeing the Nest

When you readest this, suppress thy sobs, sue out a divorce, and set thy cap for another and a more happy swain, while I roam through the world sipping honey from the bitter or sweet flowers that chance may strew in my path.
—*1824 notice from Reuben Ward to his wife in Missouri Intelligencer*

The land was ours before we were the land's.
She was our land more than a hundred years
Before we were her people.
—*Robert Frost, "The Gift Outright"*

No immigrant was more restless than Tom Paine (1737–1809) or more committed to fresh starts. And none had greater need of them. His first came at age nineteen, when he tried to run off to sea to escape his apprenticeship in the moribund business of making stays, the whalebones used in corsets (he later claimed to have been sixteen). His father came to London just in time to talk him out of it—luckily, since the ship he had planned to board was almost immediately destroyed by the French, with ninety percent fatalities. Paine remained in London, working as a scab corset maker during a protracted strike over the length of the working day (then fourteen hours). Within a month, though, he had shipped out on a "privateering" vessel—a polite word for officially sanctioned piracy—whose six-month journey netted him a tidy sum. His share of the booty allowed Paine to spend half a year in the London subculture of self-educated artisans and religious Dissenters who were busy studying everything from astronomy and mathematics to geography and philosophy.

When his loot ran out, Paine set up shop in the town of Sandwich and soon married. He was equally soon widowed, with his wife and baby dying in childbirth. For the remaining forty-nine years of his life, he does not seem to have talked or written about the event or this marriage at all. From then on, says one biographer, he "spent virtually the whole of his waking time with men."[1] Paine devoted the next several years to moving about through a series of towns in pursuit of a series of jobs, from which he was frequently fired for quarreling with his employers. Before and after his first marriage, he seems to have been a lay preacher, most likely (the evidence is sparse) for the Methodists, whose artisanal audiences tended to favor individualism as well as social justice. A long stint as an excise officer (weighing casks of beer and wine, watching for smugglers) seems to have turned him against governments, corrupt enough in that period, especially royal governments. He grew increasingly devoted to politics.

His activism did not keep him from another marriage, unfortunately, to Elizabeth, the daughter of his landlord and patron in Lewes, where he was now working. At the ceremony in 1771 Paine declared himself a bachelor rather than widower, altogether denying his prior marriage. The new one does not seem to have been much happier. Paine was absent for months at a time, and rumors spread through Lewes that it had never been consummated. His political work seems to have led him to neglect his business as well as his wife, and his personal property was auctioned off—a sign of bankruptcy—in April 1774. He and Elizabeth came to a "separation agreement," in which she paid him for certain legal rights, although these later proved unenforceable. Paine almost immediately left Lewes and never again saw Elizabeth, who on her own could not crawl far out of the poverty in which he had placed her. In London, Paine arranged to meet Benjamin Franklin, who no doubt touted America as the land of freedom, individual merit, and fresh starts. In September, Paine sailed for Philadelphia, traveling first class thanks to the settlement from his wife.

Paine could not have enjoyed his arrival at the end of November, for he was stricken with seasickness and "ship fever" (probably typhus), which had hit all 120 passengers (100 of them indentured servants from England and Germany). He might not have survived his illness without his letter of introduction from Franklin, for he was carried from the ship to the house of the captain's in-laws, where he recuperated for a month. Although Paine arrived with a vague idea of establishing an academy to teach young women, he soon landed a job editing and writing for a new journal. He poured forth essays, reportage, and poems under a variety of pen names, including "Esop," "Vox Populi," "Atlanticus," and "Justice and Humanity." Barely four months after Paine's arrival, the Battle of Lexington spread anger and shock among the colonists, including Paine, whose views became even more radically pro-American and anti-Empire. He soon quarreled with the journal's owner (himself a recent arrival from Scotland) over the terms of his contract and was fired.

Paine began writing pamphlets, and in the fall of 1775 he concentrated on one in particular. When it was published as *Common Sense* in January, 1776, it proved the best-seller of the colonial era, converting many to the cause of armed rebellion. It indeed captured and defined the common sense of the time, using the language of Protestant Dissent to portray British power as old and corrupt, feudal and clerical, and once again to present America as the model for the future. In equally American fashion, it also triggered a tangle of litigation over the rights to subsequent editions.

Paine thought his mind had a natural "bent" toward science, and he believed that Newtonian first principles could be used to derive a science of society. In Enlightenment fashion, he felt that logic could prescribe the best possible government, which might be established from scratch in America. In contrast, British government was beholden to "precedents." Just as he had taken a fresh start, so should his adopted country, cutting its ties to the "mother" land. Even language could be cast anew, and in *Common Sense* the term *republic*, previously mostly derogatory, became a utopian ideal for future governments. "We have it in our power," Paine wrote, "to begin the world over again . . . the birthday of a new world is at hand."[2] Paine's was a classic immigrant stand of "a man who knew Europe well enough to hate its society and who longed desperately enough for salvation to envision in a flash of illumination the destiny of the New World as liberation from the Old."[3]

Common Sense begins by distinguishing government from society. "Society is produced by our wants, and government by our wickedness." Thus government is at best a necessary evil, a "badge of lost innocence." In the youthful culture of America, there is more virtue and less need of government than elsewhere—especially of monarchy, for "the palaces of kings are built on the ruins of the bowers of paradise." Here, in paradise on earth, there should be no need to build such palaces. Paine even finds biblical evidence that "the will of the Almighty . . . expressly disapproves of government by kings."[4] Paine's influential arguments against monarchy shade easily into a rejection of any strong government.

Paine rarely stayed in any place long. He returned to England, but when charged with treason, he fled to France, where he also supported

the revolution. He returned to the United States in 1802. His own natural restlessness was surely reinforced by his difficult personality
(add him to our long list of difficult immigrants). Benjamin Franklin's
daughter, who knew Paine in Philadelphia, wrote to her father in 1781:
"There never was a man less beloved in a place than Paine is in this, having at different times disputed with everybody. The most rational thing
he could have done would have been to have died the instant he finished
his *Common Sense,* for he never again will have it in his power to leave
the world with so much credit."[5] She might have meant "credit" quite
literally, for once again Paine was broke; he spent the years following
the Revolution pestering Congress and state governments in the hope of
cash rewards for his (past) patriotic services. An unprecedented grant
of three thousand dollars from Congress and a New Rochelle farm from
the New York assembly did not satisfy him in the slightest, and he continued to complain bitterly, but at least these gifts covered his debts.

Paine was not the only man to abandon wife or family in coming to
America, just as so many young men headed west without theirs. We
saw that when Paine's friend Ben Franklin wished to sneak out of
Boston to escape his apprenticeship, his excuse (to hide his breaking of
his apprenticeship contract) was that he had gotten a young woman
pregnant. In the restless world of sea captains, and perhaps of colonial
America, abandoning a pregnant girl was acceptable; breaking an economic contract was not. The restless young men who were attracted to
America and to its boomtowns were escaping from many things, and
family obligations have always been high on the list.

How wise are teenaged boys? The question is absurd. They are filled
with energy and testosterone but not much else. Yet through most of
American history boys and young men (until recently boys of twelve
were young men) were treated as though they were capable of making
decisions for themselves, their families, and the rest of society. When
Stephen Demas came to the United States, he was barely a teenager, as
were my grandfather when he left home to find work and Joseph Smith
when he began playing with the supernatural. Houdini first ran away at
age twelve and began his magic career at sixteen. Relatively speaking,
Paine was an old man when he came to America at thirty-seven (although midlife is another time for new starts). Paine and Kerouac may
have been older, but they still had a teenager's attitude toward family
and responsibilities. The romantic view of children as innocent and society as corrupt has only reinforced this tendency to believe in the

young. If America itself is about youth, then the young must have a privileged status. We have trusted teenaged boys to relocate, start families, and found new religions.

Most American women have had a different view, seeing the world around them as an opportunity not for individual self-promotion but for building and maintaining social bonds. Because they have usually felt greater loyalties to family, friends, and community, including the physical locations where all these are found, they have been considerably less enthusiastic about cutting all those ties to move a thousand miles to the frontier. They have preferred, on the whole, to improve the lives they had than to start again from scratch. Yes, some women immigrated here, and many agreed to move around with their husbands, but most moved out of loyalty to their mates rather than to find a fresh start. And many resisted moving. When they balked, their men—more true to new starts than family ties—frequently went without them. Worse, the men wrote them out of their histories and novels, out of their dreams and ideals.

The historian Mary Beard complained in 1933, "As in the case of the original settlements, the westward movement of the population has been, in general histories at least, treated principally in terms of politics, religion, and economics—election brawls, revivals, corn, bacon, and wheat, the 'frontier' conceived in images of Daniel Boone and Davy Crockett—as the untrammeled habitation of rough, uncouth men, and often as if no women were there at all."[6] Following Beard, feminists have made several nested complaints about American history: women were underrepresented in many of the important events and processes of our country; women were there but prevented from having much influence over those events; those women who were there have been ignored in our later understanding and celebrations of that past. All are accurate complaints, if potentially contradictory when pushed to an extreme.

The most striking silence in both *Huckleberry Finn* and the *Narrative of the Life of Frederick Douglass* is about women. Huck Finn flees when he encounters them; he never has sexual longings or romantic interests. This is a standard of American literature, even for grown men. (Cooper's Leatherstocking rejects the "snares" of matrimony on at least two occasions.) It is easier for fictional characters to avoid women, however, than real-life men, who need but often ignore them. Frederick Douglass had a wife, but in the *Narrative* he only mentions her once, briefly. Anna was a free black who helped pay for his ticket north and later supported their family by working as a domestic and making shoes while he was away. Douglass was around for barely two years before he was on the road lecturing full-time, something he would do for the next thirty-five years.

A more complicated version of Huck Finn's dread of women appears in William Faulkner's *Light in August* after Joe Christmas rapes middle-aged spinster Joanna Burden (her name itself a hint). Sex is the only thing Christmas wants from women; otherwise he fears and loathes them. When Joanna comes alive, sexually and spiritually, she becomes a threat. "She has come to talk to me," Joe realizes in a panic one day when she shows up at his cabin, recognizing that conversation is a form of connection. Joe begins "to see himself, as though from a distance, like a man being sucked down into a bottomless morass. . . . I better move. I better get away from here." Language connects people; no doubt this is one reason that women tend to talk more than men, and why male heroes, especially those of Westerns and of authors like Hemingway, are nearly mute. And when Joanna tries to mother Christmas, an orphan, not to mention when she rediscovers religion, they fight and he kills her. Huck at least has the decency simply to flee.

Anna was frequently alone for the births, and in one case the death, of their children. She was shy and illiterate, and seems to have suffered her husband's long absences stoically. But she was deeply unhappy, not least because of her husband's suspiciously close friendships with a series of other women. Most striking of all were his silences about her. In none of his autobiographies did he give her more than a mention, a silence he also applied to his second wife. Women were crucial to his self-creation, but they had no place in his idealized version of it.

Douglass is not alone in rewriting history. In successive published accounts of Daniel Boone's adventures, Boone's patient wife Rebecca was also obliterated; even though she maintained and protected their children during her husband's long absences and helped her husband hunt when rheumatism nearly crippled him, she was rarely even named. In bragging of his exploits, Houdini too erased his wife from the story, unwilling to admit that she slipped him the keys he needed in his most challenging escapes. Even though she was an essential part of his act, he mostly mistreated her.

American men/boys, both fictional and real, tend to flee or ignore the women on whom they depend—perhaps precisely because they are ashamed of that "unmanly" and un-American dependence. Emerson and his fellow male Transcendentalists tried hard to treat women well (Emerson even attempted to persuade his cook to eat with the family), but the women in the group seem to have found them annoyingly driven by distant ideals rather than grounded realities. Margaret Fuller, for instance, "sensed that for all their enthusiasm for practical living, the men failed to grasp social needs with a realism more natural to a woman in ante-bellum society."[7] Emerson did not light out for the territories, but he could seem almost as distant when he withdrew into his own idealistic soul.

Samuel Gompers's wife, Sophia, had to put up with his primary devotion to trade unions. In the aftermath of the failed strike of 1877, Gompers was blackballed by cigar manufacturers. The family finances, already devastated by the strike, showed no signs of improvement. They were subsisting on gruel made from water, salt, pepper, and flour. A fellow worker visited Gompers's wife, carrying an offer of thirty dollars and a job if her husband would cease his union activity. When he returned home, he was stunned to find that his wife had taken the money. "What do you suppose I said to him with one child dying and another coming?," she replied. "Of course I took the money."[8] At that point, Gompers's quixotic unionism had little promise, but Sophia tolerated her husband's primary commitment to his dream.

The world of American restlessness, escape, and movement is a world defined by men. The goals of individual material success and deep inner searching, as well as the means of detachment and flight, are those of the men who have dominated American institutions and ideas throughout its history. They created most of the novels that are remembered, the laws we must obey, and the roads we take.

In addition to being written out of history, women were in fact relatively absent from many of the key places and times when American character was being defined and set into symbols. It is young men, not women, who flock to boomtowns and frontiers. The influence of respectable women, as opposed to prostitutes, would have made boomtowns less violent, brutal, and unhealthy. It's no accident that women's reform movements (like the Woman's Christian Temperance Union) have regularly attacked gambling, drinking, and prostitution, the three big boomtown vices. In 1870 Wyoming became the first state (or, in its case, territory) to give women the right to vote, an easy gesture given how few women lived there, but a recognition of their tempering influence (as well as an effort to attract more of them). Even among those who went west to homestead and farm rather than to pan for gold, men outnumbered women. Many of the settlers left wives and families behind. Some of these men never intended to send for their families; others never got around to it. In many cases, it was the wives who refused to leave their friends and family for the unknown.

Abandonment and separation are old American traditions. When the Virginia Company wrote a pamphlet in 1610 to encourage migration to its badly failing colony, it made abandonment of one's family sound downright noble. Speaking of men who had stayed or were eager to return to the colony, it boasted, "neither the imbracements of their wives, nor indulgence to their babes, nor the neglect of their domesticke fortunes, nor banishment from their native soile, nor any experimented dangers have broken their noble resolution [to settle the new colony]."9 One wonders how effective this unpleasant list could have been in recruiting migrants, unless they were already looking for a way to escape their families. Even those who intended to return home most likely died before they could. The company apparently did not even try to persuade their wives to go along. Of course the pamphlet addressed the fate of one of the few women who had migrated to Jamestown: during a particularly bad period of starvation her husband killed her and was planning, when caught, to eat her. Perhaps the Virginia Company was right to suggest that men leave their wives in England.

Promotional appeals did not change much over the next three hundred years. Most descriptions of the American frontier in the nineteenth century remained poorly disguised public-relations efforts, rarely directed to women. When they did try to appeal to women, they inadvertently revealed women's widespread hesitation to accompany their husbands into the wilderness. One chastised "modern wives, who refuse to follow their husbands abroad [west], alleging the danger of the voyage or journey, or the unhealthiness of the proposed residence, or because the removal will separate them from the pleasures of fashion and society."10 The separation, of course, was not just from fashion but from every friend and family member the wife knew—probably forever. Many a woman was expected to set off with a taciturn man whom she had just married and barely knew and whose sanity she no doubt privately questioned when he proposed venturing to the woods or prairie to live in a windowless cabin out of sight of any neighbor.

Even today, American men do not weigh their families very heavily in decisions to move. In one survey of executives, almost half said that family ties posed no obstacle at all to relocating, and only 8 percent mentioned their wives' careers as possible drawbacks.11 And, after all, if one's wife is not "transportable," she can always be abandoned, along with the kids, like a lame mule. Or she can remain to raise the kids in an unstable arrangement dubbed a commuter marriage. We hardly need research—although there is plenty of it—to show that job relocation strains marriages and families. But surveys like these may reflect men's ideals of themselves as unencumbered cowboys, ready to move at a moment's notice, more than the realities of love (and legal obligation). More men think they are ready to pull up stakes, perhaps, than really are. But plenty are all too ready.

Women have been less absent in actual fact than in the idealized stories later told by men. One reason that men have written women out of their individualistic tales may be that women have so frequently ridiculed the wilder dreams of their menfolk. We can never fully know just how many women found their husbands' restless endeavors preposterous, how many dutiful wives were appalled by their husbands' decisions to risk all their savings on unseen land in Indiana, Wisconsin, or Florida. We do know that large numbers of less dutiful ones stayed behind, either relieved to say farewell to their husbands, or hoping to join them eventually on a homestead, or simply believing that the East was a better place to raise children. Many women have responded to restless men as Jack Kerouac's aunt did to Neal Cassady: "She took one look at [him] and decided that he was a madman." Many women have been happy to see such men ride off into the sunset.

Men often returned the scorn. We can return to *Huckleberry Finn* to see Clemens's view of the culture of nineteenth-century women. They do not come off well. They wield the kind of civilization that Huck finds stifling and unnatural, the world he is fleeing. It is a private, domestic world, rule-bound and moralistic. (Although the women can be quite strong and competent, especially compared to the grossly inept men caricatured in the novel.) It is the women who love Huck, forgive him, understand and sympathize with him. They believe in his goodness and believe they can reform him. His father just whips him. Women reach out to Huck in loving connection—yet he is repulsed. To some extent Clemens is parodying women's culture, especially in the maudlin poetry of the wan young Emily Grangerford, suggesting that he himself had doubts about this form of emotional connection. He shows that this sentimental culture could be abused; even love could be used to control and repress people. But in men's restless vision, any form of connection is dangerous.

Divorce came to America with the Puritans, who as early as 1639 granted occasional divorces for adultery and desertion. From the start—and in contrast to English practice—divorcees were allowed to remarry. This shows the link between divorce and American enthusiasm for starting over: divorces reflected optimism about eventually finding the right spouse, not pessimism about the institution of marriage. It was a simple recognition that people could make mistakes in their choices, requiring freedom to try again. No less a Puritan than John Milton admitted the occasional necessity of divorce in a famous essay of 1643 in which he insisted that a loveless marriage was no marriage at all. The frequency of divorce has risen steadily since 1639, always higher in America than anywhere else.

Boomtown conditions especially encouraged divorce. With men heading (often sneaking) off to new lands, desertion was a grounds for divorce from the start, the most common grounds in most colonies. Massachusetts passed a law in 1695 that allowed petition for divorce once the spouse had been missing without communication for seven years. In Connecticut the wait was even shorter. Needless to say, it was usually the husband who disappeared and the wife who petitioned for divorce. Absent spouses rarely contested divorce proceedings. Americans continued to outdivorce other countries in the nineteenth century. From 1867 to 1907, our divorce rate was 230 times as high as that of Canada, which prided itself on being more conservative on such issues.[12]

Western boomtowns frequently came to be known for their lenient divorce laws: places like Indianapolis, Sioux Falls, Fargo, and Reno. Even southern states, which had resisted official divorce in the colonial period, caved in during these years of great westward expansion. By 1859 there was even a self-help book published, *How to Get a Divorce*. Those starting over in utopian communities regularly divorced their spouses as part of rejecting their old selves. So did Mormon converts. The territory of Utah gained a reputation as a divorce mill due to liberal Mormon policies on divorce. A couple could be divorced the same day they applied, for no other reason than that they both wished it. Brigham Young himself granted more than sixteen hundred divorces. He divorced one polygamous man from three of his wives on a single day.[13] Boomtown culture was only part of the reason for frontier liberalism concerning divorce. As territories became states, they typically adopted divorce laws that were the most liberal in existence anywhere in the world: most encouraging of individual freedoms, market contracts, and so on. Replicating the dynamic found in the settling of America as a whole, the western world's newest institutions were its most individualistic. Despite the increasing ease of divorce in the nineteenth century, it is likely that far more marriages ended by abandonment without the official closure of divorce.

Alongside boomtown pressures were more romantic ones. Few Americans have ever married for reasons of property, and arranged marriages have accordingly been rare. Americans have instead married for love, a less stable basis. Only the two individuals can judge their own hearts, and go their separate ways if love evaporates. When, as a young lawyer, Thomas Jefferson prepared a client's divorce case, he linked divorce to the freedom of contracts, which could not be enforced if neither party favored it. Freedom of the heart, like freedom of worship, depended on individual choice, just like an economic contract. Middle-class notions of a proper spouse changed in the nineteenth century, and new grounds for divorce appeared, including drunkenness, cruelty, gross misbehavior, and "intolerable severity."

Americans continue to out-divorce every other country in the world. (In one extensive United Nations data source the only exception was the tiny Pacific island Republic of Maldives.) Most advanced industrial nations have around ten or twelve divorces per one thousand marriages in a given year, with Scandinavian figures slightly higher. In the United States, on the other hand, the figure is over twenty per thousand. That works out to only 2 percent, but that is 2 percent *every year.* Eventually, 55 percent of American marriages end in divorce, compared to 30 percent of European marriages. (Americans lead the industrial world in a related statistic, which also reflects a form of restlessness: rates of adultery.) Being optimists, though, Americans believe in marriage despite the odds. In thirty years of polls, around 95 percent of Americans have said they would like to marry. And three quarters view marriage as a life-long commitment. But if you start your life over, that commitment apparently no longer holds.

Divorce is related to male fantasy. The willingness to leave one partner depends on a faith that there is a better mate somewhere down the road. Divorce is linked to a romantic belief in true love with a perfectly matched partner. I have said that men are more prone to fantasies than women, and this turns out to be true of romantic fantasies, too. They are more likely than women to say of their partners that "we are perfect for each other," and that they fell in love at first sight. Men are almost three times as likely to say they would not marry someone they did not love, even if that person had all the other desired qualities. They believe in romance and are willing to search until they find it.[14]

Restless men invented most of America's political institutions and laws, the constraints that shape so much of our lives. They also created most of the images of high culture: the "classic" films, the novels and poems read in schools, the paintings that hang in museums. And yet their influence is not what it once was. Women's impact on politics, economics, religion, and culture grew considerably during the last half of the twentieth century. From their own separate culture in the nineteenth century, women began to participate—first as consumers but soon also as producers—in an emerging national culture, including "high" culture. For more than one hundred years they have been entering the paid labor force in greater and greater numbers, gaining considerable economic autonomy as they did so. They attained national voting rights in 1920. With the exception of the famous baby boom after World War II, family size has been shrinking steadily, leaving women more years freed from the time-consuming task of raising small children. Rising divorce rates have offered a freedom that is sometimes soothing, often terrifying. Immigration was a man's world for most of American history, but since the 1930s, when immigration was drastically curtailed, women have equaled men in the ranks of immigrants, surpassing them since the 1950s. Beginning in 1946, after changes in immigration and the fatalities of World War II, women have outnumbered men in the general population of the United States—the mix that other industrial countries have faced for centuries.

In the United States, the 1950s (which culturally lasted until 1965) represented an initial triumph (short-lived) for traditional women's values of connection. Although feminists see the decade as a period in which male elites pushed women out of the workplace and back into domestic roles after World War II, the period's cult of domesticity, family, and stability reflected longstanding preferences on the part of women that had been swamped by male restlessness. For generations, women had been discouraged from working and encouraged to nurture their children and husbands, establishing strong affective bonds. To be realized, their domestic impulses needed the structural support of government policies like the GI Bill and the Servicemen's Readjustment Act. College educations, medical care, low-interest mortgages, and loans to buy farms and businesses were channeled to sixteen million veterans. All these incentives encouraged postwar Americans to settle down, work hard, and raise families. This was one of the least restless decades in American history.

One result of this (relative) surge of domesticity was a cult of childhood. Americans were reminded that children were special, innocent creatures in need of protection and nurturing, and childhood was celebrated as a time free from economic anxieties and strategizing. Like Huck Finn, they could teach the rest of us about goodness and purity. In the shadow of nuclear weapons and the "military-industrial complex," the adult world looked insane. Middle-class kids, heirs to the romantic

An immigrant named Michael Igor Peschkowsky, redubbed Mike Nichols, made Joseph Heller's *Catch-22* into a movie (along with plays like *Barefoot in the Park* and other films, such as *The Graduate*, that helped define the new sensibility of the late 1950s and 1960s). In this novel and movie, the adult world has its perverse logics—of making money through madcap bartering on the one hand, of self-destructive war on the other. Only the insane Yossarian is reasonable, and bureaucratic rules—the Catch-22—prevent anyone from admitting this. Modern institutions are horrid, much more dangerous than the government agents whom Thoreau despised. After all, these lunatics have the Bomb. When the children of the 1950s went to college in the 1960s, their romantic confidence in their own goodness would issue in a range of countercultural practices and sincere efforts to improve the insane world of adults.

tradition of Emerson and Whitman, would create the counterculture of the 1960s, critical of markets and materialism in the name of a deeper restlessness of the soul. From the ties of domesticity came a romantic generation that pursued self-fulfillment, often through movement.

In addition to children, many men also rebelled against the domesticity of the 1950s. There was a moral panic over conformity, amounting to concern that America's "organization men" would form a "mass society" not so different from communism. Psychologist Stanley Milgram, trying to show that Americans were different from the Germans, discovered that Americans too would follow orders, even when it meant administering severe electrical shocks to human subjects. Sociologists like David Riesman fretted that Americans were becoming "other-directed" conformists, unlike the "inner-directed" men who had conquered the frontier. Romantic concern over the autonomous inner self seized hold of the educated middle class. Some of the anxiety, a backlash against domesticity, was that boys were being overmothered, made into weak sissies by their well-intended moms. In the spirit of Emerson, overconformity was seen as a threat to manhood, as other-directed men were too sensitive to the desires and feelings of others. Conformity threatened restlessness, and women were to blame.

For a while, the rebels could value the family as a haven from the pressures of large organizations, but soon the family too came to be seen as oppressive. In what Barbara Ehrenreich calls a "flight from commitment," men began hating and leaving their families. Few men were willing to dump their organization jobs, but they could at least free themselves from their domestic responsibilities. Divorce rates rose dramatically in the early 1960s, with men as likely as women to break loose, following the old dream of a new start. They had always done this, but the numbers increased once again. *Playboy* began publication in 1953, helping to define the joys of "bachelorhood" as heavy consumption of hi-fi systems, blended scotch, sports cars, and large-breasted nymphs. Just as *Look* magazine was celebrating the "togetherness" of the suburban family, many men's inner boys were deciding they just wanted to have fun. Few men could afford the full *Playboy* lifestyle, but many dreamed of it. The beats lived out an extremely peripatetic version of it. There were rear-guard panics over adolescent rebellion and delinquency, although the working-class images of these delinquents (James Dean, Marlon Brando) were surprisingly sexy; but when the real rebellion came it was from the college kids of the upper middle class. The triumph of domesticity had been brief, and the new American dream of the 1960s was to escape from it. Domesticity encouraged romantic rebellion—against the conformity of domesticity.[15]

The 1950s and early 1960s were a low point for immigrants and their influence in the United States. It was easy for the romantic search to expand at the expense of the material search. In part because postwar prosperity benefited so many Americans, their sheltered suburban children could worry about more soulful things. Many native-stock Americans had grandparents or parents who had already achieved the material dream. Like Thoreau, they could look for other things.

None of this is to say that all women are alike, much less that they are all different from men. But women in America still raise most of the children and tend to most of the sick and elderly. They are still the ones who remember to call relatives, who keep track of birthdays and the addresses of friends and relatives. They are still mostly left in charge of emotional connections, leaving their husbands free to dream about moving to California and starting over. Which is exactly what many of their husbands do. Like the men who fled to Carson City when in trouble with the law back east, or those who went to Oklahoma looking for land when they could no longer support their children, men still file for divorce when family obligations become difficult, still run off to start over when they have trouble with their bosses.

Many women have tried to moderate American restlessness, but not all. We should not underestimate the extent to which American women, like their men, have been anxious to make a buck or escape their past. Many accompanied their men west, often out of concern to provide for their children. A few single women even joined in the California and

Yukon gold rushes, aiming to get rich or to find a man who already was. Women can be tough, driven, and restless, even if the general tendency is in the opposite direction.

Despite their differences, American men's and women's visions agree on the paramount importance of personal choice. Women's worlds are still composed of individuals, not structures, even if those individuals are more likely to remain loyal to families or places. The women's movement has tried hard to spread awareness of systematic oppression, but the solution is still for individual women to cast off abusive husbands, bring lawsuits against harassing bosses, and use their anger to free themselves. Individuals are expected to put their lives back in order. In addition the substantial backlash against feminism has been grounded on a denial of structural disadvantage, offering instead a view in which individual women choose to work less or stay at home more (often because of supposed biological instincts).

When American women have chosen to start over, they have been especially prone to do so in groups. Ann Lee's Shakers saw celibacy as a step toward women's liberation and equality. Many nineteenth-century communes experimented with equality for women, and almost any deviation from the normal nuclear family of that century was likely to help women (except polygamy!). This was the way to start over for those who believed in emotional bonds, for entire families—or groups of sisters or friends—could join the new communities. In addition, the communal experiments, while they believed in new starts, also promised real human connection. Few places in American society include this on the agenda.

Women, especially artists imbued with the romantic form of restlessness, are not immune to dreams of starting over as individuals—especially if they can write about it. Novelist Alix Kates Shulman wrote about leaving her busy Manhattan life for a summer alone on an isolated Maine island. In standard romantic fashion she used nature to explore her inner self: "I don't know if I'm more or less in touch with nature than I was before I came to live here, but I'm certainly more in touch with myself." She had a lot to learn—how to whip eggs with a whisk, sweep with a broom, and do without meat—after a life seemingly devoted to consumption and electrical gadgets. (Americans must apparently move to Maine to learn how to use a broom.) Part of her break was an escape from a women's movement which, she said, "exalts community and distrusts all individualists and loners." At times Shulman can sound as juvenile as any man. But in the arena of motherhood, she need not, cannot, play with her identity: "I never have any doubt who I am when my children need me."[16] What is more, Shulman tries to use the island as a starting point for working back out in a more connected way, first to the mainland, especially New York, and eventually, through increased environmental awareness, to the world. By knowing one small place well, she is better able to understand and care about the vast universe. In the tradition of Whitman and Thoreau, it is possible for patient romantics, even if they start as isolated searchers, to connect eventually with others. Parenthood, or at least motherhood, is a giant step in this direction.

Parenthood in its fullest sense is usually associated with a feeling of home: a physical setting identified with family members, a place that feels safe and familiar, stable and secure. It is where we go for holidays or when we are ill or dying. The spatial and the social are fused together. The physical layout of a house or apartment defines public and private boundaries, ties together a family as a unit, tells us where our selves end and others begin. Memories of our childhood home—its layout, and furniture, and yard—are inextricably bound up with recollections of our family and childhood. Physical places, if only in memory, support our other memories. Home is a special place that supports a sense of connection with others.

A feeling of home is not restricted to a building but can expand outward to encompass a neighborhood. In fact one of the most vibrant protest movements of the last thirty years has consisted of Not-In-My-Backyard—NIMBY for short—groups trying to preserve what they see as the integrity or safety of their neighborhoods. Tens of thousands of these groups began to appear in the 1970s, fighting nuclear power plants, hazardous waste dumps, trash incinerators, even public housing projects: anything members believed would change their immediate surroundings for the worse. Because of the decentralized political structure of the United States, they have been remarkably successful at blocking new proposals, often delaying construction projects for years in the courts. Women have been the backbone of this movement.

Mothers tend to care more about family, neighborhood, and other connections because these are important to children and their development, and women still have primary responsibility for this area of life. *Restlessness is bad for children.* Kids need tight bonds, loyalties, patience. The ones who move frequently are more likely to repeat grades and have behavioral problems, less likely to complete high school. Indeed, frequent moving is the strongest single predictor of dropping out of school. Kids slide toward delinquency when constantly torn from hard-won friends. Perhaps because they feel like "outsiders" in their new schools, they are more likely to fall in with "bad" crowds. Their academic achievement is generally lower. Children, it seems, are the primary victims of movement.

Children also suffer from divorce. Foremost is a drop in material comfort, as most children live with their mothers, whose incomes tend to be lower than the fathers', and by definition are lower than the two together. There are also emotional problems in the first year or two. In the longer term, most children adjust, but some continue to show the effects of divorce. Many boys from divorced families continue to be aggressive or delinquent, do worse in school, and report lower levels of overall happiness. Girls seem to adjust more quickly to divorce, but some of them show later problems. After adolescence, a significant proportion of them marry early, get pregnant before marriage, and choose men who are psychologically and economically less stable. Although many additional factors affect how children do, for many the impact of divorce is negative and lasting.

At the political level there is another consequence of America's high divorce rate: large numbers of noncustodial parents, mostly men, who have less interest than they should in issues of children's welfare. They see the effects of taxes on their own incomes, forgetting how important these taxes are for supporting schools, vaccinations, nutrition programs, and many other policies to help children. They easily forget what children need. The result: America has relatively low levels of spending for the young. On top of this, single parents simply have less time for the PTA and other organizations, further reducing political "voice."

But one of the main reasons kids are hurt by divorce has to do with their relocation. Broken families move more often, and more often for involuntary "push" reasons. One of the best studies of divorce and single parenting found that most of the deleterious effects of divorce were due to residential mobility, which was just as important as changes in income.[17] This is the reason that kids who live with a parent and a stepparent after divorce suffer as much as those who live with just a parent.

What do kids lose by moving? A "place" in the local culture, in the pecking order, including friendships which reinforce that place. They are still figuring out how to have their first identity, and are hardly ready to start over with a second. At a more practical level, children's and parents' networks channel information about all sorts of opportunities—about which teachers, coaches, and counselors are better; about after-school programs, sports activities, or libraries. If nothing else, being the new kid on the block can be distracting, nerve-wracking, or even terrifying.

These social networks are especially important for poor Americans, because they can substitute for money. If you can't afford child care, you can park the kids with an aunt or grandmother. If you've just lost your apartment, someone will take you in for a few months. Out of work? You can borrow someone's car to go to a job interview. Relatives and even friends will help out with extra food, hand-me-down clothes, even a small loan. Poor people can get along by pooling their meager resources. Meals and beds are for sharing.

Everyone loses the benefits of social bonds when they move, but most adults rebuild these more easily than children do. Those who care for children—still overwhelmingly women in American society—see these effects and try to repair the damage. This is the biggest reason that, even today, women tend to be less restless.

Despite the pull of their dreams, most Americans still have some hidden psychological need for community and connection, and place is important as a means of providing these. Some attachment to place may be a universal human need, but it seems to vary a lot by gender. Throughout our history, women have usually missed community the most and tried to sustain it when they could. For some of them, this meant separation from restless husbands. And when they went, they tried to establish connections with friends and neighbors, tried to domesticate the land as a habitat, tried to maintain some connection to their previous lives. They have tempered some of the worst aspects of restlessness.

Women's culture is not the only alternative in American history. Most Native Americans have retained a traditional sense of connection to their land and to the future generations who will inherit it. African Americans, forced to live separate, marked lives for four hundred years, are more likely to feel part of a binding community; when they pursue their version of American restlessness, they choose cities with African American communities and networks of relatives to welcome them. (Blacks and Indians did not come to America through voluntary immigration, and mainstream culture has punished them for this ever since.) Such countertraditions should certainly be celebrated and nurtured in order to sooth American restlessness. But it is women's tastes, preferences, and habits which have, perhaps along with environmentalism, the greatest potential as a balm for our motion sickness. Women's traditions appeal to a sense of place, community, and family that most Americans share but have usually repressed as an interference with their movement. It is no wonder restless men fear women.

The traditional activities of motherhood have left women and their culture with a sense of human connection that has resisted many of the temptations of restlessness. What is more, a concern for the next generation has often led to a concern for unknown future generations, which easily slides into a concern for unknown others of all—or at least many—kinds. In the resulting visions, humans are no longer disconnected individuals capable of walking away from everything and everyone they know; instead they are part of a place and a social network that help define who they are. Some forms of romantic restlessness, when pushed to their logical extreme, also point to connection as the source of people's final fulfillment.

A final literary example, the grim landscapes of Wallace Stegner's *The Big Rock Candy Mountain,* shows how a deep nostalgia for family and place occasionally works against restlessness. The title is taken from a folk song celebrating the dreams of the common man (the author of which, Harry MacClintock, also wrote "Hallelulah, I'm a Bum," an even greater celebration of restlessness.) Late in the novel the son, Bruce Mason, who has escaped East for college, is going home after his June exams. "Ahead of him was the long road, the continental sprawling hugeness of America, the fields and farmhouses, the towns." There follows a listing of towns, ranges, and roads, poetically Whitmanesque in the way they sweep along. "It was a grand country, a country to lift the blood, and he was going home across its wind-kissed miles with the sun on him and the cornfields steaming under the first summer heat and the first bugs immolating themselves against his windshield." The fecund vastness that had appealed to the dreaming explorers four hundred years before still attracts this young man, driving alone. But there is a problem at the center of Bruce's excitement: "But going home where? he said. Where do I belong in this?" He considers the possibilities: places he has lived, where he was born, even where his parents' ancestors were from, "in some Pennsylvania valley, where the roots first went down in this country, [or] where the first great or great-great grandfather broke loose from his Amish fireside and started moving rootless around the continent."

The glory of the open road does not entirely satisfy Bruce, and he concocts a nostalgic image of what home is: it is where your family lives, the place associated with your childhood memories, the place you have buried your dead, as well as "the last sanctuary where you can kill yourself in peace." He envies those for whom all these are the same place, who have lived in the same town all their lives. (His father, half child and half man and prone to violence, was particularly restless, seeking his fortune in the hotel business, in new farmland, and finally in rum-running during Prohibition, all the time dragging his wife and two sons from state to state.) Bruce's homelessness gnaws at the excitement he gets from "the smell of the burning oil in the motor like a promise of progress to his nostrils." He would like to "belong to a clan, to a tight group of people allied by blood and loyalties and the mutual ownership of closeted skeletons. . . . To have that rush of sentimental loyalty at the sound of a name, to love and know a single place, from the newest baby-squall on the street to the blunt cuneiform of the burial ground . . . " Family, place, and memories would be woven together in mutual support. "I wish, he said, that I were going home to a place where all the associations of twenty-two years were collected together. I wish I could go out in the back yard and see the mounded ruins of caves I dug when I was eight." He wishes he had had boyhood adventures like Tom Sawyer's and Huck Finn's, except less peripatetic.

Nostalgic doubts like these do not last long in a young man, however. "Was he going home, or just to another place? It wasn't clear. Yet he felt good, settling his bare arm gingerly on the hot door and opening his mouth to sing." American men don't have much time to ponder what they are missing. Because Bruce still has restless dreams: "Why remain in one dull plot of earth when Heaven was reachable, was touchable, was just over there?" In fact, Bruce is heading to Nevada, where his father has gone for the gambling, pure symbol of the lottery of the American dream. "It was easy to see why men had moved westward as inevitably as the roulette-ball of a sun had rolled that way. What if the ball settled in the black, on the odd, on number 64? There were so many chances, such lovely possibilities. And if you missed on the first spin you could double and try again, and keep on doubling until you hit. . . . Oh lovely America, he said, you pulled the old trick on us again." The American dream had not come true for his parents, but maybe it would for him. For most men, home, place, and family fade in the bright light of dreams like these.

The world looks different when families are your starting point. Many feminists have asked what American society would look like if our root image of society were not a market but a family: if, instead of disconnected individuals who come together to pursue their own interests, our imagination began with a group tied together by love and a sense of common interests. You are born into your family—"stuck with them," rootless males would say. Most other institutions you join voluntarily, or think you do, including your society and government. You could always emigrate, after all. But the family is different. Your parents care for you because they love you and because you cannot care for yourself, not because you have hired them to do it. The family is one of the few social institutions that recognize interdependence rather than demanding individual autonomy. It is based on primordial loyalties not freely or consciously chosen. If we thought of society as a family, saw the emotional connections between its members more clearly, we might be more eager to help those at the bottom, to restrict markets, to protect nature.

Since the late twentieth century, the biggest challenges to restlessness have come from women, whose influence has grown enormously. They have been aided by a new ecology movement devoted to reverence for nature and place, as well as by a resurgent romantic tradition which can sometimes lead to connection as well as to flight. In fact, it is the romantic generation and the counterculture it created that have encouraged a certain amount of fusion between environmentalism and feminism based on a sense of loyalty to place and to other beings. The explosion of movements for peace, against nuclear energy, and for animal protection are just a few of the results of this new synthesis. Of all the recent moderations of traditional restlessness, this may prove in the long run to be the most important.

It does not matter why women and men tend to feel and act differently, why men are so often frightened of women or women exasperated with men. The two influence each other enormously. There are so many men and women who go against type—men who are caring and connected, women who are restless and autonomous—that any talk of innate, inevitable differences is suspect from the start. What is more, differences between men and women have changed enormously over time. Whatever the reason, American women have developed a sensibility that, despite its own flaws, is suspicious of too much restless motion and starting over. It makes explicit what most Americans, male and female, feel intuitively: that we are missing something in moving about so often, that the obligations of place and community can be a pleasure, not just a burden, that we belong to the land as much as it belongs to us.

Are Americans Ready to Settle Down?

Tell me a story.

In this century, and moment, of mania,
Tell me a story.

Make it a story of great distances, and starlight.

The name of the story will be Time,
But you must not pronounce its name.

Tell me a story of deep delight.
—*Robert Penn Warren, "Audubon"*

The only political vision that offers any hope of salvation is one
based on an understanding of, a rootedness in, a deep commitment
to, and a resacralization of, *place.*
—*Kirkpatrick Sale*

Of all the Americans we have looked at, the one who best knew a
place was Henry David Thoreau. But his closest contender,
surprisingly, was Sam Clemens, who in his years as a riverboat pilot had
to learn every sandbar, snag, and shoal in the five hundred miles of the
Mississippi between St. Louis and New Orleans. "There's only one way
to be a pilot, and that is to get this entire river by heart." They know the
place best who travel ceaselessly along it—and who have a practical financial stake in knowing it well. Clemens thought he had lost something in gaining such detailed knowledge: the ability to put the details
back together. In contrast to Thoreau, whose aesthetic appreciation of
Concord seemed to grow the more deeply he knew it, Clemens had lost
the ability to enjoy a simple sunset over the river. Before, when he saw a

sunset, "I drank it in, in a speechless rapture." Now that simple aesthetic appreciation was gone; he "looked upon it without rapture, and
should have commented upon it, inwardly, after this fashion: 'This sun
means that we are going to have wind to-morrow; that floating log
means that the river is rising, small thanks to it; that slanting mark on
the water refers to a bluff reed which is going to kill somebody's steamboat one of these nights, if it keeps on stretching out like that; those
tumbling "boils" show a dissolving bar and a changing channel there.'"
In the end, "The romance and beauty were all gone from the river. All
the value any feature of it had for me now was the amount of usefulness
it could furnish toward compassing the safe piloting of a steamboat."[1]
The Americans who take careful note of place usually have an ulterior
motive for doing so. For river pilots, as for mining geologists or survey-
ors, familiarity with nature is a means to an end.

Few Americans feel tied to their geographic location, and those who
do often seem old-fashioned or misguided to the rest of us: the farmer resisting the encroachment of the suburbs, members of inner-city gangs
whose territoriality makes them loyal to their 'hood, the old lady who has
lived in the same peeling house all her life. The educated, the powerful,
the energetic Americans, those with a future, are ready to move in pursuit
of that future. They wonder why the rooted ones don't exclaim, "I've got
to get out of here and make something of myself." Millions of immigrants
worldwide are ready to risk everything they have for a chance to come
here and do just that, and millions of native-born Americans move and
start over each year. This is the modern dream, a utopia in which individuals control their destinies. Around the world, it is a powerful ideal.

Market opportunities for restless individuals have had enormous
benefits, as the story of America has been one "of great distances, and
starlight." In pursuing their own dreams, immigrants and their descendants have created jobs, inventions, and new ways of doing (and seeing)
things. It is hard not to admire the powerful and flexible economy they
have created. Huge material rewards have come from all that hard work
and willingness to exploit our natural resources. As long as there is severe inequality across nations, there will be immigrants happy to come
to the United States. They can work for wages which by American standards are very low and still make more money than they did back home.
Economically, everyone benefits—except for those native-born at the
bottom of the hierarchy whose wages are suppressed by the great supply of immigrant labor.

This is only one of the costs of our restlessness. Americans have little
respect for institutions, especially government, and so rarely work to

improve them. As long as we see and use politics as a way to enrich ourselves, it will remain a dirty word. Our ideals, Ben Franklin's influence notwithstanding, tend to revolve around private accomplishments. Constant striving for material success leaves us with deep anxiety about how we are doing. As long as we identify with those above us, we will ignore—even punish—those below us and those left behind as we move and move again. If we aren't moving up, we feel we are falling behind. And we ourselves are often caught in a trap, for the promise of moving, of starting over, is rarely fulfilled. It is exciting, even intoxicating, when one is young. As one ages, fresh starts become less plausible. The disappointments and self-blame that set in may outweigh the excitement that the dream once provided. And by the time we give up on fresh starts, we may not have put down deep enough roots to help us much in our old age. Further, with our faith in starting over, we will never develop a comprehensive view of the world that sees structural constraints as well as individual choices, and thus we will never see most of the forces shaping our lives. If we don't see them, we can't work to change them. Our very faith in individual autonomy blinds us to many of the constraints on it.

There will always be structures shaping our incentives and our movement. Inequality guarantees that it is easier for those who start off near the top to end up there. Our schooling system, while it has an appearance of merit, in fact tracks people from an early age, encouraging aspirations in line with their backgrounds. Our tax system does little to redress these imbalances. The rich and the poor are both important moral symbols to Americans, whose dreams and nightmares revolve around them. More specific forms of inequality, especially racism and sexism, further skew Americans' life chances, favoring some while hurting others. Because we refuse to see structures like these, shaping how Americans do in the great lottery, we can never force our system to live up to our own ideals. The biggest cost of restlessness is that it both hides and eats away at communal obligations.

Other structures encourage everyone to keep moving, whatever their chances in the lottery. Policies of the Federal Housing Administration guarantee mortgages for buying a new home, not renovating an existing one. To derive full tax benefits from home ownership, an American needs to move before the mortgage is paid off. Legally, it is as easy to get divorced as it is to get married. There are no legal constraints and in fact some benefits to changing your name or starting your own religion. Federal land policy nearly gives away many of the resources on our national lands, encouraging continued hyper-exploitation. Congress still loves big highway construction projects and hates gasoline taxes. Corporations still expect executives to move when asked, and moving expenses can be written off. Specialization is so extreme in many professions that one *must* search nationally in order to find a job. The military expects its officers to transfer to new places every year or two, as the best way for them to accumulate skills and experience. Corporate and government policies like these could be changed—if Americans paid enough attention to them to agitate for change.

Our culture offers other incentives for movement. A prestigious college education is something you must go away for, not go down the street for. Artistic expression, we feel, requires rejection and escape from our old selves, just as religious fulfillment often demands a new start in a new sect. Who brags to friends about staying home to read novels during vacations, rather than seeing the masterpieces of the Louvre? Will acquaintances describe us as "interesting" if we stay put all our lives? If all our friends leave home for college or retire to Florida, why should we stay behind? In our culture, every major life event, especially for the middle class, is an excuse to move: college, marriage, new children, new jobs, retirement, and of course divorce. Cultural pressures are hard to change, but we already have a number of alternative traditions and impulses more sympathetic to place and community— women's culture foremost among them.

There may be universal human impulses to be loyal to a place and yet also to see what is beyond that place. Many cultures have recognized the importance of travel as a form of education and self-improvement. Epics like the *Odyssey* or early novels like *Tom Jones* are about travel, and a number of religious traditions recommend occasional pilgrimages to important shrines. But in most of these cases, the goal is to return home, recount one's adventures, and incorporate new wisdom into one's old life. Home is never doubted, and the tension of these tales comes from the contrast between the new places and the old. Only in chivalric romance did the journey become an eagerly sought way of testing oneself, and only in the modern novel do people end up different, and in a different place, at the end—especially in American literary traditions.

National character has limits as a way of explaining a country's politics and policies. None of it is shared by absolutely everyone. A few critics or eccentrics accept none of it; a larger number, only portions. But certain ideas, impulses, and images recur so frequently that they must be widely held, reinforced by self-selection. Immigrants who believe in traditional forms of the American dream come here; others go elsewhere. Those who aren't restless stay home. The United States has a number of cultural cleavages and conflicts, today as in the past, but vast areas of agreement exist among the disagreements. Critics of traditional ideas of American success abound, for instance, but most take a romantic form of escape rather than a grounded approach of political change. The religious right may criticize humanists, but they are just as individualistic as their targets. Our economy and polity are set up to reward those who believe in the traditional dream and punish those who resist. So most follow along, at least acting as though they believe, whether or not they do. I have tried to show that many of the exceptions to American visions—communes, romantic artists, religious sects—are only partial exceptions.

Even if all Americans believed and sought the same things, though, the preferences of individual citizens are not the only (sometimes not even the main) determinant of what government actually does. In the United States, politicians spend so much time raising funds that corporations and trade groups (and some individuals) with lots of money have a grossly disproportionate influence—as most Americans know. Money helps win elections, but it has even more effect after the election is over. Politicians may appeal to the restless individualism of Americans when they need to win votes, but they usually listen to the more organized, attentive interests when they actually make policy choices. A majority of citizens might wish to curtail immigration, for instance, but too many American businesses depend on the cheap labor of new arrivals for that to happen. Most Americans, when they vote, do so on the basis of emotional symbols; after the election they ignore what government does. We already expect it to be irrelevant or evil.

═══

A sense of roots is the obvious antidote to restlessness. Americans tend to think of roots as family connections, and you can take your family with you when you go—even though many men do not. But roots also involve a sense of a place where one is "rooted," in a soil that nurtures us, as well as an associated sense of community broader than just our family. Our physical surroundings help define who we are, broadcast that definition to others, and support our daily routines. To have a place is to know who we are, for we define ourselves by our position on some (mental and physical) map of the world. Americans do care about their places: they protest against proposed incursions and invest time and money in reshaping their surroundings. They want a yard with a lawn, a few trees and shrubs. They feel betrayed when their city's baseball team moves away. They have sacred places like Niagara Falls and the Gettysburg battlefield. They take pride in their neighborhoods, regions, and country.

Americans nonetheless try to define their identity by their lack of place: we see ourselves as people who are ready to move anywhere to take advantage of new opportunities. For us the road itself is a place, in fact our favorite place. As the philosopher Susanne Langer once wrote, "Nomadic cultures, or a cultural phenomenon like the seafaring life, do not inscribe themselves on any fixed place on earth. Yet a ship, constantly changing its location, is none the less a self-contained place, and so is a Gypsy camp, an Indian camp, or a circus camp, however often it shifts its geodetic bearings. Literally we say the camp is *in* a place; culturally it *is* a place."[2] Roadsides, boomtowns, and riverboats are all places where Americans feel at home, constructing a sense of identity built around movement rather than place. We miss out on the satisfaction of attachment to fixed places, a unique pleasure like that of winning an Olympic medal or having a child. We can still be whole human beings without one of those experiences. We are missing something, but something we can live without. At least if we want to live without it. Young men often seem happy roaming about. But for those who would like to settle into a place, yet who are dragged away by employers or spouses, there can be considerable suffering.

Rootedness is part of a broader sense of limits, which Americans have hidden under all their motion and anxiety. To the extent that we are attached to a place—or to a family, an institution, a job—we limit our ability to move, retool our occupations, recreate our selves. Attitudes like these vary by social class, with more options for those higher up. For the college-educated upper middle class, movement remains an opportunity, full of potential. Movement is more frequently forced on the lower classes, who must follow the jobs just to stay out of poverty. As a result, the poor and working classes have a greater sense of their own limits and of human limits more generally. They would often be happy to remain in a community of family and friends, a network of people to help them through tough times. They have more trepidations when they move, for things may turn out badly in the next town or city.

Restlessness is not the whole of American history, and women are hardly the only ones to resist it. Recurrent nostalgia for a past time, when community bonds were stronger, is one way that loyalty to place surreptitiously surfaces in American culture: the fields and farms of yesteryear supported, we imagine, stronger connections to place and people. Those who were not voluntary immigrants, notably Native Americans and African Americans, have often felt stronger bonds of obligations and a sense of group boundaries. Certain religious groups have attained some measure of group feeling, however briefly. A number of working-class organizations, especially in the nineteenth century, pursued collective resistance and alternatives to markets. And of course there are environmentalists who, like Kirkpatrick Sale, see our salvation in loyalty to place. Many have resisted or been ambivalent about the motion of market society. I hope to tell their story in a sequel, *Yearning for Connection.*

If most Americans, especially men, reject their roots and rootedness, how could we change their attitudes and habits? Must we close off immigration, or engage in a headlong assault on the American dream? If inequality results from our restlessness, our occasional political efforts to reduce inequality can never have much effect. Only by becoming aware of the structures that encourage restlessness and their social costs can we begin to challenge them. Then we might ask ourselves, How much immigration, and what kind? How much relocation, and for what purposes? For starters, a number of minor policies and incentives could be revised. FHA policies could make it easier to renovate old houses. Job assignments could be rethought, with fewer moves expected. There could be more rewards for stability and loyalty. Corporations could be constrained somewhat in their movement of capital, since many Americans who move are simply following the migration of jobs.

If nothing else, some distance from our traditional myths might help: Americans could realize that individual upward mobility is difficult and rare, so that they would not necessarily expect it or blame themselves for not attaining it. Stronger trade unions might also lead to a livelier working-class culture and pride, as well as higher wages, counteracting some of the effects of immigration. If fewer Americans expected to move up, they might demand more from their position in the economic hierarchy. Like all humans, Americans respond to the incentives they face. We tend to deny their existence, or at least to insist they are not fixed "structures," but they shape our behavior even more because we don't see them clearly.

Ecologists such as Wendell Berry see family farming as the solution to modern placelessness, but how realistic is this? Yes, the idea of tending the same plot of land across the generations may engender deep loyalties, but this seems to me a nostalgic vision of place. Can we not feel loyalty to a place without farming it? Cities too have seasons and weather and a characteristic "feel" to them. Can't they nurture us too? Can't we value a place for its energy and life rather than its peace and quiet? For its architecture rather than its fields? Can't loyalty to Greenwich Village run as deep as loyalty to Greenwich, Connecticut? Americans have diverse tastes in place, and could settle in many different types of habitat.

There are risks to localism, including a hatred of outsiders. The promise of modern movement has been to broaden our horizons, to teach us how others live and encourage tolerance for those who are different. But in the electronic age, is movement necessary for that kind of education? We watch documentaries on penguins and peasants we will never meet. Even if some new starts are fun, adventurous, or necessary, it might still be possible to settle down afterward, especially if you can choose the place you feel most comfortable. Perhaps it is never too late to give up a migratory life and put down roots. In fact, many of the NIMBY activists mentioned in chapter 8 defend their neighborhoods so fiercely precisely because they have moved there from elsewhere, choosing the kind of place they most wanted to live. Choice does not preclude eventual loyalty.

Academics are notoriously rootless, beginning with college and graduate school but often continuing later, as the most successful are happy to move from one university to another, every few years, in pursuit of higher salaries and prestige. As a result, perhaps, they have spun elaborate theories about the importance of meritocracy (from which they think they benefit), but few about the benefits of staying put. They would claim that their real community is that of colleagues scattered across the globe, but of course that is part of the problem. Even when they are not switching jobs, they trot the globe from one conference to another rather than staying home and tending their gardens. Their ideal is the cosmopolitan equally at home in Chicago or Frankfurt; but is this person really at home anywhere? Ever since academics took over American intellectual life in the 1950s and 1960s, they have suppressed any voices arguing for allegiance to place. It is not open to debate.

The dream of escape will always be there to undermine our sense of place. It is, after all, an exciting ideal. It is the dream of modernity, of self-actualized individuals unconstrained by their pasts, or by place, with their lives shaped only by their own choices. Only an authoritarian regime could enforce total stasis. But there could be a balance between movement and place, a sense of the trade-offs, a feeling that there is at least a dilemma here. A good life could have *a period of searching, then a period of settling in.* (Many Americans do this, without admitting that they are settling in, continuing to dream of moves they will never make.)

Loyalty to place is no panacea for America's problems or challenges, only the mildest starting point. The ultimate step would be to rebuild the senses of politics and community that have been casualties of restlessness. Place loyalty is compatible with every sort of intolerance, else the American dream of movement would never have had the appeal it did. But we are unlikely to develop a sense of community without more allegiance to place. Of course other elements influence our acceptance of inequality and contempt for the poor, especially our tendency to see the economy and politics through a moralizing lens, but these are also linked to restlessness. Restlessness makes Americans anxious and fearful, and this makes them lash out at others, perceiving evil influence at home and abroad. Curbing restlessness would be a start at curbing anxiety about economic success. Only a start, but an important start.

As we have seen in most chapters, a number of recent trends promise to ease our historical restlessness. Although immigration has increased again in the last thirty years, more women and more professionals are among the new arrivals. Women are motivated partly by a desire to rejoin other family members. Professionals such as lawyers and doctors, once they find appropriate jobs, need not move as frequently in search of new opportunities; their movement tends to come at earlier ages when they go to college and graduate school, not later. Part of their economic power comes from their personal reputations, which grow when they stay in the same place. Once they find a place they like, they will probably stay there, following the search-then-settle pattern.

Economic changes may also work against migration. More women than ever before have jobs and careers, and they are less willing to follow transferred husbands. A few employers, universities foremost among them, are beginning to see the advantages of hiring both wife and husband, a form of collegiality that makes them less likely to move. Gone are the days when a family automatically followed the husband's peripatetic career. Divorce and commuter marriages still undermine the stabilizing effects of marriage, but not entirely.

Another hopeful trend is the nature of work itself. Although still small, an increasing proportion of the work force can work at home, attached to offices electronically; they may not need to move when their company headquarters do. In addition, fewer fortunes are to be had these days from ransacking nature. To get rich you need to perceive a new consumer need, or have a particular skill that people will pay to watch. Some of these entertainment jobs may keep you moving (during the basketball season, for instance, or on musical tours), but ironically a job in motion may allow you to have a stable home. You can have a home that makes up for your other movement. A "postindustrial" society, in which more and more people deal with symbols and knowledge, also stresses self-fulfillment, which—in the tradition of Thoreau—may entail the pleasures of place.

One reason for breakthroughs like those of electronics is that communications and transportation have been split apart. Two hundred years ago letters traveled on the same boats that passengers did, and later on the same trains. Only with telegraphy was it possible to communicate with people more rapidly than to visit them. Further means for doing this, from the telephone to the Internet, have made communications infinitely easier. A message that used to require a boat or train now needs only light waves. Humans cannot themselves travel at the speed of light—only their words and signals can. Today there are faster—and more profitable—ways to conduct business than moving about.

Although it has not improved as fast as communication, transportation has also grown easier, so that it is now possible to visit a place before deciding to move there. How many immigrants have found themselves in America only to regret it almost immediately? How many homesteaders bought the official publicity about arid North Dakota, only to realize their mistake once there? Even fifty years ago, how many young men and women went off to distant colleges they had never seen? Such errors can be avoided more easily today. Not everyone can afford to reconnoiter first, but more can than ever before.

Figurative boomtowns depend less on migration than literal ones do. The point of the latter is to go in, build the bridge, mine the gold, knock down the trees, then move on: in and out as fast as possible. Cities may feel like transient boomtowns, but they need not require the movement that literal boomtowns do. Our modern economy has shifted away from industries that extract resources from the earth, first to manufacturing industries that transform many of those raw materials and finally to industries that process information and symbols rather than steel and coal. In the first case, people must go where the resources are. In the second, the materials are brought to factories, but jobs are concentrated together, and people need to move to where the jobs are. In the last case, freed from physical materials, many jobs can be done anywhere. Most people in these symbolic industries still need to get together to coordinate their activities, but the places where they do that are not determined by huge capital investments. On the one hand, this frees Americans even more from a sense of place. On the other, their economic success may depend less on frequent moves, allowing them to develop a sense of place on other grounds, such as family ties or quality of life.

Restless motion has become less important to the functioning of our economy than it once was, but we still have rules and cultural images that celebrate and expect it. We cling to those images in thinking about who we are, even if they no longer help us attain our dreams. But eventually, they too can change. We need to rethink restlessness. Let me end with a few suggestions toward that end.

A VITAL FLOW

Since immigrants have made the United States what it is, those who admire our character can hardly advocate killing the golden-egg-laying goose. Most ironic are the conservatives who would restrict immigration, apparently not recognizing the greatest force for individualism, and hence usually conservatism, in American history. The most successful immigrants have made stunning contributions to our economy and culture. Even less successful ones have worked hard and contributed to economic growth. Few seem to regret their decisions to move here, and although some psychological denial may be at work among unsuccessful ones, we can assume that most are better off here. Most native-born Americans are better off because of them. Before we change immigration policies, we should be clear about the full effects that might have.

A LITTLE GRATITUDE

Americans should be grateful to immigrants for fostering the economic vibrancy they have enjoyed for so long, as well as for providing some of the most memorable Americans. But they need gratitude to more than just the immigrants who have made it big, the Astors and the Carnegies. More than ever, the lives of today's upper middle class depend on the availability of poorly paid immigrants who clean their homes, cook their meals, and tend their children. Immigrants nurse our failing grandparents through their final years. The Clinton administration made an admirable effort to appoint women, but in doing so it showed just how dependent on cheap immigrant labor affluent Americans are today. The careers of many women, especially, have been built on this labor. Many Americans today make so much money they cannot afford to take the time to scrub their own toilets, or even raise their own kids. What would happen if immigrants were not there to do it? Finally, the children of the upper middle class are free to pursue romantic self-fulfillment in greater numbers than ever before because of the hard work of newcomers. Rather than demanding fulfilling careers as our birthright, we should be aware of the economic hierarchy that makes them possible.

COMPASSION FOR THE BOTTOM

In such an unequal society as ours, the top inevitably feeds off the bottom. Our society has too many poor people, most of whom are not immigrants and are not working their way upward. The enormous disruption of moving is not normal, and poor people should not be unduly punished for loyalty to family, friends, and place. Immigrants contribute a lot to American economic growth and eventually benefit from that growth themselves. But many other Americans do not. Poor Americans, disproportionately African Americans, are usually hurt. If immigration makes the country as a whole wealthier, we should use some of that wealth to help groups that, time and again, have been hurt by cheap immigrant labor. This is an issue of sheer human decency.

APPRECIATION FOR CONNECTION

We can ignore and hide but never finally abolish our ties to places and people. We can derive more satisfaction from those connections if we recognize and nurture them, seeing them as pleasures to cultivate rather than a snare to trap us. After all, some of the greatest pleasure-seekers in American history, Whitman and Thoreau, found their deepest satisfaction in connection. If our vision of the world shifted from individuals in markets to connections among people, we would better understand problems like poverty and crime and racism. And we would feel an obligation to deal with them.

A SENSE OF PLACE

Some of the worst effects of our immigrant culture are evident in our attitudes toward the environment. A deeper appreciation of one place, where we live, usually leads to respect for other places, other habitats.

The women of the frontier were right: this is not simply a resource to use up, but also the place where we make our lives. Although the environmental movement has educated many of us about the damage we have done, there is far more to do to protect our habitats. Our own health continues to be undermined by toxins in our air, water, and soil; our pleasures are limited by the disappearance of woods and wilderness. Even as individuals, we are losing a lot due to our boomtown attitudes. Unfortunately, real environmental protection will require government intervention.

MORE VOICE, LESS EXIT

Mistrust for large organizations is always healthy. But Americans need to use that mistrust to try to control government more, instead of ignoring, denying, or trying to flee it. Government is no longer an alien imposition, as it was under George III. It exhibits who we are as a people. This is why it reflects and encourages both restlessness and inequality. We can never fully flee it, as right-wing survivalists have discovered. Better to face it head on, trying to modify it in small, and sometimes large, ways. No, we will never fully control it, both because it is a large bureaucracy and because money rules. But we will control it even less if we never try. Sometimes it is better to stay and fight than to flee.

INCENTIVES FOR STAYING PUT

The American government, like all governments, intervenes in markets in all sorts of ways, encouraging us to act in certain ways but not others. Thousands of tax subsidies and penalties, for instance, shape our choices. Among these could be rewards for stability. For instance, rent-control laws in many cities have had the effect of discouraging moving, but they were unfortunately usually tied to the property rather than the tenant, so that a new tenant could demand the same low rents. Instead, regulations could allow newcomers to be charged market rates, but then control subsequent increases: the longer you stayed in a place, the smaller would be your rent increases. For homeowners, a similar system could decrease property taxes the longer you owned (and lived in) your home. Most states already have something similar: tax breaks for those who keep their land open and undeveloped. No one will ever stop Americans' anxious movement, but there is no reason to encourage or subsidize it, and good reason to discourage it.

SEARCH THEN SETTLE

Some movement is healthy, especially if it means finding the kind of place one most wants to live. Some people prefer cities; others prefer the suburbs. Some prefer California; others, New England. Let Americans travel about when they are young, as young people do anyway, and settle somewhere new if they wish. Then let them settle into their new homes, learning about the region, exploring the neighborhood, developing friends among their neighbors. Hopefully, they will learn to like their location, and develop loyalties to it.

SETTLING DOWN MEANS GROWING UP

Americans are older than they once were, and restless movement is a young man's game. Facing our responsibilities to people and places is an act of maturity. Men may continue to fantasize, but let's encourage them to fulfil their obligations. Changes in child-support policies, the Child Support Enforcement Act of 1984 and the Family Support Act of 1988, are forcing men to pay their due. But this is only a small first step toward recognition that, as adults, we have connections and obligations to the world around us.

AMERICAN IDEALS

The United States has some moving ideals. We should try to live up to them. If we claim to believe in the meritocracy of markets, we should enact policies to encourage it. We should try to remove barriers facing poor Americans, African Americans, women, or new immigrants. Make the lottery fair. If we believe that individuals should control their own lives, we should let them do that—as long as they do not interfere with *other* people's autonomy or the resources of future generations. Rather than letting them strip-mine nature, let them read, ingest, and dress as they wish. Let them surf the Internet rather than cruise the highways. In its consequences for others, libertarianism in culture is better than in the economy.

These are hard, not easy, solutions. They are my own utopian vision, my own American dream. But like most Americans, I believe that my vision would be good for others.

SUGGESTIONS FOR FURTHER READING

Extensive literatures exist on many of the issues raised in *Restless Nation*. In the following I have tried to select books for readability, availability, and a general rather than academic interest. (Publisher and date are given briefly in parentheses; a school, state, or city name alone indicates a university press.) Most books on American character, including my own, are little more than a gloss on Alexis de Tocqueville's *Democracy in America*, available in several editions. It is a good starting point for any reader.

The earliest European efforts to figure out what America meant have received considerable attention lately, partly due to multicultural interest in what it was like to be at the "receiving" end of the great explorations. Tzvetan Todorov examines the bafflement in *The Conquest of America* (Oklahoma, 1999). Jack Greene shows how the new world became the land of dreams in *The Intellectual Construction of America* (North Carolina, 1993). Eviatar Zerubavel looks at European efforts to map the new continents in *Terra Cognita* (Rutgers, 1992). Charles Nicholl not only recounts but retraces Walter Raleigh's 1595 expedition in *The Creature in the Map* (Chicago, 1995).

As political debates over immigration have reappeared, so have books on the subject. Some of the best are Alejandro Portes and Rubén Rumbaut, *Immigrant America* (California, 1996); Sanford Ungar, *Fresh Blood* (Simon and Schuster, 1995); Sarah Mahler, *American Dreaming* (Princeton, 1995); and Mary Waters, *Black Identities* (Harvard, 2000). Among readable historical works are David Cressy, *Coming Over* (Cambridge, 1987); Alison Games, *Migration and the Origins of the English Atlantic World* (Harvard, 1999); David Hackett Fischer, *Albion's Seed* (Oxford, 1989); Bernard Bailyn, *Voyagers to the West* (Knopf, 1986); Roger Daniels, *Coming to America* (HarperCollins, 1990); and Ronald Takaki, *Iron Cages* (Oxford, 1990), and *A Different Mirror* (Little, Brown,

1993). Mark Wyman looks at the immigrants who *really* saw the United States as a temporary abode, namely those who returned home in the period around the turn of the nineteenth century, in *Round-Trip to America* (Cornell, 1993).

Two recent arguments against immigration appear in Roy Beck, *The Case Against Immigration* (Norton, 1996), and Chilton Williamson Jr., *The Immigration Mystique* (Basic Books, 1996). Both ignore contrary evidence, but Beck is persuasive about the adverse effects of immigration on African Americans; Williamson, arguing that today's immigrants undermine core American values, takes a view diametrically opposed to my own and has, in my opinion, a peculiar idea of what those core values are. Joel Millman defends immigration in *The Other Americans* (Viking, 1997), especially arguing that those immigrants with low levels of formal education more than compensate through hard work and determination, and that their family-based production units are especially efficient. He also shows how, by finding new markets, immigrants may create more jobs than they take. In *Still the Promised City?* (Harvard, 1993), Roger Waldinger gives a balanced assessment of how many immigrants to New York still believe in, and sometimes find, the American dream.

Fear and hatred of new immigrants has been almost a constant in American history. Two classic works on the phenomenon are John Higham, *Strangers in the Land* (Rutgers, 1988), and David Bennett, *The Party of Fear* (Vintage, 1990). Tyler Anbinder, in *Nativism and Slavery* (Oxford, 1992), provides a detailed history of the anti-immigrant Know-Nothings in the 1850s. Rita Simon documents a century of popular prejudice in *Public Opinion and the Immigrant* (Heath, 1985). Many of the general works on immigration also document native-born responses.

A number of writers have dealt with the idea of starting over in one way or another. On communes, see Rosabeth Moss Kanter, *Commitment and Community* (Harvard, 1972); Donald Pitzer has edited a helpful volume called *America's Communal Utopias* (North Carolina, 1997). Frances Fitzgerald's *Cities on a Hill* (Simon and Schuster, 1987) looks at four contemporary "new communities." Women are also capable of utopian dreams, and Dolores Hayden describes feminist schemes from the late nineteenth and early twentieth centuries in *The Grand Domestic Revolution* (MIT, 1981). There is even a book on names, which considers the implications of renaming, by Justin Kaplan and Anne Bernays, *The Language of Names* (Simon and Schuster, 1997). Divorce, one means of starting over, is well chronicled in Glenda Riley, *Divorce:*

An American Tradition (Oxford, 1991). For a view of American divorce in the broader context of world history, see Roderick Phillips, *Putting Asunder* (Cambridge, 1988).

John G. Cawelti describes Franklin's autobiography and later examples of the genre in *Apostles of the Self-Made Man* (Chicago, 1965). Richard Weiss, in *The American Myth of Success* (Illinois, 1988), depicts the many versions of the self-made man, economic and other, since the nineteenth century, as does Richard M. Huber in *The American Idea of Success* (Pushcart, 1987). In *The Positive Thinkers* (Pantheon, 1980) Donald Meyer concentrates on a special tradition of self-making. Judith Hilkey examines success manuals in the late nineteenth and early twentieth centuries in *Character Is Capital* (North Carolina, 1997). On autobiography as a form of remaking the self, see Thomas Cooley, *Educated Lives* (Ohio State, 1976); Herbert Leibowitz, *Fabricating Lives* (Knopf, 1989); and Diane Bjorklund, *Interpreting the Self* (Chicago, 1998).

Americans write how-to manuals for everything, including creating a new identity when starting over: Doug Richmond, *How to Disappear Completely and Never be Found* (Loompanics Unlimited, 1991); Kenn Abaygo, *Fugitive: How to Run, Hide, and Survive* (Paladin, 1994); Ragnar Benson, *Acquiring New ID: How to Easily Use the Latest Computer Technology to Drop Out, Start Over, and Get on with Your Life* (Paladin, 1996); Sheldon Charrett, *Modern Identity Changer: How to Create a New Identity for Privacy and Personal Freedom* (Paladin, 1997); and John Newman, *The Heavy Duty New Identity* (Loompanics Unlimited, 1998).

Phil Patton has written about the joys of movement in *Open Road* (Simon and Schuster, 1986), while Tom Lewis concentrates on the hidden intervention—the construction of the interstate highway system—which made this possible in *Divided Highways* (Viking, 1997). John Stover has written a fine history of American railroads, *American Railroads,* 2d ed. (Chicago, 1997), and Stephen Goddard has described their losing struggle against the automobile in *Getting There* (Basic Books, 1994). On America's fascination with the automobile, good works include John Rae, *The American Automobile* (Chicago, 1965); Michael Berger, *The Devil Wagon in God's Country* (Archon, 1979); Cynthia Golomb Dettelbach, *In the Driver's Seat* (Greenwood, 1976); and James Flink's comparative book, *The Automobile Age* (MIT, 1988). Jane Holtz Kay's *Asphalt Nation* (California, 1998) is a critique of our automobile culture. For more classic dissenting voices, read Hamlin Garland's *Main-Travelled Roads* (Nebraska, 1995 [1899]) or John Steinbeck's *Grapes of Wrath* (Penguin, 1999)—but see also Steinbeck's peripatetic adventures in *Travels with Charley* (Penguin, 1980).

James Grossman writes about the migration of African Americans to Chicago at the beginning of the twentieth century in *Land of Hope* (Chicago, 1989), and Nicholas Lemann about the broader black migration northward in *The Promised Land* (Knopf, 1991). Stanley Lieberson has exhaustively compared the economic fate of black migrants to the north with that of white immigrants in *A Piece of the Pie* (California, 1980).

Generations of historians have left us their thoughts on the settling of the American frontier. Among the most readable and interesting are, for the colonial period, Kenneth Lockridge, *Settlement and Unsettlement in Early America* (Cambridge, 1981), and John Frederick Martin, *Profits in the Wilderness* (North Carolina, 1991). On the nineteenth century, see William Cronon, *Nature's Metropolis* (Norton, 1991), on Chicago's growth and how it reshaped the midwest; Kevin Starr, *Americans and the California Dream, 1850–1915* (Oxford, 1986); and John D. Unruh Jr., *The Plains Across* (Illinois, 1993). *A Life Wild and Perilous* (Holt, 1997), by Robert Utley, describes the "mountain men" who penetrated the west in advance of the settlers. A good volume on the California gold rush is Malcolm Rohrbough's *Days of Gold* (California, 1997), but for a good account of one family's experience, see J. S. Holliday's *The World Rushed In* (Simon and Schuster, 1981). Dean May compares three settlements in the mid-nineteenth century in *Three Frontiers* (Cambridge, 1994), showing a shift from family toward individual self-interest. In *Adapting to a New World* (North Carolina, 1994), James Horn traces the strong influence of the culture that immigrants brought with them from England as they settled the Chesapeake colonies—a nice counter to national-character arguments that focus on the effects of the land and its abundance once settlers arrived. Anyone who doubts that the frontier was about money should read Patricia Nelson Limerick's *The Legacy of Conquest* (Norton, 1987).

David Courtwright has documented the links between young men and violence in *Violent Land* (Harvard, 1996). On violence more generally in the United States, read Franklin Zimring and Gordon Hawkins, *Crime Is Not the Problem* (Oxford, 1997). And on urban violence in nineteenth-century Philadelphia, see Roger Lane, *Violent Death in the City* (Harvard, 1979).

A distinct tradition has examined the mythological aspects of the frontier and the West. An early example is Henry Nash Smith, *Virgin Land* (Harvard, 1978 [1950]). Another classic is Leo Marx, *The Machine in the Garden* (Oxford, 1964), an examination of pastoral ideals in the settling of America. Richard Slotkin has written a trilogy of long books on the subject: *Regeneration Through Violence* (Wesleyan, 1973), *The Fatal Environment* (Oklahoma, 1998), and *Gunfighter Nation* (Oklahoma, 1998). Timothy Egan's *Lasso the Wind* (Knopf, 1998) contains, among other good things, a fine chapter on the Mormons. For a playful look, there is Robert Coover's novel, *Ghost Town* (Holt, 1998). In *Into the Wild* (Anchor, 1997), Jon Krakauer recounts the story of one man who escaped from civilization, fatally, in Alaska in 1992.

Markets in land, labor, and everything else have been at the center of American life since the earliest colonies. William Cronon, in *Changes in the Land* (Hill and Wang, 1983), gives an excellent account of the ecological effects of colonization in New England, especially the impact of production for markets. D. W. Meinig looks at geography and spatial flows, but not at the cultural meanings that accompany them, in his multivolume *The Shaping of America* (Yale, 1986, 1993, and 1999). Two recent historical works have given nuanced views of the rise of markets in early American history: James Henretta, *The Origins of American Capitalism* (Northeastern, 1991); and Allan Kulikoff, *The Agrarian Origins of American Capitalism* (Virginia, 1992). Charles Sellers examines the rapid expansion of markets in Jacksonian America in *The Market Revolution* (Oxford, 1991), although, like other authors with a "revolution" thesis, he exaggerates how different the "before" period was, in this case making too much of subsistence farming.

You work harder when you believe markets will reward you for it. Juliet Schor has documented this in *The Overworked American* (Basic Books, 1991). In her history of vacations in America, *Working at Play* (Oxford, 1999), Cindy Aron found that, thanks to their suspicion of "time off," Americans take their work with them on vacations, as well as using the time for spiritual, psychological, and intellectual self-improvement.

American attitudes toward market outcomes are the subject of Jennifer Hochschild's *What's Fair?* (Harvard, 1981) and *Facing Up to the American Dream* (Princeton, 1995). Richard Sennett and Jonathan Cobb explore the self-blame of the working class in *The Hidden Injuries of Class* (Norton, 1993). At the other end of the economic hierarchy, we have Sidney Verba and Gary Orren, *Equality in America: The View from the Top* (Harvard, 1985). Melvin Lerner has described the just-world hypothesis most fully in *The Belief in a Just World* (Plenum, 1980). A useful historical work is Daniel Rodgers, *The Work Ethic in Industrial America, 1850–1920* (Chicago, 1978). Herbert McClosky and John Zaller explore survey data in *The American Ethos* (Harvard, 1984), finding some beliefs that work against the dominant market vision. Michèle Lamont compares American and French attitudes toward getting ahead, morality, and culture in *Money, Morals, and Manners* (Chicago, 1992); she and Laurent Thévenot have edited an academic volume, *Rethinking Comparative Cultural Sociology* (Cambridge, 2000). Both books document American faith in markets.

On the related concept of the American dream, see Katherine Newman, *Declining Fortunes* (Basic Books, 1993); and—for what Americans have turned to when material dreams are not enough—Andrew Delbanco, *The Real American Dream* (Harvard, 1999). For a biographical twist, read Doris Kearns Goodwin, *Lyndon Johnson and the American Dream* (St. Martin's, 1991). On the rise of American psychotherapy as a means of controlling the world around one, see Eric Caplan, *Mind Games* (California, 1998); and Philip Cushman, *Constructing the Self, Constructing America* (Addison-Wesley, 1995).

The flip side of the dream—the reality of considerable inequality—has inspired a mountain of research and argument. On the causes of inequality, the classic is still Christopher Jencks and others, *Inequality* (Basic Books, 1972). Other assessments include Reynolds Farley and Walter Allen, *The Color Line and the Quality of Life in America* (Oxford, 1990); F. Allan Hanson, *Testing, Testing* (California, 1993); Stanley Lebergott, *The American Economy* (Princeton, 1976); Frank Levy, *The New Dollars and Dreams* (Russell Sage, 1998); Douglas Massey and Nancy Denton, *American Apartheid* (Harvard, 1993); Melvin Oliver and Thomas Shapiro, *Black Wealth/White Wealth* (Routledge, 1995); Jeannie Oakes, *Keeping Track* (Yale, 1985); Edward Wolff, *Top Heavy* (Twentieth Century Fund, 1995); and Claude Fischer and others, *Inequality by Design* (Princeton, 1996). Graef Crystal documents the overcompensation of American CEOs in *In Search of Excess* (Norton, 1991). Richard Merelman argues that our cultural conceptions do not allow us to see the structural realities shaping our lives in *Making Something of Ourselves* (California, 1984).

Some sadly gripping studies of poor Americans have been written, beginning with Michael Harrington's *The Other America* in 1962 (Penguin, 1981). On poor blacks, see Carol Stack, *All Our Kin* (Harper and Row, 1974). Recent works that examine policies as well as results include William Julius Wilson, *The Declining Significance of Race* (Chicago, 1978), *The Truly Disadvantaged* (Chicago, 1987), and *When Work Disappears* (Knopf, 1996); Christopher Jencks, *Rethinking Social Policy* (Harvard, 1992), and *The Homeless* (Harvard, 1994); and John Schwartz and Thomas Volgy, *The Forgotten Americans* (Norton, 1992). For a longer historical view, see Michael Katz, *In the Shadow of the*

Poorhouse (Basic Books, 1986), and *The Undeserving Poor* (Pantheon, 1989); and Jacqueline Jones, *The Dispossessed* (Basic Books, 1992).

Even though Americans do not like their government to help the disadvantaged, they do this themselves as individuals. According to Robert Wuthnow's interesting book about Americans who volunteer to help others, *Acts of Compassion* (Princeton, 1991), they do this as a form of individual self-fulfillment or development, not out of a sense of obligation to a broader community. According to Janet Poppendieck, in *Sweet Charity?* (Viking, 1998), our tradition of voluntary charity actually undermines progressive politics that might push the state to do more for those unable to fend for themselves in economic markets.

Among the vast literature on the crucial period for organized labor, the end of the nineteenth century, I recommend David Montgomery, *The Fall of the House of Labor* (Cambridge, 1987); Karen Orren, *Belated Feudalism* (Cambridge, 1991); Victoria Hattam, *Labor Visions and State Power* (Princeton, 1993); and Kim Voss, *The Making of American Exceptionalism* (Cornell, 1993). On the legal aspects, read Christopher Tomlins, *The State and the Unions* (Cambridge, 1985), and *Law, Labor, and Ideology in the Early American Republic* (Cambridge, 1993). Patricia Sexton links this history to the present in *The War on Labor and the Left* (Westview, 1991). On the development of contract-oriented law, especially as it became hegemonic in the early nineteenth century, see Morton Horowitz, *The Transformation of American Law, 1780–1830* (Harvard, 1977).

Ira Katznelson shows how the fragmentation of neighborhoods by national origins has undermined a broader working-class politics in *City Trenches* (Chicago, 1981). Michael Kazin traces Americans' deep-rooted suspicion of authority, sometimes leaning left and sometimes right, in *The Populist Persuasion* (Basic Books, 1995). For a persuasive case that our Bill of Rights was motivated by fear of government, see Akhil Reed Amar, *The Bill of Rights* (Yale, 1998). Morton Keller documents Americans' resistance to government's expansion in the nineteenth century in *Affairs of State* (Harvard, 1977).

The American Revolution gave definitive symbolic form as well as institutional support to many of the cultural meanings I discuss in this book. Gordon Wood's *The Radicalism of the American Revolution* (Knopf, 1992) is a grand discussion of many of these issues, even though, in support of the thesis embodied in his title, Wood tends to play down the migratory impulse, ambitions, and weak social structure that had already characterized the colonies. Works that established the contribution of radical political ideas to the Revolution include

Bernard Bailyn, *The Ideological Origins of the American Revolution* (Harvard, 1992 [1967]); Pauline Maier, *From Resistance to Revolution* (Knopf, 1972); and Gordon Wood, *The Creation of the American Republic, 1776–1787* (North Carolina, 1998 [1969]). Theodore Draper's *A Struggle for Power* (Random House, 1996) is a readable account of what led up to the Revolution. Edmund Morgan takes a trans-Atlantic view of the rise of popular sovereignty in *Inventing the People* (Norton, 1988). Samuel Beer looks at abiding tensions over the concept of a national government in *To Make a Nation* (Harvard, 1993). For a sweeping history of the fallout from framing the Revolution in terms of individual rights, see James MacGregor Burns and Stewart Burns, *A People's Charter* (Knopf, 1991). The founding fathers' republican sense of collective obligation (emphasized by recent historians) does not preclude an individualist vision of society and markets—out of which republican virtue must come; the obligations of citizens do not preclude suspicion of government; rather, the two go hand in hand.

Although I do not examine foreign policy extensively in this book, it fits with some of my themes. Through most of American history, we have avoided foreign entanglements, either because they are bad for business or because they might spoil the purity of Americans by exposing us to corrupt Old World states. Walter McDougall shows how our attitudes evolved from isolation to a vision that we need to share our purity with others in *Promised Land, Crusader State* (Houghton Mifflin, 1997). At first, Americans were reluctant to intervene in what would become our most popular war, World War II, as William O'Neill demonstrates in *A Democracy at War* (Harvard, 1995). *In the Shadow of War,* by Michael Sherry (Yale, 1995), shows how Americans have partly reconciled themselves to foreign intervention since World War II. Only recently has militarism become closely connected with cultural themes of masculinity and violence, as James Gibson shows in *Warrior Dreams* (Hill and Wang, 1994). On one of the few immigrants to make a mark in foreign policy (and one of the few women immigrants so far to become famous), see Michael Dobbs, *Madeleine Albright* (Holt, 1999).

There is a vast literature on the Emersonian tradition in American arts and culture. On Emerson and his contemporaries, readable works include David Leverenz, *Manhood and the American Renaissance* (Cornell, 1989); David Reynolds, *Beneath the American Renaissance* (Harvard, 1988), and *Walt Whitman's America* (Knopf, 1995). Lawrence Buell focuses on the role of place for these (and many other) writers in *The Environmental Imagination* (Harvard, 1995). Myra Jehlen has traced American individualism across a large swath of literature in

American Incarnation (Harvard, 1986). Best of all, though, are the originals: Cooper's Leatherstocking novels; Emerson's journals and essays; Thoreau's journals as well as *Walden* (Princeton, 1989), and *The Maine Woods* (Princeton, 1972); Walt Whitman, *Leaves of Grass* (Vintage, 1992).

American literature abounds in restlessness. The premise of John Steinbeck's *Travels with Charley: In Search of America* (Penguin, 1980) is that "Nearly every American hungers to move." At the opposite end of the spectrum is *Death of a Salesman*, Arthur Miller's indictment of the boyish dreams of success that constant movement does not necessarily attain. I hardly need to cite other examples, as many are mentioned in the text itself.

The studies of specific arts are endless. John Cawelti's *Adventure, Mystery, and Romance* (Chicago, 1976) provides good insight into Westerns and hard-boiled detective novels. Jane Tompkins is especially interesting on Westerns in *West of Everything* (Oxford, 1992). On the constant movement of American musicians, including country, rock, and blues performers, see Peter Guralnick's *Lost Highways* (Little, Brown, 1999) and Cecelia Tichi's *High Lonesome* (North Carolina, 1994). Daniel Belgrad has written about the romantic revival of the 1950s as a cult of improvisation: *The Culture of Spontaneity* (Chicago, 1998).

A number of writers, frequently if misleadingly labeled "communitarians," have dealt with some of the cultural traditions explored in this book. The best include Robert Bellah and several coauthors, *Habits of the Heart* (California, 1996), and *The Good Society* (Knopf, 1991). One weakness of these works, though, is that they often confuse actual social connections between people and the ways in which people talk about those connections; people may talk in a more disconnected way than they act. Like me, though, they believe that these cultural images matter enormously. Another work, an effort to revive the idea of American exceptionalism, is Seymour Martin Lipset's *American Exceptionalism* (Norton, 1996). On individualism, see Herbert Gans, *Middle American Individualism* (Oxford, 1991); and Lawrence Mitchell, *Stacked Deck* (Temple, 1998).

Because only individuals can actually have character, biographies are good sources for research into American character. Those I found most useful include Justin Kaplan, *Mr. Clemens and Mark Twain* (Simon and Schuster, 1966); Andrew Hoffman, *Inventing Mark Twain* (William Morrow, 1997); William S. McFeely, *Frederick Douglass* (Norton, 1991); Waldo Martin Jr., *The Mind of Frederick Douglass* (North Carolina, 1984); Kenneth Silverman, *Houdini!!!* (HarperCollins, 1996); Justin

Kaplan, *Walt Whitman, A Life* (Simon and Schuster, 1980); Paul Zweig, *Walt Whitman: The Making of the Poet* (Basic Books, 1984); Jerome Loving, *Walt Whitman: The Song of Himself* (California, 1999); David Freeman Hawke, *Paine* (Harper and Row, 1974); Eric Foner, *Tom Paine and Revolutionary America* (Oxford, 1976); A. J. Ayer, *Thomas Paine* (Atheneum, 1988); Jack Fruchtman Jr., *Thomas Paine, Apostle of Freedom* (Four Walls Eight Windows, 1994); and John Keane, *Tom Paine* (Little, Brown, 1995).

Other good reads include Ann Charters, *Kerouac* (St. Martin's, 1994); Robert Richardson Jr., *Emerson* (California, 1995); and Jackson Benson, *Wallace Stegner* (Viking, 1996). On two famous immigrants, see Kenneth Lynn's *Charlie Chaplin and His Times* (Simon and Schuster, 1997); and Joseph Frazier Wall, *Andrew Carnegie* (Pittsburgh, 1989). Owen Wister, an easterner who wrote *The Virginian* and saw the West as "like Genesis," a place for his own rebirth, is well chronicled in Darwin Payne's *Owen Wister* (Southern Methodist, 1985). Lyndall Gordon has written a fine book about Henry James, *A Private Life of Henry James* (Norton, 1999), in which she shows among other things that he shared the American vision of individuals as in tension with, rather than fully part of, society. In his fear of women and his utopian escapism, Walt Disney could have been Huck Finn grown up; his life is chronicled by Steven Watts in *The Magic Kingdom* (Houghton Mifflin, 1998). A walking symbol of American individualism (with a misogynist underside) is dissected in Randy Roberts and James Olson, *John Wayne* (Free Press, 1996), and Gary Wills, *John Wayne's America* (Touchstone, 1998). In *The Life of Raymond Chandler* (Dutton, 1976), Frank MacShane has written about the writer, born in Chicago but then raised in Ireland and England until he re-migrated to find his fortune (as he saw it) in his mid-twenties.

And of course there are the autobiographies, important evidence despite and often because of their distortions. Franklin's autobiography is available in many editions. Frederick Douglass's three versions of his life are also available. *Narrative of the Life of Frederick Douglass, an American Slave, Written by Himself* (originally published in 1845) is still the most popular, but the others are still in print: *My Bondage and My Freedom* (Illinois, 1987 [1855]) and *Life and Times of Frederick Douglass, Written by Himself* (Citadel, 1984 [1881, revised 1892]). There is also Samuel Gompers, *Seventy Years of Life and Labor* (Cornell, 1984 [1925]); and Alex Haley, ed., *Autobiography of Malcolm X* (Ballantine, 1992 [1965]). Americans whose lives are their main art, such as Henry David Thoreau or John Muir, are inevitably autobiographical in their writing.

In a different vein, Laura Ingalls Wilder's novels are more or less auto-biographical, with fine details of what life was like for those misguided folk who tried to homestead the poor land of the northern plains states.

One of my themes is the greater restlessness of men. Several histories of American masculinity are compatible with my descriptions, including those of Michael Kimmel, *Manhood in America* (Free Press, 1996); David Pugh, *Sons of Liberty* (Greenwood, 1983); and E. Anthony Rotundo, *American Manhood* (Basic Books, 1993). The research on women's history is vast, but a few of my favorites include Nancy Cott, *The Bonds of Womanhood* (Yale, 1977); Ann Douglas, *The Feminization of American Culture* (Avon, 1977); Stephanie Coontz, *The Social Origins of Private Life* (Verso, 1988); and Elaine Tyler May, *Homeward Bound* (Basic Books, 1988). Annette Kolodny has written about the different view women had of the frontier in *The Land Before Her* (North Carolina, 1984), and for a complex portrait, see Julie Roy Jeffrey, *Frontier Women* (Hill and Wang, 1979). Carolyn Cassady, wife of Kerouac's friend and hero Neal Cassady, wrote what it was like to be one of the women left behind in *Off the Road* (Morrow, 1990).

Finally, a number of writers have tried to show what Americans miss when they lose their sense of place, including Wendell Berry, *The Unsettling of America* (Sierra Club, 1996); John Brinckerhoff Jackson, *A Sense of Place, A Sense of Time* (Yale, 1994); and Scott Russell Sanders, *Staying Put* (Beacon, 1993). In *No Sense of Place* (Oxford, 1985), Joshua Meyrowitz blames new electronic media for our loss of a sense of place, incorrectly assuming that we used to have one. Among those interested in how meanings come to be attached to places are Kay Anderson and Fay Gale, eds., *Inventing Places* (Wiley, Halstead, 1992); and Kathleen Stewart, *A Space on the Side of the Road* (Princeton, 1996). Sharon Zukin blames restlessness on capitalism in *Landscapes of Power* (California, 1991), seeing only one direction of causality between the two. Daphne Spain examines the interaction between built spaces and gender roles in *Gendered Spaces* (North Carolina, 1992). Craig Whitaker shows how architecture (including road design) reflects American values in *Architecture and the American Dream* (Potter, 1996).

NOTES

INTRODUCTION

1. Samuel Langhorn Clemens, *Adventures of Huckleberry Finn* (New York: W. W. Norton, 1977), p. 229.

2. Frederick Douglass, *Narrative of the Life of Frederick Douglass* (New York: New American Library, 1968 [1845]), p. 92.

3. Dr. Thomas Low Nichols, *Forty Years of American Life* (New York: Negro Universities Press, 1968 [1869]), vol. 1, pp. 401–7.

CHAPTER ONE

1. Although Berkeley's poem was only published in his *Miscellany* of 1752, it is commonly thought to have been written in the mid-1720s.

2. Tzvetan Todorov, *The Conquest of America* (New York: Harper and Row, 1984), p. 5.

3. Henri Baudet, *Paradise on Earth* (New Haven: Yale University Press, 1965), p. 55.

4. Jack P. Greene, *The Intellectual Construction of America* (Chapel Hill: University of North Carolina Press, 1993), p. 25.

5. Thomas More, *Utopia* (Harmondsworth: Penguin Books, 1965 [1516]), p. 40.

6. Carl Ortwin Sauer, *Sixteenth-Century North America* (Berkeley: University of California Press, 1971), pp. 33, 96.

7. Donald A. Barclay, James H. Maguire, and Peter Wild, eds., *Into the Wilderness Dream* (Salt Lake City: University of Utah Press, 1994), p. 72.

8. Richard Hakluyt, "Discourse Concerning Westerne Planting," in Bradley Chapin, ed., *Provincial America, 1600–1763* (New York: Free Press, 1966), pp. 33, 24.

9. "A True Declaration of the Estate of the Colonie in Virginia," in David Beers Quinn and Allison O. Quinn, eds., *New American World* (New York: Macmillan, 1979), vol. 5, p. 261.

10. Greene, *Construction of America*, pp. 54–55.

11. Bernard Bailyn, "Politics and Social Structure in Virginia," in Stanley N. Katz, ed., *Colonial America*, 2d ed. (Boston: Little Brown, 1976), p. 125.

12. Edmund S. Morgan, *Inventing the People* (New York: W. W. Norton, 1988), p. 128.

13. Bailyn, *Voyagers to the West* (New York: Alfred A. Knopf, 1986), p. 251.

14. Ronald Takaki, "Introduction," in *From Different Shores* (New York: Oxford University Press, 1987), p. 4.

15. Quoted in William S. Bernard, "A History of U.S. Immigration Policy," in Richard A. Easterlin et al., *Immigration* (Cambridge: Harvard University Press, 1982), p. 85.

16. Quoted in Mark Wyman, *Round-Trip to America* (Ithaca: Cornell University Press, 1993), p. 25.

17. Sarah J. Mahler, *American Dreaming* (Princeton: Princeton University Press, 1995), p. 83.

18. Toni Morrison, *Jazz* (New York: Alfred A. Knopf, 1992), pp. 106, 32.

19. Gordon S. Wood, *The Radicalism of the American Revolution* (New York: Alfred A. Knopf, 1992), pp. 169, 189–90.

20. Thomas Paine, *Common Sense* (London: Penguin, 1976 [1776]), p. 84.

21. F. Scott Fitzgerald, *The Great Gatsby* (New York: Charles Scribner's Sons, 1925), p. 182.

22. Figures reported in Jennifer L. Hochschild, *Facing Up to the American Dream* (Princeton: Princeton University Press, 1995), pp. 21, 58.

CHAPTER TWO

1. Rubén Rumbaut reports that the 1990 census found twenty million foreigners in the United States, with another twenty-five million children who had been born here: "Origins and Destinies: Immigration to the United States Since World War II," *Sociological Forum* 9 (1994): 589.

2. Figures from Richard A. Easterlin, "Economic and Social Characteristics of the Immigrants," in Easterlin et al., *Immigration*, pp. 19–20.

3. Bailyn, *Voyagers*, p. 202.

4. Mahler, *American Dreaming*, pp. 79–80.

5. Bailyn, *Voyagers*, pp. 150–51. Another 5 percent claimed to be in trade or shopkeeping, and 2 percent in "gentle trades" such as gentlemen, public officials, clergy, lawyers, and physicians.

6. All these figures are from Easterlin, "Economic and Social Characteristics," pp. 22–23.

7. Alejandro Portes and Rubén G. Rumbaut, *Immigrant America: A Portrait* (Berkeley: University of California Press), p. 79.

8. The classic study of this phenomenon is Barry R. Chiswick, "The Effect of Americanization on the Earnings of Foreign-born Men," *Journal of Political Economy* 86 (1978): 897–921.

9. Roger Daniels, *Coming to America* (New York: HarperCollins, 1990), p. 202.

10. Michael J. Piore, *Birds of Passage* (Cambridge: Cambridge University Press, 1979).

11. These data are reported in Roger Waldinger and Greta Gilbertson, "Immigrants' Progress: Ethnic and Gender Differences Among U.S. Immigrants in the 1980s," *Sociological Perspectives* 37 (1994): tables 2 and 3.

12. Nathan S. Caplan, Marcella H. Choy, and John K. Whitmore, *Children of the Boat People* (Ann Arbor: University of Michigan Press, 1991).

13. For the best study yet, still in progress, see Rubén G. Rumbaut and Alejandro Portes, two volumes forthcoming from the University of California Press, 2000.

14. Mahler, *American Dreaming*, p. 75.

15. Quoted in George J. Borjas, *Friends or Strangers* (New York: Basic Books, 1990), p. 3, which is itself an argument (by a Cuban immigrant!) that recent immigrants are less skilled and less desirable than previous ones.

16. The Chinese were 9 percent of California's population. See Ronald Takaki, "Reflections on Racial Patterns in America," in *From Different Shores* (New York: Oxford University Press, 1987), p. 28.

17. Quoted in David H. Bennett, *The Party of Fear* (Chapel Hill: University of North Carolina Press, 1988), p. 36.

18. Quoted in Rita J. Simon, *Public Opinion and the Immigrant: Print Media Coverage, 1880–1980* (Lexington, Mass.: D. C. Heath, 1985), pp. 66, 67, 98.

19. Rita J. Simon, "Old Minorities, New Immigrants: Aspirations, Hopes, and Fears," *Annals* 530 (1993): 62–63.

20. Simon, "Old Minorities," p. 63.

CHAPTER THREE

1. Robert V. Hine, *Community on the American Frontier* (Norman: University of Oklahoma Press, 1980), p. 249.

2. Unlike the Virginia data, the New England data allow us to exclude those who died, one reason that region appears more stable (and people lived longer there than in Virginia). See David Hackett Fischer, *Albion's Seed* (New York: Oxford University Press, 1989), pp. 184, 392.

3. John B. Rae, *The American Automobile* (Chicago: University of Chicago Press, 1965), p. 193. Rae calls the automobile "European by birth, American by adoption" (p. 1).

4. James J. Flink, *The Automobile Age* (Cambridge: MIT Press, 1988), p. 361.

5. James R. Beniger, *The Control Revolution* (Cambridge: Harvard University Press, 1986), p. 189.

6. Charles B. Nam, William J. Serow, and David F. Sly, eds., *International Handbook on Internal Migration* (New York: Greenwood Press, 1990).

7. The mobility statistics come from the Kristin A. Hansen, *Geographical Mobility: March 1993 to March 1994*, U.S. Bureau of the Census, Current Population Reports, P20-485 (Washington, D.C.: U.S. Government Printing Office, 1995).

8. Andrew Hoffman, *Inventing Mark Twain* (New York: William Morrow, 1997), pp. xiv.

9. Linda Haverty Rugg, *Picturing Ourselves* (Chicago: University of Chicago Press, 1997), p. 29.

10. Hoffman, *Inventing Mark Twain*, p. xiii.

11. Quoted in Justin Kaplan and Anne Bernays, *The Language of Names* (New York: Simon and Schuster, 1997), p. 58.

12. Leon F. Litwack, *Been in the Storm So Long* (New York: Alfred A. Knopf, 1979), p. 247.

13. Ralph Ellison, *Shadow and Act* (New York: Random House, 1964), p. 147.

14. H. L. Mencken, *The American Language*, Supplement 2 (New York: Alfred A. Knopf, 1948), p. 475.

15. Kaplan and Bernays, *Language of Names*, p. 133.

16. Benjamin Franklin, *Autobiography and Other Writings* (Cambridge: Houghton Mifflin, Riverside Editions, 1958), pp. 17–18.

17. Nellie McKay, "Autobiography and the American Novel," in *The Columbia History of the American Novel* (New York: Columbia University Press, 1991), p. 27.

18. Toni Morrison, *Jazz* (New York: Alfred A. Knopf, 1992), p. 123.

19. Carl J. Guarneri, *The Utopian Alternative: Fourierism in Nineteenth-Century America* (Ithaca: Cornell University Press, 1991), p. 2.

20. Stephen E. Whicher, ed., *Selections from Ralph Waldo Emerson* (Boston: Houghton Mifflin, 1957), p. 129.

21. Robert S. Fogarty, *All Things New* (Chicago: University of Chicago Press, 1990), pp. 19–20.

22. Frances Fitzgerald, *Cities on a Hill* (New York: Simon and Schuster, 1987).

23. Litwack, *Storm*, pp. 297, 297–298.

24. Anne B. Hendershott, *Moving for Work* (Lanham, Md.: University Press of America, 1995), pp. 21, 143.

CHAPTER FOUR

1. In Clarence L. Ver Steeg and Richard Hofstadter, *Great Issues in American History: From Settlement to Revolution, 1584–1776* (New York: Random House, 1969), p. 105.

2. Edmund S. Morgan, *American Slavery, American Freedom* (New York: Norton, 1975), p. 111.

3. Werner Rösener, *Peasants in the Middle Ages* (Cambridge: Polity Press, 1992), p. 123.

4. Lynn White Jr., "The Historical Roots of Our Ecological Crisis," *Science* 65 (10 March 1967), p. 1206.

5. John Locke, *The Second Treatise of Government* (Indianapolis: Bobbs-Merrill, 1952), p. 20.

6. Locke, *Second Treatise*, 18.

7. Samuel P. Hays, *Conservation and the Gospel of Efficiency* (New York: Atheneum, 1980), pp. 19, 20.

8. David Hackett Fischer, *Albion's Seed* (New York: Oxford University Press, 1989), p. 630.

9. Pieter Spierenburg, "The Body and the State," in Norval Morris and David J. Rothman, eds., *The Oxford History of the Prison* (Oxford: Oxford University Press, 1995), p. 76.

10. Kevin Starr, *Americans and the California Dream, 1850–1915* (New York: Oxford University Press, 1973), pp. 26, 31.

11. Quoted in Starr, *California Dream*, p. 53.

12. Starr, *California Dream*, p. 65.

13. Samuel Langhorne Clemens, *Adventures of Huckleberry Finn* (New York: W. W. Norton, 1961), p. 116–17.

14. Ronald Takaki, *Iron Cages* (New York: Alfred A. Knopf, 1979), pp. 95–96.

15. Takaki, *Iron Cages*, p. 101.

16. David T. Courtwright, *Violent Land* (Cambridge: Harvard University Press, 1996), p. 3; for figures on median age, see p. 22.

17. Lois A. Fingerhut and Joel C. Kleinman, "International and Interstate Comparisons of Homicide among Young Males," *Journal of the American Medical Association* 263 (1990): 3292–95.

18. William Cronon, *Changes in the Land* (New York: Hill and Wang, 1983), p. 118.

19. Gérard Chaliand and Jean-Pierre Rageau, *Atlas Stratégique* (Paris: Librairie Arthème Fayard, 1983).

20. In 1968, Shepard B. Clough and Theodre F. Marburg claimed that Americans used 20–30 times as much water per capita as Western Europeans: *The Economic Basis of American Civilization* (New York: Thomas Y. Crowell Company, 1968), p. 29.

21. Cronon, *Changes in the Land*, p. 170.

22. Donald Worster, *Nature's Economy* (Cambridge: Cambridge University Press, 1985), p. 226.

23. J. Hector St. John de Crèvecoeur, *Letters from an American Farmer* (New York: Penguin Books, 1981 [1782]), pp. 67–68.

24. Ken Robison, *The Sagebrush Rebellion* (Blackfoot, Idaho: D and S Publishing, 1981), quoted in C. Brant Short, *Ronald Reagan and the Public Lands* (College Station, Tex.: Texas A & M University Press, 1989), p. 33.

CHAPTER FIVE

1. Quoted in the most recent biography: Kenneth Silverman, *Houdini!!!* (New York: HarperCollins, 1996), p. 50.

2. Silverman, *Houdini!!!* p. 200.

3. Hoffman, *Inventing Mark Twain*, pp. 56–57.

4. Quoted in Richard Weiss, *The American Myth of Success* (Urbana: University of Illinois Press, 1969), p. 215.

5. Philip Cushman, *Constructing the Self, Constructing America* (Reading, Mass.: Addison-Wesley, 1995), p. 138.

6. Richard Fisch, John H. Weakland, and Lynn Segal, *The Tactics of Change: Doing Therapy Briefly* (San Francisco: Jossey-Bass, 1983), p. 257.

7. Jennifer L. Hochschild, *Facing Up to the American Dream* (Princeton: Princeton University Press, 1995), pp. 21, 272.

8. Joe R. Feagin, "Poverty: We Still Believe That God Helps Those Who Help Themselves," *Psychology Today* (November 1972): 110ff.

9. Reported in *The Economist*, 22 November 1997.

10. Greene, *The Intellectual Construction of America*, p. 62.

11. Aubrey C. Land, "Economic Base and Social Structure: The Northern Chesapeake in the Eighteenth Century," in Katz, *Colonial America*, p. 357.

12. Bailyn, "Politics and Social Structure in Virginia," p. 137.

13. Data are from the General Social Survey. Reported in Dennis Gilbert and Joseph A. Kahl, *The American Class Structure*, 4th ed. (Belmont, Calif.: Wadsworth Publishing, 1993), p. 146.

14. Mahler, *American Dreaming*, p. 128.

15. Denny Braun, *The Rich Get Richer*, 2d ed. (Chicago: Nelson-Hall, 1997), pp. 106–7.

16. *New York Times Magazine*, 17 August 1997, p. 17.

17. "Surprises in a Study of Life Expectancies," *New York Times*, 4 December 1997.

18. Edward Pessen, "The Myth of Antebellum Social Mobility and Equality of Opportunity," in Pessen, ed., *Three Centuries of Social Mobility in America* (Lexington, Mass.: D. C. Heath, 1974), pp. 117–18.

19. Quoted in Wood, *Radicalism of the American Revolution*, p. 326.

20. James A. Henretta, *The Origins of American Capitalism* (Boston: Northeastern University Press, 1991), p. 271.

21. Michèle Lamont, *Money, Morals, and Manners* (Chicago: University of Chicago Press, 1992), p. 146.

CHAPTER SIX

1. Samuel Gompers, *Seventy Years of Life and Labor* (Ithaca: Industrial and Labor Relations Press, Cornell, 1984 [1925]), p. 10.

2. Gompers, *Life and Labor*, p. 8.

3. Gompers, *Life and Labor*, p. 7.

4. Gompers, *Life and Labor*, pp. 46–47.

5. Quoted in H. M. Gitelman, "Adolph Strasser and the Origins of Pure and Simple Unionism," in Daniel J. Loeb, ed., *The Labor History Reader* (Urbana: University of Illinois Press, 1985), p. 157.

6. Edmund S. Morgan, *Inventing the People* (New York: W. W. Norton, 1988), p. 144.

7. Quoted in Morgan, *Inventing the People*, p. 138.

8. Kenneth A. Lockridge, *Settlement and Unsettlement in Early America* (Cambridge: Cambridge University Press, 1981), p. 49.

9. Bernard Bailyn, *The Origins of American Politics* (New York: Alfred A. Knopf, 1968), p. 102.

10. Stephen Skowronek, *Building a New American State* (Cambridge: Cambridge University Press, 1982), p. 26.

11. Both quotations are from Leo Marx, *The Machine in the Garden* (London: Oxford University Press, 1964), p. 137.

12. David S. Lovejoy, *Rhode Island Politics and the American Revolution, 1760–1776* (Providence: Brown University Press, 1958), p. 17.

13. Ira Katznelson, *City Trenches* (Chicago: University of Chicago Press, 1981), p. 113.

14. Quoted in David Montgomery, *The Fall of the House of Labor* (Cambridge: Cambridge University Press, 1987), p. 82.

15. Quoted in Montgomery, *House of Labor*, p. 86.

16. Quoted in Gary Marks, *Unions in Politics* (Princeton: Princeton University Press, 1989), p. 189.

17. Roy Beck, *The Case Against Immigration* (New York: W. W. Norton, 1996), p. 166.

18. Randall K. Filer, "The Effect of Immigrant Arrivals on Migratory Patterns of Native Workers," in George J. Borjas and Richard B. Freeman, *Immigration and the Work Force* (Chicago: University of Chicago Press, 1992), p. 267.

19. Richard Sennett, *Authority* (New York: Alfred A. Knopf, 1980), p. 16.

20. Robert Wuthnow, *Acts of Compassion* (Princeton: Princeton University Press, 1991), p. 216.

CHAPTER SEVEN

1. Quoted in Robert D. Richardson, Jr., *Emerson* (Berkeley: University of California Press, 1995), p. 183.

2. Quoted in Richardson, *Emerson*, p. 246.

3. Stephen E. Whicher, ed., *Selections from Ralph Waldo Emerson* (Boston: Houghton Mifflin, 1957), pp. 147, 148, 150.

4. Whicher, *Selections from Emerson*, p. 149.

5. Whicher, *Selections from Emerson*, p. 135.

6. Whicher, *Selections from Emerson*, pp. 164–65.

7. "The Young American," in *The Collected Works of Ralph Waldo Emerson*, vol. 1, *Nature, Addresses, and Lectures* (Cambridge: Harvard University Press), pp. 226, 230, 234.

8. Ralph Waldo Emerson, *Nature* (San Francisco: Chandler Publishing, 1968 [1836]), pp. 5–6, 77, 78.

9. Henry David Thoreau, *Walden and Civil Disobedience* (New York: W. W. Norton, 1966), pp. 187, 115.

10. Walt Whitman, *Complete Poetry and Selected Prose* (Boston: Houghton Mifflin, 1959), p. 108.

11. Whitman, *Poetry and Selected Prose*, p. 94.

12. Whitman, *Poetry and Selected Prose*, p. 83.

13. John G. Cawelti, *Adventure, Mystery, and Romance* (Chicago: University of Chicago Press, 1976), p. 198.

14. Henry Nash Smith, *Virgin Land* (Cambridge: Harvard University Press, 1978 [1950]), p. 135.

15. Raymond Chandler, *The Long Goodbye* (New York: Pocket Books, 1955), pp. 218–19.

16. Kathy J. Ogren, *The Jazz Revolution* (New York: Oxford University Press, 1989), p. 50.

17. Simon Frith, *Sound Effects* (New York: Pantheon, 1981).

18. Leon Edel, *Henry James: The Untried Years* (Philadelphia: J. B. Lippincott Company, 1953), p. 20.

19. Robert Jones, writing in *Harper's New Monthly Magazine*, quoted in William W. Stowe, *Going Abroad* (Princeton: Princeton University Press, 1994), p. 3.

20. Stowe, *Going Abroad*, p. 7.

21. Joseph W. Reed, *Three American Originals* (Middletown, Conn.: Wesleyan University Press, 1984), p. 26.

22. Ann Charters, ed., *Jack Kerouac: Selected Letters, 1940–1956* (New York: Viking, 1995), p. 107.

23. Jack Kerouac, *On the Road* (New York: Viking, 1955), pp. 5, 8, 60, 11, 16, 29.

24. Letter to Neal Cassady, *The Portable Jack Kerouac*, p. 607.

25. Kerouac, *On the Road*, p. 141.

26. Roger Finke and Rodney Stark, *The Churching of America, 1776–1990* (New Brunswick, N.J.: Rutgers University Press, 1992), pp. 24, 30.

27. Wood, *Radicalism of the American Revolution*, pp. 331, 333.

28. Nathan O. Hatch, *The Democratization of American Christianity* (New Haven: Yale University Press, 1989), p. 210.

29. Whitman, *Poetry and Selected Prose*, p. 25.

CHAPTER EIGHT

1. John Keane, *Tom Paine* (Boston: Little, Brown, 1995), p. 52.

2. Philip S. Foner, ed., *The Complete Writings of Thomas Paine* (New York: Citadel Press, 1945), 1: 31.

3. Yehoshura Arieli, *Individualism and Nationalism in American Ideology* (Cambridge: Harvard University Press, 1964), p. 73.

4. Thomas Paine, *Common Sense* (New York: Penguin Books, 1976 [1776]), pp. 65, 72–73.

5. Quoted in Keane, *Tom Paine*, p. 206.

6. Mary R. Beard, *America Through Women's Eyes* (New York: Macmillan, 1933), p. 88.

7. Anne C. Rose, *Transcendentalism as a Social Movement, 1830–1850* (New Haven: Yale University Press, 1981), p. 102.

8. Gompers, *Life and Labor*, p. 51.

9. David B. Quinn, ed., *The Extension of Settlement in Florida, Virginia, and the Spanish Southwest* (New York: Arno Press, 1979), p. 262.

10. Quoted in Annette Kolodny, *The Land Before Her* (Chapel Hill: University of North Carolina Press, 1984), p. 93.

11. Hendershott, *Moving for Work*, p. 23.

12. Roderick Phillips, *Putting Asunder* (Cambridge: Cambridge University Press, 1988), p. 465.

13. These facts are from Glenda Riley, *Divorce: An American Tradition* (New York: Oxford University Press, 1991).

14. Men's greater romanticism, along with the statistics, is discussed in Francesca M. Cancian, *Love in America* (Cambridge: Cambridge University Press, 1987), p. 77.

15. Barbara Ehrenreich, *The Hearts of Men* (Garden City: Anchor Press, 1983).

16. Alix Kates Shulman, *Drinking the Rain* (New York: Penguin Books, 1995), pp. 62, 59, 92.

17. Sara McLanahan and Gary Sandefur, *Growing Up a Single Parent* (Cambridge: Harvard University Press, 1994), ch. 7.

CONCLUSION

1. Mark Twain, *Life on the Mississippi* (New York: Hill and Wang, 1957), pp. 36, 54.

2. Susanne Langer, *Feeling and Form: A Theory of Art* (New York: Scribner, 1953), p. 95.

INDEX

Abdul-Jabbar, Kareem, 79
Absalom! Absalom! (Faulkner), 209
academics, as rootless, 248
action painting, 210
actors, name changes by, 77
Adams, John Quincy, 167
adolescents. *See* young people
Adventists, 85
AFL (American Federation of Labor), 160, 177, 178
African Americans: in Bacon's rebellion, 97; in colonial Virginia, 55; communal ties of, 184, 237, 247; compassion for those at the bottom, 252; expatriate artists, 209; immigration's effect on, 179; jazz, 205; migration to northern cities, 31–32, 90–91; mobility of, 72, 89–91; names as source of identity for, 79–80; as percentage of population in 1790, 56; sharecropping, 31; stereotypes of, 10; as strikebreakers, 91, 177; unions preferring immigrants to, 179. *See also* slavery
Agee, William, 147
agriculture: agribusiness, 118, 123; Dust Bowl, 75, 89, 120; family farms, 74, 75, 150, 247; homesteading, 108, 123, 226; immigrant labor depressing wages in, 179; immigrants engaging in, 101; migration from country to city, 74–75, 124; movement away from, 143–44; nineteenth-century writers on virtues of farm life, 135; producing for the market, 150; rural depopula-

tion, 123; sharecropping, 31; wasteful American practices of, 117, 118
air travel, 71
Alaska, 31, 59
Albright, Madeleine, 37
Alcott, Bronson, 195–96
Alger, Horatio, 134, 135
Ali, Mohammed, 79
Alien Nation (Brimelow), 58
Allen, Woody, 77
altruism, 184
Amana, 85
America (United States): American Revolution, 33–34, 149, 156, 166, 222; Americans as quick to exit, 183; are Americans ready to settle down, 241–54; Civil War, 135, 158, 168, 171, 179; colonization of, 23–29; divorce rate in, 229, 230, 232; fragmented culture of, 8; immigrants harboring illusions about, 30, 49; inequality in, 145–49; innocence of, 18, 189; as land of freedom, xii, 18, 32–33; as land of opportunity, xii, 10, 11, 27, 35–36, 44, 59, 101, 125, 137, 139, 142, 145; living up to its ideals, 254; as a lottery, 126–56; melting pot myth, xii; mineral resources of, 117; modernity and self-image of, 5; as moral model for the world, 37–38; as most modern country, 18, 19; as nation of immigrants, 43; newness as quintessentially American, 94; placelessness symbolized by, 35; religion in, 12, 216–17; romanticism in, 192;